PROJECT HUMAN

FIRST CONTACT

BY
BEA WATERS

ALMANDEL ENTERTAINMENT
FREDERICTON, TURTLE ISLAND, EARTH

Published by: Almandel Entertainment Inc.

This book is a work of fiction.
Names of places in this book are real. Names of characters are fictional and any resemblance to real people, living or dead, is purely coincidental.

ISBN 978-1-7388822-0-5 (softcover)
For information on this ISBN, contact:
Legal Deposit
Library and Archives Canada
550 de la Cité Boulevard
Gatineau, Quebec J8T 0A7

Waters, Bea
Project Human: First Contact / by Bea Waters

DEDICATIONS

This book is dedicated to my loving husband, Mark, and my daughter Emily, both voracious readers who have supported me with critical feedback and positive vibes; to my mother, whose feminism and curiosity about life has fuelled the fire in my belly from day one; to my dad, who gave me the stubbornness I needed to push through difficult edits; to Arwen and Ryan, you are always in my heart; the only thing between us is geography. I hope you like the story.

This book is also dedicated to anyone who has ever been cast aside or isolated by bullies. Don't learn their behaviour. Don't become what you hate. Rise above, and sing a different song. Like Olivia, you will find your tribe.

ACKNOWLEDGEMENTS

Thank you to Matt Loze, who rejected my pitch for a TV series. You encouraged me to write a book, and pitch this again once the story that I wanted to tell existed on paper. It was the nicest rejection I've ever received. I hope you enjoy what your positivity helped to create.

I am grateful to my readers for their amazing contributions to my ability to properly tell this story: Jenny Vardy, Daniel Perley, Dan La Noue, and Mark Jenkins; to Jim Middleton for the cover artwork; to Erika LeClair for her proofreading skills; to Kylie Dixon for her social media training. I'm grateful to my ancestors, especially my Nan who always encouraged my creative spark. I'm grateful to all of the ARC readers who gave me kind reviews and boosted my sales, along with the podcasters who have featured me in the run up to launching this book. You've helped me to make a living as an author. I love you all!

AUTHOR'S NOTES

This fiction creates an alternate hypothesis for how humans evolved. Many artefacts that have been uncovered in archaeological digs challenge the currently accepted academic narrative of how humans and their civilizations evolved. While doing research into these findings, I found that too often, physical evidence that did not support the accepted story was dismissed, confiscated, and then went missing. No longer believing the human origin story taught by academia, I have constructed an alternative origin story which is just as wild.

This book was written in the version of English that I learned in school, some years ago. This was the language I used to write my very first novel, at the tender age of eleven. The words I use are very much a part of my journey as an author, and so this is the way I express myself. You will see colour, flavour, candour, and rancour all spelled with a u. Forward is how I spell the adjective, as in, he’s a really forward guy. Forwards, towards, and backwards are how I spell adverbs, as in, she fell backwards with a thud. If you see a word you think is misspelled, look past it, just like you look past the jerk who still owes you $20 from 5 years ago. My spelling isn't worth losing sleep over. I can only afford to make one version of this book, and I think we should all be able to come together to celebrate our common love for stories. Just like Olivia, I’m looking for my tribe: the people who accept me even if my spelling is a little strange. Peace and blessings to you all!

Glossary of Characters

Characters on Earth

Migitju (Mee-GEET-joo) – Olivia's grandmother
John Carpenter – Olivia's father
Brooke Carpenter – Olivia's mother
Dr. Retchen (RETCH-en) – Private school recruiter

Olivia's Alien Friends

AmmaNa (AH-mah-NAH) – a Jin ship Captain
Keilte (KEEL-tee) – a Teuton (TOO-tawn) student
Tuatha (Too-AH-thah) – a Deyonn (DAY-yawn) student
Rama (RAH-mah) – a Vegan (VAY-gan) student
Kyrrha (KEER-hah) – an Atlantian (at-LAN-tian) student

Olivia's Alien Teachers

Master Eldrin (ELL-drin) – an Atlantian (at-LAN-tian) professor
Master Yamma (YAH-mah) – a Doggo (DOH-goh) professor

The Council of Twelve

Queen Tara – Jin Councillor
Lord Harvarder – Teuton (TOO-tawn) Councillor
Lord Tamiel – Atlantian (at-LAN-tian) Councillor
Duchess Damia (DAH-mia) – Polarian Councillor
Fae Morgana (Mor-GAH-nah) – Deyonn (DAY-yawn) Councillor
Shakkar (Shak-CAR) – Telosian (Tel-OH-shun) Councillor
The Procyons (PRO-see-ons)
The Felicians (Fell-EE-shuns)
The Saurians (SORE-ians)
The Vegans (VAY-gans)
The Yanisma (Yan-EES-ma)
The Doggos (DOH-goes)

1 THE FAMILY SECRET

"TAKE OFF YOUR SHOES."

"Migitju, can't I keep them on this time? It rained this morning." Notes of petrichor were still in the air, and the ground was soggy but drying quickly in the late-August heat.

"Our connection with the earth is always better when we are skin to skin." Migitju waited, unwilling to go further until Olivia removed her sandals and left them at the head of the trail.

A lush, velvety carpet of bugleweed caressed her bare toes as Olivia entered the forest. Hundred-year-old maples stretched their arms up and reached for each other, joining into a canopy that left the world below immersed in shadow. She enjoyed these walks through the woods because it was so different from the landscape back home, but she wished that Migitju would get on with it and stop teaching her the same thing over and over. This summer was the first time she'd been allowed to visit New Brunswick on her own, and she appreciated all the time Migitju spent teaching her stuff, but she had so much catching up to do, and Migitju was stuck on repeat. They'd already done this tree thing at least a dozen times.

"You have to learn that fire is hot before you strike a match. Don't wanna burn yourself."

They stepped from the shadows into a clearing where the canopy opened and the blue sky flooded in, where a brook cut through the forest and made space for a small field of wildflowers. A cool breeze peeled away the sun's heat, but only for a quick moment.

"Here."

Olivia's grandmother opened a small leather pouch that she kept around her waist. From it, she took a good pinch of tobacco and placed it on the ground in front of her tenderly, with meaning. "We give a gift to show our gratitude and to remind us to give back."

Sensing that Olivia's mind was wrestling with a question, she spoke again, her way of nudging that question loose. "So many forget to give back."

"Migitju, what if I don't have any tobacco to give? They don't sell tobacco to teenagers."

"If you truly have nothing to give, you can give your words. You always have your words. But I'll give you some tobacco to take home in a special pouch so airport security won't mess with it." Migitju nodded her head like a stamp that sealed the deal. Each of the Elders Olivia had met this summer had the most endearing quirks, like Migitju's head stamp of approval. Olivia didn't want to go home.

"Quit sulking and plant your feet." Migitju hiked her dresses and stamped each bare foot firmly into the ground. They squelched down into the soggy stream bed. Olivia copied Migitju, her feet squishing through the velvety bugleweed and planting into the moist earth.

"Good. Close your eyes. Feel the ground on your soles, cradling each curve. Feel the cold earth under your toes. Feel the cold creep up into you, blurring the lines between the earth and your feet. Welcome it. You are one with the earth. Your feet sprout roots down into the dampness. Feel those roots grow. Feel them grow down, down into the earth. Feel those roots grow until they are as big as the roots of a maple."

Even though she'd done this ritual a dozen times, yesterday, the roots had somehow come alive. Like plugging a lamp into a wall, something had just clicked. Today, her roots thrummed with excitement the moment they began to grow. Energy buzzed up through her calves.

"You are tiny, but you can sense the vastness of this planet. Feel her jungles, alive and raw. Feel her plains, fertile and satisfied. Feel her deserts, scorched and resting. Feel her springs, streams, and rivers, a network of veins as complex as the roots of a tree." She could feel it all, connected to her, alive and tingling.

"Now, take the pain you have been holding and push it down through your roots. Deep, deep down that pain goes. She can take it.

She knows what to do with our pain; she can handle it."

After the grounding practice, Migitju gave thanks for the gifts and set Olivia to work harvesting wild plantain, instructing her to leave the root intact so that the plant could regrow. Among the many things Olivia had learned this summer, at the top of the list was that every teaching was followed by hard labour. Harvesting Migitju's medicines was a small price to pay for all that she'd learned about her mother's Mi'kmaq culture.

"Something weird happened last night when I was out dancing."

"What kind of dance were you doing?"

"The dance I learned at the powwow."

"Now that you're connected to the earth, she knows you. She sings when you dance. It is a special bond."

Migitju's house was a cozy two-bedroom at the end of a street with a backyard leading to the woods where her medicines grew. The second bedroom, which normally served as storage for a large variety of dried plants in bottles, all of which were labelled with the moon and its phase at time of harvest, had been cleared out to make room for Olivia. To accommodate her supplies, Migitju had secured a baby barn, which had quickly evolved from simple storage to being her favourite workspace. But Migitju wasn't ready to retreat to her workshop just yet. The ritual of drinking tea still happened in the kitchen.

Migitju put the basket of wild plantain on the kitchen table and shuffled over to the stove to turn on the heat under the kettle. The house was small but cozy, and it always smelled of sage and cinnamon. Streaks of sunlight sliced through the small window above the sink, landing on a hand-chiselled totem on the sill.

"Did your mother tell you that our ancestors came from the stars?"

"What, like stars fell to Earth and became people or something?"

Migitju chuckled. "No, no. We used to live up there." She pointed to the roof and the sky beyond. "And then we came to live here."

"You believe in people from outer space?"

"You don't?"

"Have you actually seen an alien, Migitju?"

"Only believing in what you can see with your eyes means you only experience a fraction of what life has to offer." She handed Olivia a piece of quartz that came to a point like a pencil sharpened with a pocket knife. "Close your eyes and empty your mind. Listen to the crystal. Ask it to tell you its story."

Olivia cupped the quartz point between her palms, closed her eyes, and waited quietly. Nothing. She tried harder, focusing down into the heart of the crystal. It was frustrating. She didn't want to let her grandmother down.

"What do you hear?"

"What am I supposed to hear?"

"The star people taught us how to flinch. I thought maybe, but no… That's not how it works, is it?"

"How does it work, Migitju? I want to flinch!"

"Put it aside for now. I'll show you when the time is right."

"But I go home tomorrow."

Migitju sat at the table with her cup of tea, sipping silently. Olivia put down the crystal, once again drawn to the totem basking in the sun. The faces of the salmon, the bear, and the eagle stared at her from the wood, wanting to tell their story. She traced her finger over their hand-carved edges, careful not to pick up a splinter.

"What's the deal with this totem?"

"Ask it yourself."

"But I just tried with the crystal, and I couldn't hear anything. Please tell me."

"I don't give you the answers so you have a reason to try again."

Holding the totem in both hands, Olivia closed her eyes, took a deep breath, and let it out slowly.

Migitju put a hand on her shoulder. "You have to ask it a question. You'll only see answers to questions that you ask."

"Who carved your faces?"

As the question left her lips, a jolt ran through her like she'd touched an electric fence. The blackness of her mind exploded into a million points of light that swirled around her until they reformed themselves. She was in a kitchen, but it wasn't Migitju's kitchen. An old man with a face full of laughter carved the outlines of an eagle, a bear, and a salmon into the bark of a chunk of maple. Once he had scored the outlines, he began chipping away at the bark with his pen knife.

"Did Grampy Chester make this totem? I think I can see him."

"What is he doing?"

"He's using a knife to draw the spirit animals into the wood."

"Good. What is he wearing?"

"He's wearing a white sweater with red, black, and yellow stripes."

Migitju clapped her hands together and danced a victory circle around her kitchen. "I knew you could do it! Didn't I tell you?" She rummaged in a drawer for an abalone shell and untied a bundle of dried sage from a nail in the door frame. "We must keep our gifts a secret from the dangerous men. Smell the air."

"It smells sweet and spicy. Like jasmine and cloves. What is it?"

"That smell follows your power as a fart follows beans. We must always hide the smell... To stay safe." She lit the bundle, and the smell of sage tickled Olivia's nostrils. "We thank the Creator and ask for protection."

"Protection from what?"

"From anyone who recognizes that smell."

Olivia copied her grandmother, washing her face, head, and arms with tendrils of the white smoke that spiralled up from the aromatic bundle.

"Now, let's have tea."

Migitju poured boiling water over fresh mint leaves she had picked two days ago, when the moon was full. Olivia caught a glimpse of her reflection in the shiny silver of the kettle.

"Migitju, why do I look so weird?"

Olivia had high cheekbones, almond-shaped eyes, and skin the colour of warm ochre. But that was where her resemblance to her family ended. Her nose and cheeks were full of freckles. And while both her grandmother and mother had long, sleek raven feathers framing their faces and her dad's hair was a mousy brown, Olivia's face was framed with a bush of fiery red curls.

Migitju grinned, her cheeks scrunching into acorns that almost hid her topaz eyes. She leaned in with a secret. "Our family has special blood. It doesn't always show, but it's always there. You look just like my grandmother." She twisted her fingers lovingly through Olivia's ringlets. "She had hair just like yours."

"Really?" Olivia had always felt like a mutant with her red curly hair. "Do you have a picture of her?"

"We didn't get pictures taken back then. But it's why my parents moved us from Gold River to Elsipogtog. Bad men wanted to snatch up those who could see, those who could heal. Our brothers and sisters in Elsipogtog welcomed us and protected us. My parents even changed our family name because the Department of Indian Affairs started keeping birth records. It was the only way to hide."

"Does Mom have these special gifts too?"

"Your mother was learning about her gifts. Then one day, while she was grounding, my Migitju appeared and swung an axe at her head. She thought it was only a vision, but when she showed me where it happened, the axe was still there, stuck in the tree. She got scared. She thought that using her gift was too dangerous. She took off, and before I could bring her home, she met your dad and got married."

"Wow. Mom never said anything…"

"The best way to keep a secret is don't talk about it."

"Migitju, why can't I stay with you? I hate it there."

"I'm always with you, little one. You just close your eyes and call me, and I'll be there. It's another one of our gifts."

2 THE SLAUGHTERHOUSE

OLIVIA STARED AT the front doors of Swift Current High School from the passenger seat of Big Blue, her dad's pickup truck, and began chewing on the inside of her cheek. Ever since she'd flinched with Grampy Chester's totem, she couldn't turn it off. Her mind bubbled with questions on a constant simmer, and because of the questions, everything she touched yanked her into a flinch. It was only a matter of time before they came for her, pitchforks in hand, ready to burn her alive.

Four. Long. Years.

How could she avoid flinching for four years when she couldn't even stop it for one day? Olivia cowered safely inside Big Blue as her peers plodded forward, cattle herding themselves into the slaughterhouse. Everything about this parade made her stomach do little flips. She wasn't ready for this. Not one bit.

"Get going, then. Carpenters aren't late."

"Um, Dad, could we look into homeschooling? At least see what it's like?"

"Homeschooling's for hippies. Carpenters aren't hippies."

His fingers drummed on the steering wheel in time with the country song on the radio, something with stupid lyrics about praying away your troubles. Olivia wanted to scream. Praying didn't work. If it did, Miley and her gang of mean girls would have gone poof a long time ago. That was his answer to everything—to pick up the Bible and be inspired by the Lord. Now, if the Bible had a recipe for exorcizing a demon named Miley Brewster, that would be of interest. She tried appealing to his sense of duty.

"I need to learn how to run the farm, you know, so I can take over. I don't have any brothers, so it'll have to be me. I should be learning the trade. It's more practical."

"That's a good idea, pumpkin. I'll teach you all about the farm."

Could it be? Could it be that she'd hit the jackpot for once in her life?

"We'll do it next summer, instead of you wasting your time back east. But not today. No daughter of mine's gonna be a dropout."

Maybe she could fake a heart attack. She was, in fact, only inches away from a panic attack.

"What if I transfer to Waldeck? It's not that far. I really, really don't want to go to Swift Current High. Please, Dad!"

"It's just a building, pumpkin. Nothing's really changing."

And that was EXACTLY the problem. Nothing was changing. Everything would be exactly the same as last year. Why couldn't she go to a school where the kids liked her? Why couldn't she grow up in a town where being odd wasn't a death sentence? In a bigger city, there'd be other outcasts like her, and at least she'd have someone to talk to. In Waldeck, she wouldn't have any friends, but at least she'd have a chance to avoid the crosshairs. Even in Big Cove, she didn't have any problems with any of the other kids—they had claimed her as their own. It was just this town. Miley hated her, and that meant everyone else did, too. But he couldn't see it. Not his precious Swift Current.

"You're going to Swift Current High. If you have problems, we'll deal with them, just like we always do."

Great. His way of dealing with problems was to blame her, apologize for her "different ways," and then pretend nothing had happened. He never gave a shit about how she felt. He never stuck up for his own daughter—family was less important than his place in town. Miley would throw mud at her and call her a "dirty Carpenter" and he'd tell her to laugh it off. He didn't care if she was hurt, if she was okay. He only cared about how it might damage his reputation. She'd spent fourteen years being blamed for everything. What had she done in a past life to deserve this kind of torture?

Once she entered that slaughterhouse and she started flinching with things, her reputation as the town weirdo would be cemented.

Maybe it was better this way. Maybe once her secret got out, as it inevitably would, he'd be held accountable for his weirdo daughter and finally understand how she felt. He'd be ostracized, just like she was. He'd be forced to move to another town, maybe even another province. He'd be forced to start over.

Defeated, she stuffed her flaming-red curls into a brown beanie cap and slid out of Big Blue, clutching her stomach, ready to hurl at any moment. Sure enough, as she passed a garbage can, she ejected a steaming slurry of that morning's oatmeal. It was a small blessing. Throwing up outside was way better than doing it in class with an audience.

She skipped visiting her new locker, prepared to carry her whole day in her backpack to avoid flinching, but as she approached homeroom, flinching with her locker was suddenly the least of her problems. Miley Brewster, the self-appointed queen of mean, was sitting in judgment over everyone and everything.

"OMG, your outfit looks like someone vommed sparkle. Way to fail extra!"

What was so great about her, anyway? Her two-inch lashes? They were as fake as her blonde hair. Her sharp wit? Nope, she didn't have any of that. Her sparkling personality? That couldn't be it—the only thing that sparkled about Miley was the fake sapphire hanging around her neck. She claimed it had belonged to her great-grandmother, but that couldn't be true. What old woman in her right mind would give such a precious jewel to such a nasty bitch? Maybe the grandma had been senile at the time. Maybe Olivia would flinch with it to find out the truth and then call the little twerp out on her bullshit.

Miley had always been a bitch. She'd made it her personal mission to ruin Olivia's life and had gotten progressively better at it year after year. The only time she'd ever been reprimanded was in grade five when a teacher overheard her call Olivia a half-breed. She was punished in some way because she never said that word again. But her torture tactics didn't stop—she just found other ways to say the exact same thing. With Miley in her homeroom, it would be another friendless year. Nobody would dare to be her friend, because Miley would target them as well.

"Omigod, girls, it's the… Wait, what do we call you? We aren't allowed to call you what you really are because it's 'insensitive.'"

Her gang of plastics quickly averted their faces, trying to hide their collective embarrassment at her use of air quotes. Somehow, despite all of her attempts to look perfect in every way, she managed to make herself look like a total loser all on her own. Olivia grinned. Hooray for small miracles.

Noticing the grin, Miley got all fired up. "What's so funny, you stupid savage? Oh, riiiiiight, I'm not supposed to use that word. Too bad. It's not like anything I'm allowed to say fits whatever it is you are."

"Why don't you call her by her name?" offered a small, round-faced boy from the third row. "She must have a name. We all do."

Miley swivelled around to the little pipsqueak who had dared to speak out of turn.

"No, I think I'll call her Gingervitis, because she's a red-headed disease." Her eyes narrowed at the boy who had intruded on her fun. How did he not know that was against the rules? Hadn't he gotten the group text?

White-blond hair crowned his head, cut straight around like he was wearing a mixing bowl. He looked at least two years too young to be in high school, and he wasn't at all bothered by the venom in Miley's stare.

Miley sized him up. She knew everyone in town, but she didn't know this kid. "Who are you, anyway?"

"The name's Van Houten. Percy Van Houten."

"Mmhmm. You're obviously new in town, so you get one warning. Stay out of my business and stay out of my way. Or else."

She returned her attention to Olivia, determined to do maximum damage before the first bell. "Look, girls, Gingervitis got a new hat. Hiding those red pubes you try to pass off as hair doesn't change a thing. You're still a disease."

Janelle and Kerry hooted with laughter.

Olivia kind of wished she was carrying a disease—something like

Ebola—deadly and easily shared with Miley and her thugs.

Once again, the little blond boy piped up.

"The concept of a human as a disease does have its merits. Mao Zedong, Stalin, Hitler, and Pol Pot are all great examples of what can rightly be considered a disease to the well-being of *Homo sapiens*, because, much like a disease, their nature was to end many innocent lives. I am, however, amiss to see how our classmate fits into that category."

Miley blasted Percy with a glare that, if it had been a solid object, would have knocked him out cold. Percy returned an expression that seemed to say, *you don't have to thank me, I'll correct you anytime*. Incredulous, Miley looked to her gang of plastics for support. They all shrugged their shoulders, utterly confused by the lack of understanding this boy had for the way things worked in Miley's town.

The bell cut Miley's onslaught off short. Their homeroom teacher glowered over them.

"I am Mrs. Hammond. I am one of the toughest teachers at Swift Current High, and if you do not pay attention, you will repeat my class next year. With me. Nobody wants that, yes? So let's set some ground rules and try to have a successful year."

Olivia shuffled into a seat in the back of the class and tried to disappear. Mrs. Hammond seemed strict enough that Miley might wind her neck in a bit. Maybe she wouldn't want to get in trouble and embarrass dear Daddy Brewster. Maybe science class wouldn't be so bad.

Math was next.

It wasn't her most or least favourite subject, but that wasn't her focus. She sat at the back, watching the door. Watching for her. And this time, she finally got lucky. The bell rang, and Miley was somewhere else.

The day became a blur of being slammed around like a bumper car in the halls as she kept her hands secured in her pockets to avoid touching stuff. She couldn't flinch with something if she didn't touch it. At least, she assumed as much. It was cool to have such a strange power, but it sucked that she didn't know how to control it. It sucked that the only person who could teach her about this was on the other side of the country.

Thankfully, the rest of the day unfolded without flinching and, to her absolute amazement, without Miley. Mrs. Hammond's class was the only place where she'd have to deal with the brat. Miley hadn't been torn into little plastic bits in a freak harvester accident, but in the real world, this was probably the best outcome she could hope for.

The last bell of the day brought a promise of alone time, of peace. No worrying about what people might say to her face or behind her back. As soon as Big Blue jolted to a stop beside the house, she jumped out, grabbing the new backpack her grandmother had made for her, and darted for the barn. Her dad moved to block her, but he was too late.

"You're not going to make friends if you spend another year in that barn," he called out. He didn't really care that she wasn't making friends. He only cared that the town might whisper about what that strange Carpenter girl was doing in that barn. More to the point, he cared how it reflected on him. She'd been happy this summer in New Brunswick. She wasn't ready to come back to a life where she was everyone's burden.

"The barn isn't the problem, this stupid town is! If you take away my barn, I'll run away from home, just like Mom did when she was my age!"

His expression shifted from condescension into shock, finally settling on hurt. It was too bad that their arguments had to go this far, but it was the only thing that worked. She just needed a few hours. Time to recharge.

The barn smelled of dry hay and motor oil, welcoming her home. It wasn't fair that she had to suffer another year in this town, but at least she had her loft. She collapsed into her beanbag, running a finger over the paper spines of the only friends she had ever known, checking to make sure they were all still there. Her collection contained stories of adventure on the high seas, of time travel, of dystopian worlds that couldn't possibly exist populated by the most authentic people ever, and of discarded places that could only be found by discarded people. She had missed them all. She'd been gone so long that a substantial layer of dust coated their skins. But cleaning them up would have to wait until tomorrow. Tonight, she had other plans.

From her backpack, she fetched a small pouch made of soft deerskin and decorated with beads made from the quills of an unfortunate porcupine. It was beautiful. She ran her fingers over the detailed stitching and inhaled deeply, the combination of leather and tobacco prickling at her senses. Migitju had been correct: declaring it to be a ceremonial pouch had saved it from being taken away when she'd gotten on the plane in Moncton. She was so glad to have this gift from her grandmother.

"Thank you for the gifts, Migitju. Thank you, thank you, thank you."

She held the pouch in both hands and asked the only question she could think of. *How were you made?*

The blackness behind her eyelids shattered into a million pieces and reformed themselves into Migitju's kitchen. She was holding two pieces of leather and stitching them together with two long strips of leather that she crisscrossed on the outside of the seam. In front of her, on the table, was a fresh, steaming mug of mint tea and an assortment of porcupine quills.

Migitju finished the seam, and as she put the pouch down to reach for more leather strips, the vision evaporated. Her grandmother's kitchen was gone; Olivia was back in her loft, her nose filling with the sweet and spicy scent of jasmine and cloves. Heeding Migitju's warning about the smell, Olivia put an abalone shell in the middle of the carpet and lit a bundle of sage, washing her face, head, and arms with the tendrils of white smoke that spiralled up from the aromatic herbs. It made her feel safe; it made her feel connected to her grandmother and to a culture she was only just learning about. It was one more reason she had for protecting her place in the loft. Her father would never let her burn sage in the house.

"That's a smell that brings me back."

Olivia jumped, unaware that her mother had crept into the barn. "Oh. Hey, Mom."

"Dad said you were up here pouting."

"What does he know about smudging? He thinks it's the same as burning incense."

"Mom must have shown you some things this summer." Brooke sat cross-legged on the carpet next to Olivia and pulled the smoke towards her, washing her head, her face, her neck, and her shoulders. "Do you know why we smudge with sage?"

"Migitju says it's to cleanse away the negative energy that sticks to us."

"Mmhmm. So, you gonna tell me what it is you gotta clean away before you come say hello?"

Olivia hesitated, picking at a frayed edge of her rug.

"Miley again?"

"She's always on me, like a barnacle on a lobster boat."

"Are her words powerful enough to change who you are? On the inside?"

Brooke fluffed Olivia's curls tenderly and wrapped her in a big hug. "I missed you. I'm glad you spent the summer with Mom, but it's not the same around here without you."

"Why do we have to live so far away from Migitju?"

"This is where your father and I decided to settle down. A fresh start."

"No offence, Mom, but I doubt you had any say in it. I'm old enough to know better."

"You're wrong. I'm exactly where I want to be."

Olivia turned back to the sage bundle, watching the glowing embers slowly consume the dried herb. Trying to talk to her mom about this stuff was pointless.

"What else did you do this summer?"

"I learned about the star people who brought us here. I went to a powwow and learned to dance like our ancestors, and Migitju taught me how to flinch. Stuff I should have learned from you."

Brooke shifted uncomfortably, thought for a few moments, and then got up, brushing non-existent dirt from her pants. "Make sure you give those ashes to the earth before supper. We're having stew."

Olivia wished her mom would teach her about their Mi'kmaq

culture. It sucked that she was only just starting to brush the surface of it. Maybe that was why she always felt so out of place—because she belonged somewhere else. But bringing it up at supper would just cause a fight. Supper was Dad's time to talk about whatever was in his head. She was expected to listen and learn from his immense wisdom. Except he never brought any wisdom worth learning.

With supper finished, Olivia ventured into the backyard. The rainbow sky was already fading into the deep indigo of twilight. Normally, she'd take her bike out into the corn field, but the stalks were heavy with cobs, and she wanted to say hello to them, inhaling their crisp smell. She followed the stars, knowing which ones pointed in the direction of her special place, and after quite a hike, she popped out into a large, circular clearing. She came here often to daydream, to count the stars, and to dance. It was her own personal crop circle.

Her dad claimed he hadn't planted the circle with corn because he needed a turnaround for the tractor, but Olivia knew better. For some reason, corn just wouldn't grow here. No matter how much he planted, no matter how much fertilizer he used, only clover and alfalfa would take.

She needed to unpack the day's confrontation with Miley, and this seemed like the right setting. Was she convincing enough in her aggression? Did Miley buy it? Would she be scared? Bullies were supposed to shift targets when challenged. Was Miley a normal, garden-variety bully, or was she some kind of teen sociopath who'd hunt Olivia down and slit her throat in her sleep? What would her next move be? What should Olivia's next move be?

Her mind was full of questions, with no way to answer them. All she could do was guess. One thing was certain. No matter how many times she told herself to ignore the entitled little bitch, Miley always got to her. Miley was getting to her right now, taking up space in her head without paying any rent. Why was Miley so good at getting under her skin? It was like she could crawl right in with Olivia and see exactly what would hurt her. Maybe, if Miley got right up in her face tomorrow, she'd grab the bitch by the wrist and flinch with her to find out her deepest, darkest secrets. Then she could use them to take Miley down once and for all. Superheroes weren't coming to save Olivia. She had to do this on her own.

Getting all worked up again wasn't helping. Since an empty mind was always better for figuring out problems, Olivia dug her MP3 player out of her pocket and popped in her earbuds. As the music started, her feet shuffled forward: right, right, left, left, right, right, left, left, the way Migitju had shown her. Soon, every piece of her was in motion.

Her hips tossed left, then right. Her shoulders twisted rhythmically, tracing figure eights in the air, following the melody. As the buildup of the verse gave way to the celebration of the chorus, her hands twisted upwards, stretching, reaching, as if she could pull a song out of the stars and down into her body.

That's when it happened.

A warm gust swirled around her ankles, even though the night was perfectly still. A bright glow appeared at her feet as energy flooded from somewhere deep in the earth, swaddling her in its warmth.

As her dance intensified, the wind climbed her legs like vines up a tree, engulfing her torso and erasing the evening chill. It shot upward into the sky in a clockwise spiral, catching her hair in its pull. If one of the faithful flock of the Swift Current Baptist congregation had been there to witness it, the sight of her hair twisting and dancing against gravity would have surely sent them running to the minister to demand an exorcism. But out here, under the cover of the cornstalks, it didn't matter if her dancing made strange things happen. Nobody could see her. Out here, all that mattered was the intoxicating energy of the song.

As the song reached its crescendo, there was nothing but the dance. She was standing in a shower of love, the day's problems washed away as if they had never existed. She was pure bliss. The spiral of energy shot upward, slicing deep into the void of outer space, taking out every satellite in orbit over North America. But Olivia knew nothing of these details.

She didn't notice when the sky vanished behind a saucer half the size of a football field. Already feeling as light as air within her own dance, she didn't feel her feet leave the ground. She kept right on dancing as her body floated up, disappearing into the belly of the ship. Seconds later, as fast as it had come, the saucer vanished, leaving a deserted circle in the field below.

A TALL, SLENDER man with a marble face and peppercorn eyes admired a map of the world hanging on his office wall. Clusters of emerald pushpins like broccoli flowers dotted the map at Peru, Mexico, Egypt, Arizona, Iraq, India, Easter Island, and South Africa. Single pins dotted the landscape in too many places to name. He studied his wall of trophies with pride, licking his lips with a quick flick of his tongue. He popped open a small container full of more pins, these ones bright orange, and stabbed one into the southeast of New Brunswick, Canada. He tapped it thoughtfully.

"It is too bad I missed you."

"Energy fluctuation detected," said a calming female voice as a computer screen flashed, jolting his attention away from his trophies.

"Display target."

A map of North America appeared, a light pulsing over the Canadian prairies. The display zoomed in on Saskatchewan, the blip pulsing like a heartbeat.

"Interesting. The same as New Brunswick, but now in the prairies. Trinity, is the Canadian military capable of producing this?"

"Negative," the system responded.

"The Americans?"

"Negative."

He tapped on the blip. "Produce coordinates." The screen displayed a field just east of Swift Current, Saskatchewan: 50.305460 degrees north, -107.804224 degrees west. He strode across the room to a huge black desk standing atop four obsidian claws, and his finger stabbed a button next to a speaker. "Retrieval mission. Four agents. Two vehicles. One hour. Heading north."

His finger let go of the button, and his lips parted in a grin, revealing two rows of razor-sharp opals. Hunting was his favourite part of the job.

3 THE GOLDEN ONES

OLIVIA WAS SO fully present in her own moment that she continued dancing, oblivious as the ship left Earth's orbit. When the song ended and she tried to open her eyes, they fought back, protecting themselves from a flood of blinding light.

"How can…? I was in the dark…in the cornfield…"

Squinting behind a shield of eyelashes didn't work either. There was nothing but brightness. It was like that scene in the movies when the main character dies and the director tries to show what the afterlife looks like. The bright room never seemed believable, but now that she was faced with the blinding light, she couldn't help but wonder, *am I dead?*

She thinks that she is dead.

The voice was thick like molasses, filling every inch of the room.

"Who's there? Are you an angel?" She pinched herself. "Ouch! Yep, I'm still alive. So that's not it. What is this place?"

She changes her hypothesis as new details arrive.

She does not cling to errors when assimilating facts.

"I can hear you! So instead of talking about me like I'm not even in the room—whoever you are—would you PLEASE turn down those lights?"

The brightness bursting through her eyelids faded. Finally able to open her eyes, Olivia squinted at her surroundings. She could feel someone staring at her, and sure enough, two bulbous, almond-shaped eyes came into focus. They were the black of empty space, surrounded by a golden face that glowed like a sunrise over the ocean. Instead of eyebrows, five golden antennae protruded above each eye, swaying to and fro like grass in a breeze. Below the eyes, a delicate nose sat atop a small, lipless mouth. A mass of golden hair crowned the being's head like a swirl of frosting topping a cupcake. A being made of gold? How had she gone from a cornfield in Swift Current to this place, wherever she was?

You sent a beacon into space

that we could not ignore.

"What do you mean, beacon? I didn't send a beacon."

We saw it from a nearby star and followed it back to the source.

This is the second time that you have called us to your field.

"I…I don't understand. I was in the cornfield, dancing. And when I opened my eyes…" Maybe she'd been knocked out, and she was hallucinating. That had to be it. She was in a coma, and her brain was trying to cope. "Who are you?"

Our people are the Jin.

The golden lips didn't move, not even a twitch, but Olivia heard the voice as clearly as her own. They said they came from a nearby star. Of course, the star people had to exist if Migitju said they did, but this was next level! Why were they here? What did they want with her? Was she being abducted? Would Migitju's star people do that? Abduct humans? As she tried to make sense of it all, two more faces joined the party. Six large ebony eyes studied her with intensity, unblinking, eager to take her in. Their stare was intense, but she sensed no threat from them, only curiosity. Her own fear quickly gave way to curiosity, too.

"How do you talk without…without moving your mouth?"

Our people have evolved.

"But how does it work?"

By thinking, you create

an image in your mind.

Your thoughts are broadcast out

by way of frequencies.

Our brains receive these waves

before you choose your words.

Your waves reveal the truth

in ways that words cannot.

"But why can I hear you if you don't make any sound? I'm not telepathic."

We push the frequencies you need to hear into your brain,

and this allows your brain to hear the thoughts that we transmit.

"How do I know which one of you is speaking—er, I mean… pushing at me?"

We three are intertwined,

so only need one voice.

"Do you have names?"

The delicate lips of the middle face finally moved, stretching into a smile.

If you require a name,

you may use AmmaNa.

Olivia took a deep breath in and out, trying to stop her heart from beating right through her ribcage. This couldn't be real. There was no way she'd just been beamed up by telepathic aliens—the odds of this happening were just too astronomical. It had to be some kind of trick. She grabbed AmmaNa's arm, expecting it to dissolve, but it wasn't a hallucination. The texture of AmmaNa's golden skin was rougher than she expected, like a leather jacket that had been left out in the sun.

Are you real?

She didn't mean to think the question. Her brain was just like that. Always full of questions. A jolt passed through her body, like being zapped, and millions of cells absorbed the shock like it was fuel. Before she could retract her hand, the golden beings shattered.

A thousand shards of light rained down around her, leaving Olivia in an empty void. The shards skittered around the floor like a swarm of ants and then began assembling themselves like a puzzle on autopilot. Crisp and detailed images emerged from the chaos. Memories.

Sand stretched out to the edges of the horizon. She choked, her lungs full of dust. Hundreds of Jin appeared. They sprayed a pink mist across the barren landscape, and the fire in her lungs cooled. They joined hands and began chanting, the low drone of their chant settling across the land like a blanket. Vegetation sprouted from the cracked earth, and in seconds, a field had grown up around them. The field sighed, exhaling a million tiny puffs of steam that floated skyward and joined to form the first cloud. The cloud burst open, soaking the parched land.

You create life?

The image of the chanting beings shattered, and once again, the shards rearranged themselves to show her something new. She was in a cavernous room bigger than a football field. Gigantic blocks of pink feldspar cut into odd shapes fit perfectly together to form the walls of the cavern. Streaming down from holes in the ceiling, the natural light was amplified by a hundred torches burning around the room. Jasmine and cloves saturated the air.

The room was being used to host some kind of alien science fair. Hundreds of beings milled around the cavern, most of them humanoid despite physical traits that clearly were not human. Some had blue or red skin; some had heads that were too large for a human; others had hands with seven digits or three plus a thumb. Dozens of felines joined the crowd, walking upright on two feet and gesticulating with hands like a humanoid, but their pointy, fur-covered ears and catlike noses set them apart. On the edge of the crowd, a group of tan-coloured felines mingled with a group of canine humanoids without issue. The diversity of beings was amazing, and yet, they all had a singular purpose for attending this event.

In the centre of the massive cavern, the contents of twelve pools were evaluated by various groups of judges. Some of the judges were massive boulders, as tall as they were wide, who shook the floor as they moved. Some were humanoids with gills that gently fanned open and shut in a constant rhythm, as if they were underwater instead of on dry land, but it was obvious they were made for a wetter environment. Instead of skin, they were covered in obsidian scales that shimmered with ethereal glints of multicoloured light and shadow as they moved. Another group of judges had long red manes of hair that didn't just grow from their heads but sprouted all over them, covering their chests, shoulders, and arms in a furry layer of armour. But amongst all of this splendour, there was one special being who drew Olivia's eye away from the others as it floated from pool to pool. It had a human form, but unlike humans, every inch of its skin sparkled in the torchlight. It wasn't a golden sparkle like the Jin; it was a multicoloured glitter that trailed behind it as it moved, leaving a cloud of shimmer in its wake. Protruding from its shoulder blades, large iridescent wings fanned gently as it glided across the stone floor. Everything about it was mesmerizing, captivating.

The pools began to hiss and spew steam, pulling Olivia's attention away from the magical being. Working in trios at each pool, the Jin had dipped their hands into the water, causing it to bubble into such a frenzy that all but the Jin backed away from the splash zone. Massive plumes of steam floated up to escape through the holes in the ceiling, and as the steam subsided, each trio of Jin lifted a being from the froth, a human baby ready to gasp its first breath.

Three of the babies were black like ebony, three were the colour of frost on a windshield, three had skin painted with goldenrod flowers, and the final three had been dipped in henna. The four colours of the medicine wheel hanging on Migitju's wall had been born from these twelve pools, adored and attended by the gathering.

A crowd of Jin cooed over a goldenrod child with inky hair. A group of red beasts gathered around a henna child whose hair was as fiery as Olivia's. The Jin handed a frost baby to a tall albino with alabaster skin, angular features, and pointy ears. The obsidian fish people sang a chorus of long, harmonic tones to all three ebony infants. And among all of this, the magical being with the wake of shimmer floated from baby to baby, blowing a breath full of sparkle into each one's nostrils. The babies wriggled and cooed, reaching for the being as it floated away.

Is this how life on Earth began?

Olivia cursed her wandering thoughts. She didn't want to leave the grotto, but it was too late. The vision had already splintered into a tornado of light that swirled around her, stretching upward and raining down to form a new vision.

She stared at a peaceful blue orb from outer space: Earth. Its continents were different, but it was unmistakably her home. Another planet, this one large and brown, hurtled towards them. The Earth's orbit pulled it far enough away to dodge the brown planet and cross right into the path of one of the planet's moons. The moon ripped through the Earth's atmosphere, friction igniting the air and the land below. Trees exploded into flaming splinters. Within seconds, an entire rainforest was reduced to a scorched trail of ash. Pulled down by Earth's gravity, the moon smashed into the Pacific, releasing a mushroom cloud of steam and debris. The Earth shuddered. The continents moved, leaning away from the impact. The ocean sprinted to the furthest corners of the Earth, racing over the land in giant, rolling waves, drowning everything in sight. When the waves receded, all that was left was devastation.

Stillness. An exhale.

A bell-shaped saucer landed on a plain in the middle of a vast expanse of scorched land. The Jin exited their ship, their golden skin sparkling in the sun, bringing with them a small horde of human children. They sprayed the land with their pink mist, joined hands with the children, and chanted. Life sprouted all around them.

The Jin built massive pyramids, ornate temples, and cities. They taught the children to cultivate crops, to write with pictures, and to track the procession of the stars. Olivia tried to move in for a closer look, but she felt a sharp pinch on her bicep, and everything fell out of focus. She couldn't hold onto the image. She crashed backwards, landing with a thud on the floor of the spaceship.

She clutched at the throb in her arm. They'd injected her with something. One of the Jin pried away her hand to spray a cooling mist where she'd been poked. All she could do was gawk. No words came. Nothing could follow what she'd just experienced. These aliens were real. How could aliens be real?

All day she'd been dreading the possibility that she'd flinch with something—a locker, a jacket, a pen borrowed from someone—but instead, Olivia had to be all extra and flinch with aliens. On their ship, of all places. The pungent smell of jasmine and cloves overwhelmed her nostrils, stronger than it had ever been. Migitju's warning rolled around at the edges of her thoughts: "The best way to keep a secret is not to talk about it."

You saw as the Yanisma do.

This is a rare ability.

How do you come to know this way

of seeing through a flinch?

The question made her think of Migitju, of Grampy Chester's totem, of her very first flinch.

You held a piece of wood

and saw someone long gone.

The elder was impressed

and danced around the room.

"How…? How do you know…? I haven't told anyone about that day."

When thoughts form in your mind,

they form in our mind, too.

"What? So, basically, you can read me like a book?"

It isn't like a book.

Before your brain makes words,

your thoughts are given life.

We see them in that form

like images on-screen.

The way that we communicate ensures we know the truth.

"So not like a book, like a movie. Great, just peachy. I've always wanted someone to see all of my deepest, darkest secrets without my permission."

But hadn't she just done the same thing? Hadn't she just grabbed hold of this being she'd only just met and flinched to see the deepest, darkest secrets of the Jin? But that was exactly why she was trembling. Flinching could only show moments that had actually happened. That meant that the moon, the destruction, the babies in the birthing pools… All of it had to be real. The immensity of this revelation flooded into every corner of her body, drowning her in equal amounts of terror and wonder.

The Jin had said that she could see as the Yanisma did. Who were the Yanisma? Were they the bad men Migitju was afraid of? She hadn't described the bad men… What if they had golden skin? Where would they take her? What would they do to her?

We have no plans to do you harm.
We came because you called us here.
We are not meant to interfere
until the project is complete.

"The project? What project? What are you talking about?"

Nobody was there to answer her question. The golden Jin were gone. Olivia was sitting alone on the ground in the middle of her crop circle, staring at an inky sky full of twinkling stars.

4 THE FLINCH

OLIVIA ATE HER oatmeal in silence, nose buried in a book to avoid conversation, but she wasn't reading. She was playing last night's events over and over, trying to make sense of them. Maybe she'd fallen asleep in the circle. An alien encounter was definitely strange enough to be the material of dreams. But the images were still crisp, not at all like a dream that skittered away within minutes of waking up. One nugget rolled around in her head, bumping into stuff and refusing to go away. The golden ones had said they weren't supposed to interfere until the project was complete. What did that mean? What project were they talking about?

Thankfully, breakfast unfolded normally, her mom chewing quietly on a slice of toast while Dad sipped his coffee, too interested in his newspaper to notice that Olivia had been reading the same page for fifteen minutes. He was such an old fart. Who even read the newspaper anymore?

As soon as he disappeared into the bathroom, she kissed her mom, grabbed her backpack, and slipped out the back door, speeding away on her bike. By the time he emerged, she'd already be halfway to school. Being trapped in Big Blue with his holier-than-thou lectures about life was not on her list of things to do today. Or any day. But especially not today, after what had happened the night before.

She had to be mistaken. It couldn't have been real. The universe was big, and it made sense that other life existed out there, but if they came to Earth, they'd meet with someone important: a leader, a scientist, a Nobel Prize winner. No intelligent life would come all this way to make first contact with her. It didn't make sense.

Focusing on math and social studies was impossible. She was too busy watching the sky, trying to make out shapes hiding in the clouds.

Luckily, Miley was not in either class, and unlike Mrs. Hammond, Mr. Strickland and Ms. Waddell didn't care that she wasn't paying attention. The first part of the day turned out to be relatively peaceful. It should have been a sign. Unfortunately, the only sign Olivia noticed was the sign on the wall next to her locker, glittering down at her, taunting her.

CHEER TRYOUTS: MAIN GYM — AFTER SCHOOL

Dancing was everything, and cheer was kind of like dancing. It was choreographed like dance. It was a whole team, moving in unison, supporting each other. Maybe this was her chance to be part of something.

"That's not for you," snapped Miley, loud enough to attract attention from everyone in earshot. "Just because we're, like, in a new school or whatever, that doesn't change anything. There's no room for freaks on the cheer squad. It's for, you know, like, girls with *po-ten-shall.*"

The little blond boy was nowhere in sight, but his interference had proven that Miley wasn't made of steel. He'd said all the things Olivia had wanted to say, and it had gotten under Miley's skin. Maybe it was time to try things Percy's way.

"*Po-ten-shall?* That's, like, a really big word, Miley. Can you, like, spell it?"

Miley's angular eyes twitched at the corners. Was this brat actually talking back to her? "I don't need to spell it. My phone has spell checker."

"So you have the potential to spell, but your phone has made you so stupid that you'll never develop that potential into real skill. Got it. Anything else?"

Miley's jaw sagged in disbelief for a few moments, and then snapped shut as she heard giggles from nearby tenth graders directed at her. The corners of her eyes twitched once again. "Come on, girls, let's get away from this freak before we catch something."

A swish of brand-name jeans and fashion magazine haircuts marched away, spewing a mess of insults about Olivia and her hair to appease their wounded leader. Miley would make the cheer squad just because she was a Brewster.

So much for joining a club.

Olivia slammed her locker shut and shoved through the double doors into the dust-filled air, heading straight for the back side of the field house. Its solitude brought the promise of an excellent lunchtime hiding spot. Her hunch was confirmed as she rounded the building and found two seniors in football jackets also using this spot to avoid detection. Doug, the school's quarterback, was holding a small kid upside down over a large metal trash can, assisted by Jeb, Swift Current's star running back.

Jeb looked up and snarled. "Git lost. This's none of your business."

They dwarfed her by at least a foot, but both boys had their hands full…for the moment. Among other things she'd learned this summer, her cousins had taught her how to play poker. Olivia had learned that being timid was a sign of weakness, and it had cost her money every time. The only nights she'd walked away a winner was when she'd been upset and taken her aggression out on the game. This situation was the same. The last thing she wanted was a confrontation, but she'd walked smack into one, and she had to deal with it. Spending another year as everyone's punching bag was not happening. Not this year. She dug into her pocket, palming her cell.

"Get lost or what?"

"Git lost or you're next."

She whipped out the phone and pointed it at the bullies. "Record video."

"What do you think you're doing?"

"Maybe you decide to put that kid down, and maybe I decide not to show this video to anyone."

Doug sneered. "You don't scare us, you little freak."

Olivia wielded the phone like a powerful weapon, its tiny eye capturing millions of pixels of incriminating evidence. Her heart pounded in her throat, but that didn't stop her.

"If I put this video online, the media sees it. If the media sees it, the RCMP have to get involved. And if the cops get involved, there's no way Coach Patterson can let you play football this year. That means no scouts, no scholarships, and no way out of Swift Current. You'll be selling cars for Murray Freeman till the day he gives his dealership to Eddie. You pick on Eddie, too, don't you? And he'll end up being your boss. Looks like a pretty bleak future. A couple more almost-made-its wasting away in Swift Current. So, if you look at things from my side of this phone, you both have a very good reason to be scared of me. Now put that kid down, and gently."

The boys gritted their teeth, each looking to the other for direction, the phone watching their every move. Neither one had ever faced this kind of audacity in a freshman, and they had no idea what to do with it. Unwilling to test her threat, they hauled the kid out of the garbage can and plopped him on the dirt. It was Percy.

"You're gonna delete that video."

"No, I'm not. I'm keeping the video. You two goons leave both of us alone, and it never sees a torrent. You mess with either of us—anyone in this school messes with us—and all bets are off."

"Give it here."

Jeb advanced on her, but Olivia took a pace back, maintaining the distance between them. Her stomach rolled around like she was on the Tilt-A-Whirl, but thankfully she hadn't eaten lunch yet.

"This uploads in real time to a server I run at home. That's the thing about being a geek—I actually know how to use this stuff, unlike you meatheads who just take selfies. You so much as touch me or my phone, and the cops will be busting down your door before your mama has dinner on the table."

Jeb's sneer melted into horrified shock. He looked to Doug. "Is that even a thing? Can she do that without plugging it in?" Doug hiked his shoulders. Jeb hated backing down from a fight, but the thought of not playing football was worse. "This isn't over, you stupid little freak. It's nowhere near over." The goons vanished around the building.

Olivia gripped her stomach. There was a dead moment before it felt safe to exhale.

"Your help is appreciated, though not at all necessary," a squeaky voice admonished from the grass. "I'm glad to see that you're choosing to defend someone, even if it's not yourself. It's progress, anyway."

"I'm just sick of being picked on, you know? Being different doesn't make me a disease. I didn't choose to look like this."

"Have you ever considered that being different makes you special? They're status quo. The future is never created by the status quo. If it was, *Homo sapiens* would still be living in caves without books, or the wheel, or cell phones. Status quo is overrated."

She'd never considered that. She'd always figured that the popular kids went on to rule the world.

"Those two may become football stars, but they won't cure cancer, or solve climate change, or help humanity level up." Percy crawled around on all fours, patting the parched ground. "Could you please help me find my spectacles? I tossed them off when these boys grabbed me so that they wouldn't get nicked, and now I cannot find them. They really are irreplaceable."

Olivia spied a glint in the grass and retrieved the glasses. They were quite large, but to her surprise, when he put them on, they seemed to disappear into his face.

He offered his hand. "Percy. Percy Van Houton."

She pulled him up from the ground. "Yeah, I caught your name in class. I'm Olivia."

"I have to ask, Olivia, is your phone really downloading in real time?" He whispered the question in case the goons were still listening.

"No, that was a total bluff. I figured they only know how to send texts, take selfies, and watch football. It was a calculated risk."

"Well done, Olivia."

"You really pissed Miley off yesterday. That's probably why those jerks came after you."

"It's important to speak up for someone whose ability to speak up has been compromised. Besides, the risk was worth it if my example has helped you learn to cultivate a little self-confidence."

"Okay, you're not hearing me. Miley's dad has a lot of pull in this town, and she's on a lifelong power trip. She'll be gunning for you."

"I can handle myself." Percy looked around to see if anyone else was in earshot before he continued. "It is important to know how to fight your battles, but it is equally important to know that you do not have to attend every battle to which you are invited. It is best to choose wisely. Rarely does one have the endurance to fight them all."

Olivia peeked around the corner of the field house to make sure Jeb and Doug hadn't prepared an ambush. In the heat of the moment, defending Percy had seemed like the right thing to do, but it was foolish to think that they would let this go. As she trudged back across the sun-baked field, it felt like walking into a hornets' nest.

She slipped into chemistry and sat in the third row against the window. Outside, a pair of black SUVs parked in the bus lane. A tall, slender man in a cashmere sweater got out and strode up to the front door. She was so busy watching this unusual arrival that she failed to notice how the cacophony of ninth graders shouting over each other was missing one distinct voice, how a certain person was not holding court and judging everyone.

As the bell rang, Miley sprang from her seat, trading places with Rebekah. She was now sitting directly behind Olivia. The door slammed shut.

"SILENCE." Mrs. Hammond did not wear a friendly look. The sourness in her wrinkles had been forged over many decades of being forced to do things one does not enjoy doing, like putting up with teenagers or teaching anyone anything. "Open your text to the periodic table."

She clicked a button and a large grid appeared on the board behind her. "Every piece of matter on Earth comprises these elements." She punctuated the statement by smacking the board with a stick. She was a teacher in the wrong time, one who wished she could have lived a hundred years ago when teachers were still allowed to beat their students. "In my class, you will learn the individual elements, their characteristics, and why they are organized thusly."

"Hey, Gingervitis, check out the pig fetus on the shelf. It looks just like you. You could be sisters."

Sitting behind her, Miley was impossible to ignore, and Olivia found it impossible not to look at the fetus. A large glass jar to the left of Mrs. Hammond's desk contained a pinkish-grey figure with pointy ears and a fully formed snout. Why did Mrs. Hammond have that as a decoration? Yuck.

"When did you go get yourself cloned?"

Oh, if only that were possible. Olivia closed her eyes, dreaming up an army of clones who, on her command, would surround Miley, squish her into the ground, and destroy her.

"Hey, Gingervitis, where'd you get the lame-ass hat?"

Olivia took some deep, calming breaths. She wasn't about to give Miley the satisfaction of a response, and giving Mrs. Hammond a reason to notice her didn't seem like a wise move.

"Did you hear me, Gingervitis? I asked you where you got the lame-ass hat. Did your mama take you to the Walmart?"

Rebekah giggled, loving the heat of the burn. Like Miley, she was too good to shop in town—she always went to Regina for brand-name stuff. But Olivia knew all about Rebekah's favourite brands and had no interest in being a billboard for clothing made in sweatshops by slaves half their age. Mrs. Hammond, oblivious to the conflict brewing in the back of her class, droned on.

"The first element on the periodic table is hydrogen. It has the lowest atomic weight, and with only one electron, it is highly unstable. It's a powerful atom because it's able to bond with almost any other element. Give me an example of a molecule containing hydrogen."

Normally, Olivia avoided answering questions in class. Being smart just gave them another reason to hate her. But today, she put her hand up. Miley was up to something, and pulling Mrs. Hammond's attention to this side of the class was the only short-term fix that came to mind. A bony finger pushed a pair of rectangular spectacles up her long, hawkish nose, forming a capital T in the middle of her face.

"Yes, you in the brown hat. Name?"

"Olivia Carpenter."

"Olivia. Well?"

"Water forms when two hydrogens bond with one oxygen."

"Correct. Do you know why they bond?"

"Oxygen is missing two electrons, and hydrogen sort of has an extra one. So they get together and they share."

Mrs. Hammond flipped through her lesson plan, pursing her lips. She hadn't expected that anyone would know the answers before she, herself, had taught those answers. She scanned down her class list, and sure enough, Olivia's name was on it.

"What a nerd!" Miley sniggered, but her chance to needle Olivia was cut short as Mr. Dick, the vice principal, burst into the class.

Annoyed with the interruption, Mrs. Hammond smacked the desk with her stick. "Mr. Dick, I expect a knock before an intrusion."

"And I expect to spend my days running a school, but here I am, running errands for a man in a fancy sweater who thinks he's important. We all have our crosses to bear." Without waiting for her reaction, he turned to the class. "Zackary Griffin. Olivia Carpenter. Follow me." A collective "Oooooh" followed them out of the class, punctuated by another smack of Hammond's attention stick.

Mr. Dick led them to the office and pointed to chairs outside Principal Peabody's room. A rapid-fire *clackety-clack-click-clack* filled the room as the secretary's typing competed with the industrial clock hanging overhead.

"Mr. Dick, I must know why I've been pulled out of class," Zack protested. "This is highly irregular for a student of my standing."

"A recruiter is here from some school for gifted kids. Apparently, being vice principal means I'm the one who has to play fetch when someone walks in wearing cashmere." He disappeared into his office, grumbling to himself. "Six years of uni to be a glorified errand boy. I need a transfer."

After a long moment sizing up his competition, Zack unleashed his opinions. "So what if you know why hydrogen bonds to oxygen? That doesn't make you intelligent, it just means you can read."

Olivia didn't hear him; she was still thinking about Jeb and Doug. Part of her was proud that she'd found the courage to stand up to them. A much bigger part was obsessing about their inevitable retaliation.

"Sorry, what?"

"Exactly. You have the attention span of a gnat. An academy for the gifted will never debase itself by recruiting someone like you. That's why they do interviews."

Great. Even the biggest nerd in town hated her.

Principal Peabody's door opened. Zack popped out of his chair, offering himself up despite the lack of invitation. "The early bird gets the worm," he chided as he disappeared behind the door.

"The early bird gets the worm, yes, but the second mouse gets the cheese." Percy Van Houten swung his legs back and forth under his chair like he was warming up for a marathon. She hadn't even seen him arrive. "Rushing into decisions before one has all of the relevant information is rarely a prudent move." He pulled an apple out of his pocket and tossed it up and down, watching it rise and fall. He seemed much too young to be in high school, but much too old as well.

"What are you in for?" Olivia nodded at the sombre surroundings.

"Oh, I'm just here for moral support." He looked at the principal's door like he was looking through the solid wood. "It's really hard to keep one's cool with bullies like Miley doing all they can to push one's buttons, but there are evils far worse than Miley Brewster." He contemplated his apple before pocketing it, then removed his glasses, folded them, and put them in a case. "I didn't show you the proper gratitude for your help today at lunch. I know it wasn't easy for you to stand up to those boys. Take these." He put the case in her hand. "When you need to see people in their true form, these will help."

"But I don't need glasses."

"You need them more than I do."

"Um, do you want to be friends?"

"As lovely as that sounds, if you truly knew me, I doubt you'd want to be friends. But I'll be around if you ever find yourself in need of assistance."

Before she could ask what he meant, Zack strode out of the principal's office carrying a manila envelope. He smirked at Olivia, dangling it in front of her like the last piece of candy on earth. "Academy for the gifted, here I come."

"Olivia Carpenter?" Principal Peabody called from the door.

"Good luck, loser."

The principal's office was a lot smaller than she expected for the person burdened with running the town's only high school. A tall, slender man sat next to the large desk. He had a full head of black hair, combed and gelled so that not one single strand was out of place. It reminded Olivia of the plastic hair on her childhood toys.

"Good morning, Olivia. My name is Dr. Retchen." His voice was smooth. Velvety. Coaxing. "My academy is an exclusive facility for students who are special. Students who are different. Are you different, Olivia?"

The question stung. She was about as different as they came. Might as well own it. "Everyone thinks I have leprosy, but I don't seem to have any bits falling off. Maybe that's my special gift. I'm a carrier. Armadillo girl."

"Most of our students are…unique. With us, they find fellowship. They find acceptance."

Olivia tried but couldn't imagine what that felt like.

"Let's talk about you. What exceptional things can you do? Things others cannot do?"

She could flinch. But as much as she hated the prospect of staying in Swift Current, she could not betray her grandmother. She'd already slipped once last night—or had she? Had that even been real? But the fear that she'd let her secret slip out once was enough to make her double down on her promise to Migitju.

"The only exceptional thing about me is how much everyone in this town hates me."

"Many special gifts remain hidden until they are activated. Tell me, Olivia, does anyone in your family have any special talents?"

"Dad's family is still in Barbados, and Mom's family lives back east. I get presents at Christmas, but I'm not close to any of them."

He made some notes in a file on his lap. "Does anyone in Dad's family practice magic? A Caribbean grandmother who reads cards?"

Something about the question was off. This had nothing to do with being smart. It was what he'd ask if he were running a school for wizards. Olivia shrugged and grunted to dodge the question.

"And Mom's side… She's from Big Cove?"

A lump appeared in Olivia's throat, making it difficult to swallow. She hadn't told him where her mother was from. She'd been purposefully vague, but if she had named Migitju's community, she would have used its real name: Elsipogtog. How did he know so much about her?

"How is it that a little native girl has red hair and freckles?"

While most of her hair was hidden under her beanie, there was no way to hide her eyebrows and her freckles. But why would the colour of her hair matter? This summer, Migitju had taught Olivia about more than just flinching. She'd also taught Olivia to follow her gut, no matter what. And right now, Olivia's gut was telling her not to trust the man with the weird hair like a plastic toy.

"Maybe the stork dropped me off at the wrong house."

His eyes narrowed. He was not happy with the answer. "What do you know about free energy?"

"Nothing's free. If energy was free, Dad wouldn't swear at the power bill every month."

"Have you ever heard of Nikola Tesla?"

"I heard that Thomas Edison stole his inventions and that boxes of his research disappeared after he died. Being smart is overrated."

Dr. Retchen pulled a blank card out of his folder. "What's on this card?"

"Nothing."

"Try again."

"Is it a perfume card? I'm a bit congested today."

He put the card away. "Olivia, are you a believer, or are you a skeptic?"

"I only believe in something if I can prove it exists, but I always believe in the possibility."

"That isn't an answer. It's a clever way of dodging the question."

"Not really. Let me give you an example. I don't believe you're a doctor because I haven't seen your degree, but I guess it's possible. I do believe you're searching for someone with rare abilities because you asked me if my grandmother reads cards. That's a really weird question unless you're recruiting for Hogwarts. But I didn't get a letter by owl, so that possibility is unlikely."

"Very astute, young lady."

"Astute? Yes. Special? No. I'm good at observing stuff. It's something we loners do a lot of. Since we don't have anyone to talk to, we spend our days watching." She stood and stepped to the door to signal that the interview was over. "Sorry for wasting your time. I hope you find your rare gift."

He was on his feet in a flash, like a used-car salesman, unwilling to let a deal walk away until it was dead for good. "Don't discount your potential so quickly. Here, take this package." He produced a manila envelope, just like the one Zack had waved around like a trophy. "Take it home, look it over with your parents, and we can meet for dinner to discuss your potential."

Olivia let a huge breath go, releasing the tension she'd carried into this meeting. Maybe she'd misjudged him. Maybe he was just looking for gifted students after all. Maybe he was gifted himself and, because of it, came across as a little weird. Olivia knew all about weird.

As she claimed the envelope, she quietly wondered what the other children he'd recruited were like. In the brief moment that her guard was down, Retchen's other hand darted out of nowhere, clasping around hers in an unexpected handshake, and the world shifted into the black void of a flinch.

The void shattered, leaving her in a lavish bathroom, staring down at a large claw-foot tub with shiny brass fixtures. A healthy sprinkling of shallots and garlic rained down on the naked butt cheeks of a henna-skinned boy, followed by a careful drizzle of oil. The boy's skin shone like a glazed turkey.

"Prepare my roasting spit."

Three grey aliens, short with large heads, waxy skin, and huge oil-slick eyes, scampered out of the room to do his bidding. They looked just like the aliens she'd seen in TV shows and on posters.

"It's time to tenderize." He produced a black cattle prod that shot bolts of lightning from its end and jabbed at the boy once in each leg, once in each buttock, and once in each shoulder. The body twitched with every shock.

The vision shattered into a million tiny shards, and Olivia was once again standing in the principal's office, bewildered. What had she just seen? What was he doing to that boy?

"What just happened, Olivia? Where did you go?"

Olivia yanked her hand away and grabbed the doorknob, swinging it open to create a draft, but it was too late. The smell of jasmine and cloves filled the air, and Dr. Retchen inhaled deeply, his eyebrows arching toward his strange hair. For the first time, Olivia noticed that his eyebrows weren't real. They had been drawn with eyeliner.

"This meeting has been fascinating, Olivia Carpenter," he clucked. "We'll talk again soon, I'm sure of it."

5 ADDING INJURY TO INSULT

OLIVIA RETURNED TO class, shaken by the flinch. A boy being marinated… A roasting spit… Retchen was going to eat him.

This was the stuff of nightmares, but it had to be real. Migitju was adamant that flinching only showed memories; anything revealed in a flinch was true. That's why it had to be kept secret—seeing through lies made her dangerous. Was Retchen the infamous Slenderman? She'd flinched right in front of him. Had he seen her vision? Did he know that she knew? Would he have let her walk away if he did?

"The disease returns."

Miley's insult was lost to the horrific image of bug-eyed aliens skittering away to prepare a roasting spit. Swift Current was a crap town, and Miley was a crap person, but at least she wasn't eating people.

Refusing to be ignored, Miley grabbed at Olivia's hat, yanking it off her head and stuffing it under her butt. Olivia's red curls exploded outward in all directions. The class burst into sniggers, all of them well accustomed to this long-standing war.

Snapping back into reality, Olivia spun around.

Miley wore an innocent pout, the hat nowhere to be seen. "Can I help you? Do you have a problem?"

"Girls! Why are you interrupting my lesson?" Mrs. Hammond's sharp tone cut through the sniggers like a hot knife through ice cream.

"Miley stole my hat. Give it back, you jerk!"

Miley's face clenched. She let out a faint squeak before pulling the hat out from under her butt and handing it back to Olivia. "Smell that. Fresh from the cleaners."

"There," said Mrs. Hammond. "Now cover that mess on your

head so that we can resume our discovery of the periodic table."

"Yeah, Olivia, put your hat back on." Miley's eyes twinkled. "I dare you."

"Put on the fart-hat, fart-head," Rebekah whispered.

"Mrs. Hammond, may I change seats?"

"Absolutely not. I've had quite enough disruptions to my lesson already."

"But Mrs. Hammond, I'm not the one who's—"

"ENOUGH!" She whipped her desk with the pointing stick as punctuation and turned back to her lesson, leaving Olivia at the mercy of her nemesis.

Olivia stuffed the hat into her backpack and did her best to ignore the snickering all around her. The manila envelope demanded her attention. Would Retchen snatch her away in the middle of the night? Would she even have a choice? Migitju's family had hidden her from the priests who came to the reserve to steal children for their evil schools. But how could Olivia hide now? He knew her name. He knew about her family. She stuffed the envelope into her backpack too, terrified of what might be inside.

"Mrs. Hammond is right. That is a mess on your head. Let me help." Before Olivia could react, Miley grabbed her by the hair, yanking her head backwards.

SNIP.

Olivia spun around to find Miley clutching scissors in one hand and a large ball of red curls in the other, her smirk daring Olivia to react.

All of her life, Olivia had been taught to knuckle under, to put up with the abuse. She was done being terrorized by this bitch.

Olivia snatched the scissors and grabbed Miley by the throat, pointing the blade at Miley's eye, then her cheek, then her lips.

"Give me one good reason not to butcher your face." Olivia's words escaped in a low hiss that proved she meant business. Miley's smirk vanished, replaced by a mask of terror. She'd never seen this strength in Olivia. She'd never pushed far enough to awaken that beast until today.

"I'm sorry. Don't cut me. I'm so sorry. Please. I won't. Never again."

Olivia took a deep breath, the scissor blade pushing into the fleshy part of Miley's perfect cheek. She didn't actually want to hurt her, or anyone else; she just wanted the torture to stop. And this was just like a game of poker. If Olivia backed down now, Miley would start up where she left off tomorrow. She had to make it clear that she was done being Miley's punching bag.

The answer came in a flash of evil genius. Olivia let go of Miley's throat and grabbed as much hair as she could.

SNIP.

A large chunk of Miley's blonde locks fell to the floor, leaving the queen of mean with no bangs. Every set of eyes in the class gawked at this unexpected retaliation.

"Olivia Carpenter!"

Having already passed the point of no return, Olivia marched up to the front of the class and dropped the scissors on Mrs. Hammond's desk. Being nice to this crappy excuse for a teacher was pointless. Clearly, she cared more about her damn periodic table than anything else.

"She did it to me first, so I returned the favour. It's called payback." Olivia twisted her head around to display the gaping hole in her bush of curls.

"An eye for an eye makes everyone blind."

"You're the one who turned a blind eye to the danger I was in. I asked to switch seats five minutes ago. I asked you for help, and you ignored me."

"If I had to address every single request—"

"Then you wouldn't have as much time to spend droning on about your stupid periodic table! Keeping me safe is part of your job. I'm going to report you and get your ass fired."

Leaving Mrs. Hammond with no rebuttal, Olivia went back to grab her backpack. Miley's mascara had blackened her cheeks, completing her new freak-show look. Olivia whipped her phone out and snapped a photo. "From now on, every time you come for me, I'll come for you twice as hard. Got it, bitch?" Olivia cleared a large glob of phlegm from her throat, formed it into a huge ball, and spat it directly into the tiny bristles that used to be Miley's bangs.

"Olivia Carpenter! You sit down right now."

"Go to hell."

Cutting class on day two was not a good look, but she really needed a few hours on her bike to figure things out. Nobody was going to stop her. After what she'd just done, they wouldn't dare.

She slammed her feet into the pedals, pushing as hard as her legs would allow, the wind swirling her butchered hair into a tangled mess. She pressed harder and harder against the wind, pumping a healthy dose of pain into her quads. The burn in her legs reminded her of every time she had pedalled away the rage boiling up inside her after a round of Miley's bullying. Trying to find her centre. She'd been trained to take the crap and just be nice, to meet the violence with a smile. But today, when Miley had butchered her hair, the rage had boiled over, and that plastic bitch had learned what it felt like to be the victim. The scissors directed at Miley's eyeball had only stopped millimetres from their target. Only a breath away from carving her up like a jack-o-lantern. She was going to take a lot of shit for doing that, but…

It felt good to fight back. Exhilarating.

Maybe Miley would pick on someone else now that Olivia had threatened to chop up her face. Maybe being the scariest bitch ever was the answer.

Zipping through the flat countryside, taking detours through fields, she circled the outskirts of Swift Current until her legs were spent. She hit the highway and headed home with just enough calm built up to face her dad, but she skidded to a stop at the apex of the last hill before Eagle Crest Farm.

Two black SUVs were parked in her driveway. The pipeline guys were back. Her dad was going to be in a mood. Then again, when wasn't he in a mood?

She doubled back and cut down a dirt road that linked into the depths of the corn fields and approached the house from behind. Emerging into a graveyard of tractors, she snaked between the metal carcasses until she found Ol' Red, the pickup truck that had been the family's transportation before Big Blue. At ten, her father had started teaching her how to fix engines, and keeping Ol' Red going had become an obsession. She patted its chassis and used it to prop up her bike before jogging around the barn toward the open kitchen window. John Carpenter's voice cut through the late afternoon, strong and annoyed.

"I'll talk it over with my wife when she's feeling better. Unless there's anything else?"

Chairs scraped against the kitchen floor, and a few moments later, two car engines rumbled into action. This wasn't the first time a pipeline company had made an offer on the back end of Eagle Crest. Their new west-to-east line required a connection right through the prairies to Ontario. Thinking the farmers of Swift Current were easy prey, they'd been here a dozen times, and despite the fact that her dad kept saying no, they kept on coming back. Their continued attempts to wear down the will of John Carpenter showed that they didn't have a clue.

Olivia walked through the kitchen door, steeling herself against his inevitable tirade. This time she'd be strong. This time she'd speak up for herself. This time she would say everything she'd always wanted to say. She was done with Miley's shit, and she sure as hell wasn't going to apologize for growing a backbone. It was time to go all in. If her parents weren't going side with her, then she'd divorce both of them and look after herself.

"Where on god's green earth have you been?"

"Riding my bike on the outskirts, trying to calm down. Miley attacked me, and I had to cool off."

"So cutting class was your solution?" Yep, exactly as expected, he was going to try and find some way to blame this on her. She was ready.

"I knew there'd be trouble, but you wouldn't listen. I tried to find other solutions, but you sent me into that slaughterhouse anyway."

"So it's my fault you assaulted Miley with a pair of scissors?"

"Miley brought the scissors."

"Bringing scissors to a school isn't a crime. You also threatened Mrs. Hammond, but I guess that's Miley's fault as well?"

"No, that's Hammond's fault. She should have protected me."

"The problem always centres on you, but it's always someone else's fault."

"Miley sat behind me and cut a huge chunk out of my hair, see? All I did was retaliate. But that's the problem, isn't it, Dad? I'm the problem if I retaliate, because if it's not white, it's not right."

"Oh, for god's sake, why does it always have to be the race thing?"

"Because Miley's a god damn racist, that's why! Don't you remember the one time she actually got in trouble? For calling me a half-breed?"

"You won't let me forget it. You won't let anyone forget it. How do you think it makes me look when the whole town has to relive the story of Miley calling my daughter a half-breed?"

"How does it make you look? I don't know, Dad, how does it make you look when you side with a bigot? Makes you look like a bigot yourself. There. I said it. Should've said it years ago."

Her accusation struck him, a hard slap across the face that left his cheeks red. And then, with no rebuttal, he did like he always did when he was losing—he invoked the teachings of his almighty saviour. "Why can't you forgive, like Jesus teaches, and turn the other cheek?"

"Because when I turn my head, she attacks me with a pair of scissors!"

"Enough! This is all a part of your plan to get kicked out of school. You're lucky that your mother doesn't want to put you in a private school, or I'd enrol you tomorrow."

"Private school?"

"The headmaster just left."

Olivia swallowed hard. The black SUVs weren't from the pipeline company? Retchen had come here, to Eagle Crest? "The creepy guy in the cashmere sweater?"

"Why would you invite him here?" Brooke Carpenter emerged in the stairwell, her hair looking like she'd been dragged by a tractor.

"Why would you bring that man to our house?"

"I didn't invite him. He showed up at my school this morning. He gives me the creeps. I didn't give him our address, and I don't want to go to his school. I don't want to be anywhere near him."

"He says you hate it here and that you'd rather be with the gifted students at his academy."

"I never said that! Are you gonna believe some random over your own daughter?"

"Enough!" John Carpenter pounded his fist into the table, making its legs wobble. "Actions speak louder than words, and your actions are not those of someone who wants to be part of our community."

"I don't want to be bullied! Look at what she did to my hair!" She turned her head to show the gaping hole in her curls.

"Hair grows back. Reputations stick. Maybe a fresh start would be good."

Did he really want to send her away? If her mom's anxiety was the only thing protecting her, how long would that last? He was determined. He was inflexible. He'd keep hammering away at her until he got what he wanted.

She needed to know how far the conversation with Retchen had gone. Two glasses sat on the table, one on the placemat opposite her father. She took a deep, calming breath, and instead of grabbing the water, she put her hands on the placemat beneath it.

What did Retchen say at this table?

An image burst into the blackness of her mind. Dr. Creepy McSlenderman sat facing her father, wearing a smooth mask of calm.

"It's quite common, Mr. Carpenter. Gifted children act out because they're not being challenged. Imagine having to sit in class all day and learn nothing. Olivia's chemistry teacher reported that before she had even finished teaching her first lesson on the periodic table, Olivia already understood how chemical bonds between atoms are formed." He paused while John contemplated this. "Tell me, Mr. Carpenter, does Olivia like to read?"

"She's always got her nose in a book, unless she's tinkering with my old pickup or stargazing."

"Fascinating. An interest in stargazing shows an expansive view of the universe, common among gifted children. Her love of books is probably why she's so far ahead of her peers. I see this all the time, Mr. Carpenter. Your daughter told me that she doesn't fit in, that kids in this town treat her like a disease. At my academy, she'll be among friends. Kids who are gifted, just like her."

Olivia ripped her hand away, knocking the glass over. It toppled off of the table and crashed to the ground, splintering into hundreds of shards. The air filled with the scent of jasmine and cloves. Brooke sniffed the air. Her eyes grew large like full moons.

"I'm not going anywhere with that…monster."

"Well then, you better hope Peabody lets you back in. Tomorrow, you'll apologize to Miley, and Mrs. Hammond. And you'll say it like you mean it. You'll be lucky if Miley's father doesn't press charges."

"But Dad, you're not listening!"

"No daughter of mine is going to be a high school dropout. That family tradition ends with your mother."

"John, that isn't fair," Brooke whimpered from the stairwell. "You know why I left."

"Yes, Brooke. You had a dream about your great-grandmother swinging an axe at your head, and the next day, you found the tree with the axe stuck in its trunk. You decided that it wasn't dream, that your life was in danger, so you ran. It all sounds so logical when I say it out loud, doesn't it? I love you my dear, but you aren't emotionally equipped to handle this. You need to sit this one out."

Brooke choked back the words she desperately wanted to say and retreated up the stairs. A door slammed.

"If Peabody won't take you back, Dr. Retchen is saving you a spot. Those are your choices."

"So that's it. Either I willingly put up with abuse from the Brewsters, or you'll ship me off somewhere so you can save face? You're that starved for their acceptance? You really suck. You suck at being a dad, and you suck at being a human." Olivia raced up the stairs, desperate for her mother's protection.

Brooke was at the window, watching the highway for headlights.

"Why would you bring that man here?"

"I didn't, I swear. He's dangerous. Mom, I saw things..."

"What do you mean?"

"I flinched with him by mistake, and..."

"What!? Do you ever think first? I left home to get away from all of this crazy stuff, and you invite it right to our doorstep."

"I didn't mean to. I can't control the flinching. It just happens. Please, Mom!"

"I won't let him send you away, Livy, but your dad wants you in school, and I can't argue with him on that. You'll have to make nice, at least for the next few years."

"You want me to apologize when Miley attacked me first?"

"Sometimes you gotta give something up to get what you want."

"Like you gave up being native to marry Dad?"

"How dare you! You don't know anything about what I've suffered." Brooke crossed her arms and flattened her lips. "You need to think about what you want. We can talk tomorrow."

Olivia punched through the kitchen door and headed straight for the loft, tears screaming down her face. She sat in the middle of the carpet, hugging her knees and rocking. Her books waited silently, offering no comfort. Her crystals didn't know what to say.

Retchen ate children. Just thinking about him made her feel like something icky was climbing up the back of her neck and she convulsed a few times to shake it off. She wasn't going to his academy of marinated children. End of story. But that's what her dad wanted. It was his new way out. It wouldn't matter if she apologized to Miley and put up with all of her torture and more. He wanted to ship her off. He'd find a reason, and he'd get his way in the end. He always did. Her mother could only protect her for so long. Eventually, he'd wear her down.

That was something she'd started to notice a few years back. Whenever Mom said no, Dad worked at her and worked at her until he wore her down. She never actually consented to anything with him; she just gave up. Olivia couldn't imagine her mom ever agreeing to send her away, but she also couldn't imagine her mom ever getting the final word. Olivia couldn't risk being handed over to Creepy McSlenderman. Flinches didn't lie. She'd seen what she'd seen.

What if she ran away? For years, Dad had been saying, "The apple doesn't fall far from the tree," like he was expecting her to follow her mother's path. So what if she called his bluff? Proved him right? Why not? Migitju was the only family who would understand this danger. She needed help from her grandmother, and New Brunswick would be a wonderful escape. She'd learned so much about her heritage this summer, and she had so much more to learn.

The warmth of the idea swelled in her and through her, and in the short moment between two beats on a drum, she had her answer. All she had ever wanted was to find her clan—a community that accepted her and loved her just the way she was. Maybe she could find that in New Brunswick.

She loaded her new backpack with things that mattered for a cross-country trip: her collection of crystals, a few bundles of sage and sweet grass, a large bag of trail mix, a first aid kit, her bank card, her MP3 player, her journal, and four books: *Lightfinder*, *Shadows Cast by Stars*, *A Wrinkle in Time*, and *The Hitchhiker's Guide to the Galaxy*. None were her favourites, but they all felt appropriate for the journey ahead.

With a compass hanging around her neck and a change of clothes balled up inside a woollen blanket that she secured to her backpack with some twine, she crept to the door of the loft and listened. She'd head east on her bike, going from town to town, sleeping rough in old barns or in fields under the stars. She still had a few weeks before the nights got really cold. At that point, she'd ditch her bike and take a bus the rest of the way. Her plan was both terrifying and exhilarating.

It would have been really useful to have a phone, but her dad forbade it until she was old enough to sign the contract herself. He knew everything, and once he made a decision, that was it; it was done. No room to bend, no room to learn, no room to grow. It was always his way or the highway. He was unbending, but his spirit had forged in Olivia a spirit to match.

Tonight, she chose the highway.

Olivia whipped through the cornfield on her bike, heading east. It didn't matter that she had no map—all she had to do was follow the stars and stay off the highway. Nobody would come looking for an indigenous girl; the cops wouldn't waste their time. The more distance she put between herself and Swift Current, the better chance she had of pulling this off. Her feet pushed her excitement into the pedals, the wheels following hardened tractor ruts with ease. She was used to this terrain and held back nothing, pedalling with such enthusiasm that her foot slipped and her ankle scraped against the chain.

She yelped and toppled over, crushing a pile of corn stalks as they broke her fall. Blood rolled down her ankle, soaking into her sock.

Great.

She gritted her teeth against the sting of the wound, but the sting to her spirit was worse. How come she couldn't even get out of the backyard without messing up? She hugged her knees, hot tears flowing over her strong cheeks.

The first star twinkled overhead as Olivia finished cleaning grease out of the wound. As she bandaged her ankle, she thought about her tradition of making a wish on the first star to appear. Memories of wishing for straight hair, for a new bike, or for the last book in a great trilogy all seemed frivolous. Tonight, she wished for something really important.

"I wish I could find a place with people like me."

She laid her head back and watched as the wishing star's playmates appeared one by one. Soon, the sky was full of twinkling points. Some twinkled with such intensity that they were hard to watch for more than a few seconds; some emitted such a dim light that she could only be sure they existed if she didn't look directly at them. She picked a bright one in the east.

"Migitju, get ready. Here I come."

Close your eyes, little one. Close your eyes and feel the heartbeat of the land.

Olivia closed her eyes and listened for the heartbeat. She listened for a long moment…but all she heard was crickets. She popped in her earbuds and turned on the music she had brought back from the powwow. She had all night to put distance between herself and this town, but right now, she needed to recharge her spirit. She climbed to her feet, and despite her ankle, she started dancing the circle. She felt Migitju with her, smiling, encouraging her.

Swift Current disappeared. The mean kids and their insults disappeared. Miley's scissors disappeared. Alone with the infinite universe, she danced for the perfect system of chaos that gave her life. This chaos wanted her to exist, despite the people around her, and so Olivia danced for that infinite universe, letting her emotions flow out of her body, through her limbs, down into the ground.

A warm wind blew through the corn. Two beams of light emerged from the ground near her feet, twisting into a spiral that encased her body. The spiral of light grew and grew, and then, in the space between two drumbeats, it shot up to meet the stars.

DR. RETCHEN LEANED into his reflection in the small, dimly lit mirror of his motel bathroom. He was beyond frustrated. His interviews had been unsuccessful. He wasn't any closer to finding the source of the energy fluctuation, and he only had a few days before the local authorities would come asking questions. He needed to solve this mystery and get back to the safety of his cave.

The Griffin boy couldn't be the answer. Despite his obsession with building rockets and aliens, his interview had revealed nothing more than a book-smart braggart. He wasn't special. If he had the ability to raise a giant plume of energy, he would have claimed it. The Carpenter girl's handshake had delivered a small shock, but with hair like hers, she'd always be carrying a bit of voltage. She'd also carried a certain perfume, a scent he felt he should recognize, though he couldn't quite remember why. But he was sure that the girl was hiding something. Could she create that kind of energy fluctuation? Doubtful. He'd had one of his men poke around the farm while he'd kept John Carpenter occupied, but all the agent had found was a teenage hideaway full of books and crystals. Hardly the type of workshop necessary to build any kind of advanced technology.

He dipped an eyelash into a small pot of glue and touched it to his eyebrow. The acrid smell of the solvent brought a welcome sting to his nostrils. It was one of the few comforting smells in a world full of flowers and coffee. Just as he touched the false lash to his brow, his Zen was interrupted by a ruckus outside. Retchen dropped his tweezers, leaving his right eyebrow only partially formed, and headed out to investigate.

"It sounds crazy, but I swear I saw it!" The cook and two waitresses from the motel's restaurant stared eastward at an empty sky. Retchen tried not to seem too eager. He put on his suavest character, adjusting everything about himself, down to his tone of voice and choice of words. Normally, being polite to people like this was beneath him, but he knew how to put on a convivial facade when there was a potential benefit. And in this situation, he'd do whatever was necessary to capture his prize. The hunt was everything.

"Why all the commotion, ladies?"

The older of the two waitresses jumped at the opportunity to tell her story. "Well, about five minutes back, this big white light shot right up into the sky. Right over that way. And then a giant yoo-foe appeared. And then the yoo-foe shot straight up and out of sight, and the light vanished."

"Beg pardon, Martha," he read from her name tag. "A yoo-foe?"

"Yeah, a big, giant metal thingy. Looked like a pancake with a nipple on top. Made the ground glow orange. Wouldn't have believed it if I hadn't seen it myself."

"Really?" He poured all of his attention into the waitress. He'd learned long ago that playing up to a gossip was the best way to learn a small town's darkest secrets. Her kind just loved the attention. "And you say there was a big white light. Did it come from the yoo-foe?"

"Nope. The light came first. Right, Megs?" She elbowed the other waitress.

Megs was rarely called upon to confirm any of Martha's stories and was determined to be a good sidekick. "Yup, just like Martha said. The bright light came first, then the yoo-foe came down and shut it off."

"We saw it through the window," Martha jumped back in, nodding with conviction. "Sure as I'm standing here, the light went up from the ground. Like someone was growing a beanstalk up to the clouds."

"Like a beanstalk? Well, then. Any idea where it came from? Surely someone like yourself who knows all the goings on would know who might be testing strange devices in the backyard."

"If anyone's building weird stuff, it's the Griffin kid. He really upset old man Douglass when one of his rockets blasted right through the top of the old man's silo. That kid's the strangest we got here in Swift Current. But he ain't built no giant yoo-foe. Woulda taken him years to build something that size. I woulda known about it. I say it's military."

"Hmm. The Griffin boy. Thank you, Martha. Megs." He flashed them a genuine smile, giving a rare glimpse of his teeth. Martha was too busy staring at the sky, but Megs caught a glimpse of his pearly whites. It had only been for a second, but she was sure she had seen his sharp, pointy teeth instead of square white Chiclets.

Back in the privacy of his hotel room, he grabbed his phone. With nobody to charm, he reverted to his preferred use of the English language. "Swift Current, Saskatchewan. Bell-shaped saucer. Multiple witnesses. Send the Greys. Retrieve the human. If they resist… convince them."

The moon was on the horizon, large and bright and missing only a sliver at ten o'clock as Retchen's black SUV sped along Highway 4. The GPS directed him onto a tractor path through a field that would bring him to the exact coordinates of the original energy fluctuation. He didn't hesitate, not at all concerned about trespassing. Wolves, eagles, and grizzlies didn't bother with the imaginary lines of ownership created by humans. Top predators were above such things. The saucer that had brought him to this useless town had found something interesting enough to return for an encore. Whatever it wanted belonged to him, and he would take it back, whatever the cost.

The SUV inched forward at a snail's pace over the potholed path, tossing its driver around like laundry in a dryer. Retchen reached up and smoothed back a chunk of black hair that had come unglued from the rest.

He was closing in.

"You have arrived at your destination," the GPS sang as the farm road opened up into a large, circular clearing. He threw the vehicle into park and skittered around, searching, sniffing, touching, the beam of his flashlight flitting back and forth, hoping to land on any clue that might bring him closer to his prey.

At the edge of the circle, the moon glinted off something metallic. A blue bicycle lay against the corn stalks, abandoned. He crouched down to examine it. His nose twitched. He inhaled deeply, finding the unmistakable scent of human blood. He sniffed around, quickly locating the source: a few drops and a scraping of flesh mixed with the black grease on the chain.

He licked his lips and smirked. "I can do a lot with a little DNA."

6 THE QUANTAGATE

AS OLIVIA ENDED her dance, she opened her eyes to three golden faces with ebony eyes. Until this moment, she'd convinced herself that the whole thing was a dream, that she'd fallen asleep in the crop circle. But she was not dreaming or hallucinating.

ALIENS WERE REAL!

And since her flinch with AmmaNa had really happened, that meant ALL OF THE ALIENS AROUND THE TWELVE POOLS WERE REAL?! How was this possible?

Olivia drank in large, gulping breaths and sat on the floor to stop herself from falling over. Aliens were supposed to be a hoax.

How is it that you're skeptical?
We left behind our monuments
and clues to point you to the stars.
It makes no sense that you are shocked
to meet us once again.

Migitju had been right about the star people, about flinching, about everything. And thinking of Migitju brought reality crashing back in. Olivia was on the run. And in true Olivia form, she couldn't even run away without screwing it up. She fought back her tears, unwilling to cry in front of strangers.

A child so young with so much pain;
you should not have to live like this.
You should be cared for and be loved.
We see your tears and understand.
Can we do anything to help?
Do you have somewhere safe to go?

Six large ebony eyes watched her, full of compassion. The Jin wanted to help, but could they travel backward through time? Retchen had smelled her flinch. Even if she made it to Migitju's, would she be safe there? How many heartbeats did she have left before she was marinating in his tub?

The Jin were horrified as these thoughts ripped through Olivia's mind. They saw it all without words, and they believed her. AmmaNa's compassion wrapped Olivia in a hug.

We see this man who hunts you down.

We cannot let him have his way.

We must protect you at all costs;

your life means everything.

We must consider implementing guideline number twelve.

The Jin clasped their hands, forming a ring. Something emanated from each of their golden bodies, a ripple on a pond, passing through the air between them. The ripples collided, becoming one, and then flowed outward through the rest of the room. Olivia felt it pass through her in the space of a breath.

Guideline number twelve has been accepted through debate.

That ripple she'd felt was a telepathic debate? Not bad.

"What's guideline number twelve? What did you decide?"

BANG!

They all crashed to the floor, thrown sideways by something smashing full force into the ship.

That was your only warning.

The voice sounded nothing like the soothing voice of the Jin. It was nasal and menacing. A large window appeared in one of the ship's walls, and outside, against the backdrop of a beautiful blue planet, a small swarm of saucers hovered in battle formation. From the closest saucer, a grey face, covered mostly by huge, oil-slick eyes, glared at the ship's passengers. It was the same creature she had seen in her flinch with Retchen.

Return the girl to the surface or we will vaporize your vessel.

Every cell in Olivia's body screamed that these creatures planned to hurt her. Her brain went into panic mode. The time to consider options was gone. All she could think of was escape.

We need to get away from them, now!

The ship lurched backward. Olivia flew across the lab, her shoulder slamming into the window. The Earth receded. Within seconds, Mars sped past.

The swarm gave chase. It caught up as Mars shrank to the size of a red marble. The ship suddenly dodged sideways, just missing a stream of weapon blasts. They swerved hard the other way and then dropped hard. Olivia grabbed a railing along the wall just in time to avoid being flattened on the ceiling. A boulder the size of Manhattan filled the window, and suddenly, the violent jerky manoeuvres made sense.

They had entered the asteroid belt.

The Jin ship swerved easily around the minefield. The swarm was not so lucky. Olivia counted three explosions before another massive asteroid tumbled in front of the window, blocking the Greys from view.

BANG!

One of the swarm's weapons landed a shot. The ship shuddered and adjusted its course, heading deeper into a minefield that moved and swelled around them. It was a strange thing, fleeing one danger by speeding directly towards another kind, but ever since she'd begun sticking up for herself, danger had been demanding her attention.

The little monsters wouldn't let up. They zigged and zagged with frightening urgency around the moon-sized boulders, remnants of a planet long-since obliterated. Olivia and the Jin were trapped. Leaving the cover of the asteroids meant there would be nothing protecting them from the little grey monsters who were willing to give their lives for her capture. Olivia tasted the panic rising from her stomach. She wanted to get away from these monsters, no matter what the cost.

We need to get far enough away that they can't find us, NOW!

The ship lurched downward, dropping below the asteroid belt. The moment they were clear of the minefield, the engines went into hyper-speed. The sun, still a visible star from the asteroid belt, vanished. The planets Olivia could name vanished. The saucer swarm was nowhere in sight. Surrounded by a black sky dotted with millions of twinkling stars, the ship stopped as effortlessly as if it had just been puttering along.

Olivia's stomach was all kinds of twisty. The Jin pulled each other up off the floor, their little mouths agape like doughnut holes.

Our ship obeys as you command.
How can this be? You are not Jin.
You have now shown abilities
from three out of The Twelve.

"The Twelve… Does that have something to do with the twelve pools I saw when I flinched with you?"

You saw as the Yanisma see:
you found an ancient memory
so far removed that us three kin
have never seen its truth.

"How did those monsters know I was on your ship?"

They likely saw the beacon that you sent up now three times.

This beacon again. Migitju had told her to keep the flinching a secret, so instead she'd gone and lit up the sky with a neon sign that led the monsters right to her? She had to get control of herself.

"What is guideline number twelve?"

You brought us here with beacon bright;
your life is clearly under threat.
We choose to break galactic rules
to save a Terran life.
It is of great concern to us
that Greys know where the Terrans live.
They were not meant to find this place;
they must have come to interfere.
And now they seek you, Terran child
because you have the gift of sight,
because you take command of light.
They are prepared to start a war
to claim you as their own.

"Wait, did you say 'start a war'?"

We must take action straight away,
there is no time to wait.

Three golden bodies turned, a trio of synchronized swimmers. As they approached the wall, a door opened where no door had existed. Olivia jumped up to follow as the path ahead, bathed in blackness, lit up to greet them; a cocoon of light followed them as they moved. They didn't seem to be running, but she couldn't actually see their legs, shrouded under long robes that swished against the floor. When Olivia finally caught up, she was shocked by their height. Looming over her, they had been imposing, but now that she was on her feet, their frosting-swirl hair barely reached her shoulders.

As they faced the wall to their right, it sensed them and opened, revealing a laboratory in complete disarray. Test tubes, Petri dishes, Bunsen burners, vials, tongs, and a myriad of other scientific equipment littered the floor, tossed around during the chase. The Jin busied themselves with cleanup, replacing the items with care on the empty workbench, and Olivia took the opportunity to explore the alien lab.

Four of the six walls were brightly lit, draped with sheer green curtains. But upon closer inspection, Olivia noticed that these weren't curtains made of fabric but plants draped from the ceiling. One vine, dotted with small yellow flowers, split off into smaller and smaller vines until they were no more than threads. It looked like a tree in the winter; all branch and no leaf. But as she drew closer to investigate, an abundance of broad, flat, transparent leaves appeared, encasing and protecting the intricate web of green veins. Once she was aware of them, they were impossible to ignore. Their glassy surfaces glinted all around her.

A thick vine nestled among the transparent leaves sensed her presence and bristled outward, sending a mass of spiky quills in her direction. As long as she stayed close, the porcupine plant stood at attention, ready to defend against the curious and the hungry. This vine was not the only plant that reacted to her proximity. As she moved along the wall, a braided curtain pull sprang to life. It unfurled, revealing thousands of filaments as fine as strands of hair. They reached for her, twisting around and around like corkscrews. Their movement was hypnotic. Olivia lost herself in the swirly dance that twisted around…and around…

We must return you to our hive
to keep you safe, and tell our queen
the project now involves the Greys:
the end result may not be clean.

Olivia snapped out of her trance and jumped back, free of the plant's hypnotic spell. The filaments relaxed and settled back into the braided cord. Alien plants were interesting enough, but their caretakers were infinitely more fascinating.

"You're taking me to your hive? I'm going to meet Jin royalty?"

It is not safe to take you back.
Our ship is not equipped for war.
We're duty-bound to save your life:
you are too precious to ignore.

It was overwhelming to find someone who finally cared about her safety, but heading into outer space with aliens she'd just met was nothing like going cross-Canada. What if she got trapped and couldn't come back? But the Greys would help Retchen find her. They'd found her tonight, even on this ship. Even the Jin were scared of them. The vastness of outer space was her best hiding spot.

They ushered her toward a giant snow globe perched on stilts at the far end of the lab. It was both beautiful and mysterious.

This globe is called a quantagate.
This gate is how we travel home.

It was a dazzling centrepiece, but it didn't look like an escape pod. It had no chairs, no control panel. It was empty. Olivia chewed on the inside of her cheek. "This ship is nice and reliable. Let's just take the ship."

Thank you, crew member number four. The voice that answered was nothing like the Jin; it came from the ship.

"Call me Olivia."

Thank you, Olivia. Should I prepare a hibernation pod?

"Why would I need to hibernate?"

The Jin hive exists in the Pleaides, four hundred light-years away. I can travel much faster than the speed of light, but it would rip your fragile biosystem to shreds. Since we are limited to the speed of light, it will take us four hundred years to reach our destination.

"Whoa. So, if we go by bubble, how long does it take?"

When travelling by quantagate,

we land as soon as we depart.

"You mean, we leave here and we're instantly four hundred light-years away? I doubt that."

Have you been taught about a concept called a tesseract?

"Um, is that when you take a cube and cube each of its sides?"

You are so close, but not correct.

The cube is an unnatural shape.

List off dimensions that you know.

Begin where life began to grow.

Their golden skin sparkled with excitement as they waited for her answer.

"The first dimension is a point. The second dimension is a line that grows out of that point. The third dimension squares the line." Olivia thought out loud, reciting what she'd learned in geometry.

No, no, no. You must go back.

Dimension one, a point in time.

Dimension two expands from there.

Did life expand along a line?

Or did it expand everywhere?

"The universe started with the big bang. An explosion. So it must have expanded all around."

Because we need to choose a shape,

what shape does logic then dictate?

"A circle?"

And if dimension two is round,

dimension three must therefore be…

"A sphere?" Olivia asked in disbelief. She had never liked school; it had always seemed like they were just filling time. She learned best by reading. But this was huge. This went beyond school; this was a completely different way of thinking. Humans used squares for everything. They built square homes full of square rooms and square windows, laid out on square city blocks.

You have been taught that squares are truth?

"It's in everything we build."

It's not your fault that you believe
when you are told this is the truth.
We left behind so many clues
in standing stones and monuments,
but to your eyes, those clues must be
still shrouded in a mystery.
We understand that it is hard
to recognize what you were taught
was based on incorrect belief.
But it is crucial to your growth
to unlearn what is incorrect.

"Everything we know is based on straight lines. They join together; they form corners. Geometry, architecture, beds, chairs, tables…"

And yet on Terra, land or sea,
you will not find a natural square.
Your sun, your planet: both are round.
The world you see will make more sense
once you adjust your paradigm.

"Wow. Just wow." Olivia's mind conjured images of all the round things that had improved life on Earth. The wheel made it easier to travel. The pulley made it easier to lift heavy objects. The water wheel had harnessed power centuries ago, and now, wind turbines were freeing the world from oil and coal. Life kept getting better, thanks to round stuff!

Now think once more to what you know
about the cosmos up above.
The planets orbit round and round,
the galaxy is spinning too.
Electrons orbit much the same
around an atom's nucleus.
Within dimension number four,

each moment adds another shell.
The quantagate will let us move
across the stars in just one shell,
and that is how time does not pass
despite the distance being great.

"But how does it work?" How could an empty globe take them across the rings of time?

We have two gates, and they are twins;
their quanta linked when they were born.
No matter where we move this gate,
erd will always find erd's mate

Olivia circled the quantagate, studying its surface. It looked like glass, but she couldn't see through it to the other side, and it didn't reflect her face. Meanwhile, AmmaNa checked a curious gadget with dozens of interlocking copper gears and nodded to her crew.

The time is right for us to leave.
Before we go, you need our tech.

She pressed on the wall, and a drawer popped open, revealing two slate-grey beans she popped into Olivia's ears. At first, they were way too big to fit, but the beans came alive and began wriggling forward, stretching themselves until they fit so snugly that Olivia couldn't even feel them.

These buds will translate all you hear
so that you understand your peers.

Peers? The Pleiades had teenage aliens? But before Olivia could ask about this detail, AmmaNa turned to her shipmates. It was the first time Olivia had seen them move independently.

This mission that we undertake
is dangerous for each alike.
This child is precious— worth the risk.
We promise not to leave you here,
but if we are apart too long,
the ship will know to bring you home.
Prepare the hibernation pods.
Engage defend/evade.

The walls turned from white to a deep blue. Two beds appeared from the wall, and AmmaNa's companions climbed in and lay down, crossing their arms. They didn't look like they were hibernating; they looked like dead Aunt Tabitha. Except dead Aunt Tabitha didn't sparkle and was four times their size.

"Why are you going to sleep?"

The Jin exist as hive.

We must have three to thrive.

With only two, we sleep.

"You hibernate? What happens if you're alone?"

We don't exist as one.

If left alone, we're done.

"Don't you ever feel the need to be by yourself, alone with your thoughts?"

We live as a community

or do not live at all.

A crystal shell grew up from the sides of the bed, encasing the Jin. AmmaNa stepped up to the quantagate. Were they really going to teleport four hundred light-years across the galaxy? Was this actually her life right now? Olivia hesitated.

The hibernation has begun.

We must go now for I am one.

AmmaNa stepped into the gate. But what would happen on the other side? Would AmmaNa hit the hive right away, like planetary wi-fi? Would she have to plug in? There were too many unknowns, sending Olivia into a panic. She needed to process all of the possibilities. She needed to ask questions. She needed more time. But the clock had run out of ticks. AmmaNa disappeared. Olivia was alone with the globe. She clenched her fists, took a deep breath, and hissed it out. This plan was full of unknowns, but how bad could it be?

"Goodbye, ship. Thank you for saving us. Time to go make some friends in the Pleiades."

7 SITA, MOON OF BODIE

THOUGH IT LOOKED like solid glass, when Olivia's palm made contact with the quantagate, its skin folded inwards and consumed her hand, pulling her in. In moments, her body was suspended in the jelly, floating forward on the momentum of her last step. Ahead was a black emptiness. From inside the jelly, the outside world didn't exist.

Emerging on the other side felt like being squeezed out of a tube of toothpaste. Unfortunately, her trajectory on the way in dictated her trajectory on the way out, and the only way for Olivia to avoid a face-plant was to tuck into a somersault. AmmaNa's landing required no such acrobatics. Clearly, this wasn't her first trip through the jelly.

The quanta leaves us feeling strange
but is the fastest way to jump.

From this end, the gate radiated just enough glow for Olivia to make out the walls of a cave. AmmaNa felt her way forward, turned a sharp corner, and once again checked her gadget made of clicking copper gears before pulling back a thick curtain of vines.

"Oh, wow!"

Olivia understood how Alice must have felt arriving in Wonderland. One half of the sky was full of stars, closer and brighter than the Sun, as if stepping through the quantagate had caused her to zoom in on the galaxy. The thirty-or-so stars gave off as much light as three full moons, bathing the alien landscape in their blueish-white glow. The other half of the sky was obscured by a nutmeg-coloured planet with huge rings and four visible moons.

We orbit outside Bodie's rings,
as do a myriad of moons.
Five hives exist on other moons,

all loyal to our Queen.

"Is there a hive on Bodie?"

Its soil is rich for growing food
we cultivate to feed our brood.
We cannot stay on Bodie long,
the gravity is much too strong.
We only build a brand-new hive
when we are certain we can thrive.

A moment of calm fell over Olivia. She stood there quietly, in awe of the beauty surrounding her. A majestic pink river separated the path from vast orange fields swaying rhythmically in the warm breeze. She bent down and swirled her hand in the water, releasing a citrusy aroma. The river's colour wasn't the only surprise; the water was warm and inviting, like a fresh bath. She lost herself for a moment, wondering what gave the river its odd colour, and when she looked up, AmmaNa was disappearing over the horizon.

"AmmaNa! Wait up!" Olivia called as she jogged to catch up.

We must make haste to reach the hive.
Without them, I will not survive.
You, too, will be in danger soon,
for once the white star fills the sky,
your flesh will bubble, roast, and fry.
Our golden skin reflects her light
and even we hide from daylight.

"What's this about my skin bubbling and roasting? That detail would have been good to share before we left the ship."

AmmaNa didn't answer. Her pace was brisk, her eyes fixed on the road ahead. Something about her was different. Olivia couldn't tell if it was because of the twilight, but she didn't seem as golden as she had been on her ship. Her skin was no longer sparkling.

"AmmaNa, are you okay?"

We must make haste...

The voice was nothing more than a whisper. AmmaNa's pace began to slow.

"AmmaNa?"

Must reach the hive or I will die.

Her tiny frame buckled. She dropped to her knees.

"AmmaNa!"

All at once, reality slammed into Olivia like a truck. AmmaNa had said the Jin couldn't survive on their own, but she'd split away from her crew to bring Olivia here. She was risking her own life for Olivia's safety.

Olivia bent down, and with AmmaNa clutched to her side, she pressed forward. She pushed the pace as much as she could, but AmmaNa grew heavier with every step. And then, AmmaNa stopped taking steps.

Olivia tried to drag her along, but it was like dragging a duffle bag full of corn. She wouldn't make it to the city in time; she couldn't even see a city yet. The Jin had saved her life today, and Olivia vowed to spend every ounce of energy she had, repaying that kindness.

"Are you strong enough to climb on my back?" Without waiting for an answer, she flipped her backpack around to hang from her chest, dropped to her knees, and pulled the child-sized being on top of her, wrapping her arms under AmmaNa's legs, just like her father had done when she was little, before he'd started hating her.

"Hold onto my neck. Don't let go!" Olivia leaned forward, balancing AmmaNa's little body on her back, and ran with a determination she had never known before. She was desperate to reach the hive no matter what the cost. She ran as fast as her legs would move, and when she felt AmmaNa's body go limp, she somehow found the strength to run even faster. Up ahead, glints of blue sparkled high in the inky purple sky, but Olivia didn't see them.

She refused to acknowledge the burn in her legs or her lungs, missing the outline of the city as it emerged from the twilight. She was so focused on running that she almost ran into a wall, stopping only a few paces short. High above her, a skyscraper towered into oblivion, made entirely of crystal. There was no way in; the path ended at a smooth crystal wall flanked by ornate carvings of bees pollinating flowers. She tried to scream for help, but her lungs refused to work, overwhelmed from the sprint. She pounded her fists on the wall.

AmmaNa, still draped over her back, was motionless.

Desperate, Olivia searched for a way in. The wall in front of her looked just like the walls on the Jin ship. Maybe the answer was to be like the Jin. She closed her eyes and focused her thoughts on the wall.

OPEN THIS DOOR OR AMMANA WILL DIE!

The wall slid aside, revealing a tunnel into the crystal mountain. Olivia stumbled over the threshold and careened headlong into a small army of Jin. She dropped to her hands and knees, presenting AmmaNa's lifeless body, praying that she wasn't too late.

Please help her.

The Jin reached down and lifted their sister off the strange red-haired creature who had found a way into their city. AmmaNa's limp body twitched as her lungs took in a small breath.

"We made it," Olivia whispered. "We made it to your hive. You can wake up now."

But AmmaNa didn't wake up. Her chest rose and fell ever so slightly, but her eyes remained shut, and the gentle voice to which Olivia had become accustomed was silent.

"AmmaNa, you have to be okay." Tears flowed down Olivia's cheeks. *Please help her.*

All at once, the Jin pointed at her, their faces angry, accusing. A horrible screech blasted into her mind like a train's brakes screaming against metal rails, sparks flying in protest.

"Stop!" she cried, clutching her ears.

But they didn't stop. The noise grew louder and louder until her brain refused to work any longer and she collapsed into darkness.

WHEN OLIVIA CAME to, she ached all over, her head still throbbing from the awful scream. She went to rub her temples, but she couldn't move her hands more than a few millimetres before they hit something solid. She tried to roll over, but she was pinned down. She couldn't even turn her head. Every movement was interrupted by the same solid shell. She was trapped, encased in a crystal cocoon.

Outside, a Jin face glared at her. Its expression was nothing like the warm greeting she'd received back on Earth. And sure, arriving with AmmaNa on the verge of death would raise concerns, but the Jin were telepathic. Surely they could understand that she was trying to save AmmaNa's life.

You came in through the quantagate.
The Jin would only use that gate
if faced with ultimate distress.
We never would have brought you here
unless our lives were under threat.
You could be friend, you could be foe.
There is no way for us to know.
Until we can assimilate,
your pod will stay on hibernate.

The voice carried the reprimand of an angry parent, wary of her child's new friend. Pretty standard mama-bear stuff. And with a mama bear involved, this wasn't going to turn out well for Olivia if AmmaNa didn't recover.

The golden face vanished.

Olivia lay trapped, a fly waiting for the spider to return. Panic churned in her stomach. The more she tried to fight it, the more the panic swelled, creeping up her throat. She couldn't be sick, not while she was a prisoner in this shell. She inhaled deeply and exhaled slowly, growing roots down through her feet, her back, and her head, like a toppled tree demanding to survive. The roots connected her to the moon, to her ancestors, to her own sense of calm. The panic subsided, giving her the focus she needed to plan her escape.

The prison holding her was made by the Jin. It followed that the only way to get out was to think like them. Since the Jin did everything by telepathy, maybe escaping this cocoon was as simple as thinking the right command. What was the opposite of hibernation mode?

Wake-up mode. Pod, wake up. Pod, activate wake-up mode.

Nothing happened. Maybe she was overcomplicating things. What did she really want?

Open this pod.

Inches from her face, the shell splintered into a complex

latticework. Individual crystals turned and climbed over each other like a million ants skittering away from a predator until the cocoon had completely disappeared into the bed beneath her. Watching this behaviour up close was amazing. She understood: the crystal was alive.

Freed from her prison, Olivia jumped up and hunted for AmmaNa. Her friend was resting peacefully in the next pod over. Olivia gave the command, and the crystal cocoon skittered away. The sparkle had returned to AmmaNa's skin, and her antennae swayed rhythmically back and forth.

"AmmaNa, are you okay? AmmaNa, please, you have to wake up. I'm all alone. I don't know anything about your world." She nudged her friend's arm gently a few times, but AmmaNa didn't respond. Olivia chewed on her cheek, the gravity of her situation feeling much heavier than AmmaNa's limp body ever had. She didn't know anything about the Jin. What if being alone had damaged AmmaNa forever? What if she couldn't wake up?

Olivia shivered. Beyond her, the room housed rows upon rows of pods. It was creepy to walk amongst the cocoons. Some were occupied by fully grown Jin, and some contained tiny Jin that were still developing. Less of a prison and more of a hospital wing, but without any nurses.

Olivia returned to her friend's side and gave her golden hand a squeeze; she didn't know what else to do.

If you can hear me, hurry up and get better, okay?

She let go of the small hand with only three fingers and a thumb, placing it tenderly back next to its unresponsive owner.

Engage hibernation mode.

As quickly as it had opened, AmmaNa's cocoon skittered back into place.

Olivia's stomach growled. Searching the edges of the room, she found a buffet table full of trays piled high with lumps of honeycomb. Hunger took over and she helped herself, assuming this was likely a first meal for Jin waking up from hibernation. The honeycomb pieces looked solid, but when she picked one up from the tray, it melted into a gooey, gluey mass of honey, oozing over her hand like a fresh batch of slime. It was messy, but delicious! Her taste buds knew the fruitiness of blueberry honey and the tang of cranberry honey, but this honey was next level. This tasted like bees had pollinated a maple-flavoured peach. The strange sensation on her tongue sent a rush of energy to every corner of her body and left her buzzing and wanting more. For her second attempt, she squatted low enough to pop the honeycomb directly from the tray to her mouth. As it melted in her mouth and not in her hands, the fatigue in her muscles from carrying AmmaNa evaporated. In moments, she was better than new. Her mind felt clearer and calmer than it ever had.

As she assessed her situation, she came to the inevitable conclusion that she was utterly alone, stranded on a planet in a far-away star system, in the lair of a host who saw her as a threat. Her only ally was in a coma. Things were bleak. She was very likely in danger. She needed to get out of here. She needed a door.

She walked the perimeter of the room, studying her prison. The walls radiated enough light to see clearly, just like the ship, but as dragged her hand along the crystal, it glowed brighter under her touch and made her hand tingle in the same way that her tongue had tingled from the honeycomb.

How did that work? Where was the light coming from? Were the walls all made of these tiny, skittering crystals? Much of it felt jagged, but when she reached the section next to the table, a hexagonal patch felt smooth like glass. It reminded her of the wall that had blocked her entrance into the city. She faced it and focused her thoughts.

Open.

Just as the cocoons had, the wall obeyed, skittering away to reveal a small alcove. The alcove opened onto a concourse that wrapped around a massive cavern, home to a thunderous pink waterfall. She poked her head out to examine the falls, and her face was immediately wet from its mist. The water plummeted into oblivion far, far below, generating a low, continuous rumble that vibrated up through her body. Beyond the concourse, an endless honeycomb of hexagonal windows, some with balconies and some without, wrapped around the waterfall. The layers of windows stretched upwards, continuing past the vanishing point. Some were connected with staircases, and others were isolated. But as she marvelled, Olivia noted a repeating pattern in the construction of the stairwells. It would have been beautiful to stand and stare at its majesty—if she had been a welcome guest.

She followed the concourse around the waterfall, feeling and asking for another door, but with no luck. None of the stairs came to this level, either. She did find multiple spots where an archway opened up to the cavern and a long drop if one were to slip. Two of these archways opened to a platform overlooking the waterfall, but even the platforms were dead ends. They brought her a few steps closer to the waterfall, but no closer to freedom.

Standing on one of these platforms, Olivia gripped the railing and peeked over. The water fell into a darkness that went on forever, maybe all the way to the centre of the moon. Above her, a thousand golden bodies buzzed about their daily routines. All at once, they stopped what they were doing, raised their hands, and pointed directly at her.

You had no right to leave your pod.

We must insist that you return.

Go back to the infirmary

and wait for us to come to you.

Spiders crawled up her spine. A thousand Jin, all using one voice, demanded her compliance. She'd come here for protection, but AmmaNa was wrong. The Jin weren't going to protect her. She had to protect herself. Under no circumstance was she returning to their cocoon room.

Above her, the Jin zipped from balcony to balcony using platforms just like the one she occupied. Maybe the platforms operated like the walls. It was worth a shot.

Take me to the surface.

The platform underfoot came to life. It floated up past layer upon layer of the crystal city, passing Jin who pointed angrily as she disobeyed the voice. She went up, up, up, past hundreds of layers of hive, until finally, the lift poked out onto the surface of the moon.

The view was stunning. All Olivia could do was gasp.

8 THE CRYSTAL ACADEMY

OLIVIA RUBBED HER eyes to make sure she wasn't hallucinating. She stood at the edge of a canyon, a gaping wound that ripped five hundred stories down into the moon's belly. The wound stretched across the moon's surface with a cut so wide that from the canyon's floor, its edges had been hidden beyond the horizon. The river, too wide to swim across, now snaked across the canyon floor like a piece of thread. Buildings dotting the orange fields had transformed into grains of rice.

It was the perfect hiding place for a quantagate.

Olivia had found an elevator directly to Bodie's rings. From here, she could see gaps in the rings where three of Bodie's shepherd moons had cleared out enough elbow room in the disk for their orbits. Sita was just beyond the outermost ring but close enough that Olivia could see what it was made of, a miniature asteroid field flowing like a river around the nutmeg planet.

On top of the plateau, a pink lake sprawled away from the canyon. Its surface was calm and glassy right up until it met a crack in the plateau near the lift. There, the lake plummeted into the hive, becoming the waterfall around which the city had been built. Around the vast lake, a ring of pyramids poked their tips through a multicoloured garden of shrubs. Olivia counted twenty-seven peaks in total, much smaller than their Egyptian counterparts, and instead of limestone, they were made of polished white crystal.

She climbed down a small flight of stairs and set off along a path toward the first pyramid. As she drew near, she heard chattering noises, the sound of people socializing. An assortment of beings came into view, gathered near the pyramid's entrance.

She froze. There were so many different…aliens.

She wasn't hallucinating. She was looking at real, live, walking, talking aliens… So many different kinds. She'd seen many of them in a flinch, but her mind hadn't translated that into reality as fully as actually seeing them did. As different as they all were from each other, they all wore the same teal uniform. These were the peers AmmaNa had mentioned, the reason Olivia had translation worms in her ears.

Right. Worms were currently nesting in her ears. All of this was next level. But the worms weren't eating her brain—yet—so she gritted her teeth and decided to go with it. She had to talk to them. She needed allies. Making an ally would greatly improve her chance of surviving on this rock, and though she was shit at making friends, her gut told her this was the best way forward. Her nerves buzzed like an angry hornets' nest, but she'd had lots of practice keeping her cool back home, playing the part she was expected to play.

She shuffled closer to the group and found a blue bush full of indigo teardrop fruit to study while she mustered up the nerve to make eye contact with someone. But the longer she stood there, the more out of place she felt. Everyone else was being social. Everyone else looked like they fit in.

"Whoa. Can you tone down the anxiety?" The complaint came from a curvy being with sparkly skin and gossamer wings poking through its tunic. Its head was a ruffled mess of bright blue hair cropped in a pixie cut.

"Sorry." Olivia's cheeks burned as she backed away.

"What's wrong with you? Cut that out!" The sparkly being recoiled, shielding itself behind a tall boy with broad shoulders.

"Take it easy, Tuatha," he said over his shoulder. "She's obviously new here." The boy sported a long mane of tomato-red hair that also grew from his shoulders and the backs of his arms like fur, covering skin that was a deep shade of orangey-pink. He was definitely related to the red giants she'd seen in her flinch, except that he was only half their size, dwarfing her nonetheless at six feet tall.

"I am Keilte." He bent at the waist in a half bow, his catlike eyes crinkling at the corners with kindness. "Are you a new student in the

Guardian program? Are you joining our pod?"

Olivia tried to act casual. "Um, yeah. I just arrived. Haven't got my uniform yet."

He pointed at the curls sticking out from under her beanie. "We don't have any redheads at the Crystal Academy, other than us Teutons." He ran a large, meaty, fur-covered hand through his own hair and nodded towards his crew. "You can sit with us if you like."

This total stranger was welcoming her to sit with them? Gratitude washed over her like a tidal wave.

"Sparkling stars, you're doing it again! I mean, that one was nice, but for real!"

Olivia didn't want any trouble, but she didn't know what the problem was. "What am I doing wrong?"

Tuatha's voice came from behind Keilte's broad shoulders. "You keep exploding with emotion. It's too much!"

"Deyonns are empaths," Keilte explained. "They can smell our emotions and it affects them, but I've never seen Tuatha like this."

"Oh, sorry. I guess I'm not really in control of my emotions. They just kind of happen. I didn't mean to offend you."

"Ew! Emotions that just happen? Is that contagious?"

"No. I'm not contagious, I was just born this way."

"How can you not be in control of your emotions?" asked a blue-skinned boy with four arms and chocolate eyes. "They're yours."

"Who cares about her emotions?" The rebuke came from a girl whose frosty tone perfectly matched her hair and skin. Her angular features and diamond eyes were striking. "The real question is why are you here? The Guardian program is the most elite training program in the whole galaxy. Nobody joins a Guardian pod halfway through the term."

"The Jin brought me here."

"How touching. The Jin are taking in strays." She threw her pointy nose in the air. "Guardians aren't strays. Only the most talented among us are given the opportunity to learn from the Masters. We were chosen because we're the best of the best. Strays aren't chosen. They just tag along."

Even though she wasn't Miley Brewster, Olivia couldn't help but see the similarities. Apparently, snotty girls existed everywhere, even on the other side of the galaxy.

"Ho, ho! Princess Frosty-face thinks she's already a Guardian!" Tuatha chided. "You haven't actually been chosen yet. You're still just a student like the rest of us."

"Ignore Kyrrha," Keilte said. "Atlantians don't like anyone who isn't Atlantian."

"Did you say Atlantian? As in, the City of Atlantis?" The similarity piqued Olivia's interest.

Kyrrha lunged at her, stopping only inches from her face. Her milky cheeks turned blue. Olivia could feel the frostbite in her glare. "What do you know about our lost city?"

"Back off, Kyrrha." Keilte pushed his hulking torso between Olivia and the ice princess. "Don't make me put my hands on you."

"Oh, please! I could toss you aside without even trying."

"Where are you from, anyway?" the blue boy asked. "You look Hopi, but they aren't redheads."

"The Hopi?" Olivia was shocked to hear about people from Earth, but of course they knew the Hopi. She was the one who didn't know anything about the galactic community. "I think we're cousins with the Hopi, so to speak."

"They have a lot of colonies. Which one are you from?"

"Easy, Rama. Give her a chance to—"

BONG.

Everyone turned to face the pyramid's doorway. A tall man with long snowy hair and icy skin looked over the teal students with disdain. His sharp, angular features made him twice as severe as Mrs. Hammond. If Kyrrha was Atlantian, he had to be as well. He clapped twice and disappeared back into the pyramid, the pod following quietly and in single file.

"This isn't over, stray," Kyrrha hissed as she pushed to the front of the line.

Keilte and Tuatha waited with Olivia, joining at the end. "She can't stand being overlooked, so just pretend she doesn't exist. It's what she deserves. And don't challenge her in front of Master Eldrin. He dotes on her."

The air changed as Olivia entered the pyramid. It smelled of petrichor, just like Migitju's yard after a rain, and was full of static that she could feel in her hair. It felt like a thunderstorm was about to explode all around them.

Master Eldrin scrutinized the procession of students from his raised podium as they filed in and sat on benches arranged in three horseshoes. Olivia hid in the hulking shadow of her new friend, avoiding Master Eldrin's icy gaze. He clapped twice, and everyone sat. In moments, Kyrrha was back on her feet.

"Yes, Kyrrha?"

"Master Eldrin. It seems that a stray has joined our pod. She says she's supposed to be here, but she doesn't have a uniform. Out of respect for the integrity of the Guardian program, I wanted to make sure that you were aware of this intrusion." She sat again and stared directly at Olivia.

The rest of the class followed her gaze. Great. Just wonderful.

Master Eldrin's angular eyes narrowed in on Olivia, scanning her outfit. "A new arrival. Interesting. Stand."

She stood as ordered, and he sized her up for a long moment with eyes like shards of ice. She held her breath and bit her tongue, not wanting to give him any more reason to dislike her than Kyrrha's bratty introduction had already done.

"What do you call yourself?"

"Olivia. Olivia Carpenter."

"A carpenter?" His tone betrayed his distaste. "We don't teach carpentry at the Crystal Academy."

Kyrrha sniggered loudly enough for everyone to hear but composed herself quickly after a stern look from her elder.

"Oh, I'm sorry. I don't build things. Carpenter is a family name."

"Your family is important enough to have its own name? Interesting. Are you royalty?" The tone of his voice gave away that he didn't believe for one moment that she was royalty and wanted her to admit it. To him, a title held value. Great, more elitism. Keilte had warned her, to be fair.

"I don't believe in royalty. We're all made of the same atoms."

The corners of his eyes twitched, and he pressed his lips together hard enough to make them vanish. Obviously, he did not agree.

"I don't accept new students midway through a term. Explain yourself."

"The Greys tried to kidnap me, so the Jin brought me here for protection."

There was a general gasp, followed by muted whispers. Master Eldrin clapped his hands twice, and the room fell silent.

She swallowed hard, aware she had blatantly left out that she had escaped from her prison in the Jin infirmary and had found this place on her own. It was a calculated risk. She needed help, and if it was a choice between being locked in a Jin prison or pretending to be a new student, she chose the latter.

"I was not informed that I would be babysitting a refugee. Sit."

Her bum hit the seat before he had finished his insult.

"In my class, the rules are simple. When I ask you a question, you stand to answer it. Class began late because I was otherwise detained, and we have already wasted enough time with your arrival. We have lessons to commence. Tell me, new girl, can you name the eleven interstellar tribes of the Pleiades?"

Olivia almost choked. She opened her mouth, but thankfully, Keilte elbowed her lightly before she could speak, nodding at her to stand. She jumped to attention. "No, Master Eldrin, I cannot. This is my first time in the Pleiades, and I have a lot to learn."

"Kyrrha?"

Kyrrha stood and began reciting: "The eleven interstellar tribes of the Pleiades are the Yena from the Alcyone system, the Sau'k from the Sterope system, the Elohi of the Asterope system, the Hyadeans and the Jin from the Merope system, the Taygetans of Tageta, the Solatians of Pleione, the Atlantians of the Atlas system, the Engan from Electra, the Celestes of the Celeano system, and the Maya, also known as the Hopi, of this, the Maia system." Looking very pleased with herself, she took her seat.

"Well done, Kyrrha. Girl With Two Names, I expect you to learn and recite these eleven tribes for our next life studies class. I imagine you can handle a simple list if you're Guardian material. Any questions?" he asked, his icy stare drilling into her soul.

She was still standing, and she had a ton of questions, so she blurted out one that seemed appropriate to the current discussion. "Are there any tribes in the Pleiades that are not interstellar?"

It seemed like a fair question. After all, Olivia had just met her first interstellar beings only a few days ago. But the giggles that rippled across the pyramid told her this was another rookie mistake.

"This quadrant is bubbling with life in every corner, and we, the interstellar tribes, look after all of them, protecting and directing their evolution as needed. How can you be sitting among us and not know this? Where are you from?"

"I—I—I come from a system hundreds of light-years away. I don't know about the Pleiades because I've never had any reason to. That's why I'm here, to learn about—"

But her explanation was cut short as the white walls of the pyramid began flashing red. The pyramid detected an impostor and was raising the alarm to flush her out.

"Time to go." Master Eldrin pointed at the door.

Everyone jumped from their seats and headed for the exit, pushing past Olivia, who was confused by this behaviour and momentarily frozen.

"The lesson's done. Let's go." Keilte pulled her out into the garden, where streams of colour flowed from each of the pyramids. The colours gathered on platforms around the lake that looked much like the one on which she'd arrived, each with a golden escort waiting.

"Is this a fire drill?"

"It's not a drill. Maia's rising. We have to get underground."

9 THE ARCHIVE

"HURRY UP! WE have to go!" Keilte pleaded.

Olivia shook off her bewilderment and followed him through the garden to the closest lift. They crammed onto the platform with the rest of the teal pod, but nothing happened. The lift didn't move. One by one, the other platforms disappeared until theirs was the only one left.

Rama gripped the railing with all four hands. "Where are the Jin?"

"I don't know. They're always here to take us down to the dorms," Master Eldrin replied, confused.

"But you can move the lift, right? Atlantians can move stuff."

"This lift isn't an object; it's part of the moon. Jin technology only works by Jin command."

"I'll fly down and let them know we're stuck," Tuatha offered, fluttering into the hole where the lake became the waterfall.

"Why do we need to get underground?" Olivia asked quietly, not wanting to annoy Master Eldrin any more than she already had by joining his pod and claiming two names.

"Maia, the star that we orbit, is rising. Her rays are hot enough to melt flesh. If we don't get underground, we'll be roasted alive."

"Has…has that ever happened?"

"The golden skin of the Jin people reflects light, and even they hide."

"Yeah, their skin survives, but their insides melt," Rama added, his voice squeaking.

Olivia thought of the little bag of chocolate coins she'd forgotten on the dash of Ol' Red last May. Despite being in the sun all weekend, they looked just fine, but when she peeled back the foil, the coin inside had been reduced to a puddle of chocolate goo. She shuddered. What if she hadn't joined a pod? What if she had wandered off, like she used to do back home?

"How long do we have?"

"Long enough to get underground safely. Not long enough to wait around for help. Now stop asking questions and let me think," Master Eldrin snapped. "I could try shearing the lift away from the rock, but if I can't manage this much weight, we'll plummet to our deaths anyway."

"Normally, the Jin escort each pod to the dorms," Keilte whispered. "This lift shouldn't be on the surface without a Jin to run it."

"I saw stairs. Can't we take the stairs?"

"The stairs don't reach the surface."

"What's taking Tuatha so long?" Rama whined, his panic having raised his voice by an entire octave.

"Everyone stay calm."

With thousands of Jin roaming this city, surely one could be found to help. But maybe this was purposeful. Maybe the Jin refused to bring the platform down because they wanted to keep her on the surface, to turn her into a pile of goo.

No. She wouldn't go out like this.

Hoping that everyone was too distracted to notice, she looked down, closed her eyes, and focused on the platform.

Take us to the Guardian dorms.

The platform came alive, floating gently down into the honeycomb city and its promise of safety.

"Tuatha must have found help," Olivia told Rama, purposefully seeding the idea in his head. Back on Earth, rumours had a way of confusing the truth if they infected enough people before the facts emerged. Maybe the same would work on Sita.

"Well done, Tuatha!"

"Tuatha saves the day!"

Olivia watched over the side of the lift as the massive, hexagonal honeycomb swallowed them deeper and deeper, back into the belly of this hive full of Jin who wanted to lock her up. The platform slowed to a halt, and the students dismounted quickly, keen to relay the traumatic story of their near brush with Maia to all who would listen. Only Master Eldrin and Keilte hung back.

Master Eldrin's eyes narrowed as he studied her. "Do you even know where your pod lives?"

After her treatment by the unwelcome party at the front door, Olivia had planned to ditch this place at her first opportunity, but apparently, sleeping rough in the fields was not an option on Sita. It was a rookie mistake to think this place was just like Earth and that she could roam as she pleased.

Master Eldrin interpreted her silence correctly. "Fine. Follow me."

With Keilte tagging along, Master Eldrin led her into a massive complex of tunnels and chambers, all cut into the crystal. While the central chamber had the vibe of a hive, the academy's living spaces reminded her of an ant farm she had seen in cross section, thrumming with excited chaos. Skirting quickly through a common room, he brought them to a long hallway decorated in flourishes of teal.

"Do you have any questions?"

She had so many, but the last question had been a disaster. Staring at the floor, she shook her head. No questions.

"The first days are pretty overwhelming, Master Eldrin. I'll help her get settled in."

Relieved of his duty to get Olivia situated, Eldrin strode away in a swirl of white capes.

Keilte brought her to an unoccupied room at the end of the hall and showed her how to close the door via a panel embedded into the crystal. "I'll let you get sorted," he offered, ducking out.

Privacy.

Maybe now she could relax. Every inch of her body had been fuelled by adrenaline since she'd woken up in a crystal prison. She tried to plant her feet and grow roots to release the panic overwhelming her other senses, but growing roots on Sita wasn't at all like growing roots back home. The crystal gave her nothing. Frustrated, she went back to the basics with some of Migitju's deep breathing, and once she had created some peace, she took a look around.

The space was comfortable, larger than a hotel room, with a bed in the corner, a study nook, and a private bathroom. Best of all, it wasn't full of Jin hibernating under sparkly prisons made of skittering crystal.

In the bathroom, a steady flow of pink water flowed from a hole in the ceiling to a fixture shaped like a lampshade. It poured out over the fixture, splashing to the floor in a wide circle, where it swirled around and disappeared into another hole. It made sense: since the city was built around a waterfall, some of that flow was diverted to personal quarters for use.

Grateful for solitude that didn't involve a cocoon, Olivia helped herself to the longest shower ever. It was the perfect place to contemplate her new reality.

The galaxy was full of aliens far more advanced than humans. Last week, she would have laughed at the idea of an alien university, but here she was now, hanging out with intelligent life on the other side of the galaxy. She needed to learn more about how humans were connected to the star people, about why she could flinch and why she could command Jin tech. Where did these powers come from, and why did she have them? She recalled that in her flinch with AmmaNa, the Jin had behaved like midwives, plucking the babies from the birthing pools while everyone else watched. Did aliens even need midwives?

Too many thought-tangents.

Focus, Olivia. Focus.

The Crystal Academy had to have a library. She needed to find it and start her research. Surely it would have translation technology that would allow her to read alien languages. The worms in her ears worked perfectly.

Digging around in a cupboard, she found a simple linen tunic and pants dyed teal. Made to fit a student twice her size, her reflection drowned in folds of cotton. She bunched the extra fabric up as much as she could with the help of a belt, and though she still looked foolish, at least now she matched the rest of her pod. Small victories.

Feeling refreshed, she ventured into the hallway and almost tripped over Keilte, who was sitting on the floor with a small crystal torus perched in his hand. Light swirled above it, changing patterns as he flexed his fingers.

He grinned. "You look fantastic dressed like one of us."

"Not really. This tunic is huge."

"That is why I waited. You need a Teuton to help make it fit."

The light swirling above his torus intensified, and Olivia was so spellbound by its beauty that she didn't notice her clothing shrinking until her tunic and pants fit her perfectly.

"Whoa, what the heck?"

"My people can harness energy and use it to transform matter. Matter becomes energy, energy becomes matter. Soon, you will be able to do this transfer, too. That is what we come here to learn—the mastery of universal law."

"Wow. Thanks. And I'm really glad you're still here, because I have to get Master Eldrin's assignment done. Is there a place where I can do some research?" It seemed like a plausible excuse.

"We have a whole research level. Come on, I'll take you."

He led Olivia away from the symphony of social commotion back towards the lift and the rumble of the waterfall. They took the concourse past three archways, then made a sharp right turn into an alcove. A stairwell shrouded in darkness suddenly lit up when his foot hit the first step.

"The same thing happened on the Jin ship, like the walls sensed our approach."

"The crystal is home to tiny living organisms. They give off light, amplified by the prismatic nature of their homes."

He led her past a series of rooms, some occupied, some vacant, the whole place as quiet as midnight. "This is where we come to study," he explained. "We have access to this entire level by stairways. The next level up is where the Masters live, but that level is off-limits unless you're invited. Since you need to learn the basics of our galaxy, including memorizing the eleven interstellar tribes of the Pleiades, I brought you to one of the astronomy research rooms."

Olivia sighed. Except for a table near the wall, the room was empty. This looked nothing like a library. "No books?"

"I thought you wanted to do research. What would you need a book for? We have plenty of books in the reading room, but… I'm confused."

"Oh, well, where I come from, if you want fast information, you get it from the web, but if you want to make sure it's true, you have to look it up in a book."

"We keep all of our knowledge in the archive. Let me show you." Keilte sat at the lone table. "You put your hand on the panel and ask the archive to show you whatever you need to learn. Archive, display the Pleiades cluster."

The room dimmed, and a hologram appeared, filling the air with bright blue stars floating around their heads. From Earth, only seven stars of the Pleiades were bright enough to be seen without a telescope, but now that she was standing in the middle of an accurate hologram, there were too many stars to count.

"Wow. How many stars exist in the Pleiades cluster?"

"The Pleiades cluster comprises 113 stars."

Olivia had meant the question for Keilte, but the answer came from the archive.

"That's so freaky. That's the same voice on the Jin ship."

"What is freaky is that you can run the archive without touching the panel." His hand was still resting on the table, a dim glow emanating from beneath his palm. "How do you do that?"

He took his hand off of the panel. "Archive, display Teutonia." Nothing happened. He stared at her, waiting for an answer.

"I don't know, Keilte. Maybe there's a certain tone to my voice that resonates with the archive." It was a flimsy excuse, but she'd never been very good at inventing lies on the spot.

"Right. It must be a random coincidence. Like how you ended up on the surface without an escort. You came without a little cluster of Jin to introduce you to our pod, and then, when we needed to get below ground, our platform was already on the surface with no Jin pilot."

Olivia wasn't prepared for this direct confrontation.

A beast fighting for a bone, he pushed harder. "Tuatha was unable to find any Jin to help us. Either that lift moved all on its own, or the new girl is able to command Jin tech."

"Master Eldrin said only the Jin can command Jin tech," she tried to deflect, but he wasn't having it.

"Master Eldrin thinks just because Atlantians cannot master the ways of the Jin that nobody can."

"Has anyone ever done it?"

"We all get Jin abilities when we eat from the Tree of Life, but it only lasts five minutes."

Great. Could this get any more complex? She knew nothing about this place, and she'd almost melted trying to go it on her own. An ally would make her life much easier. Maybe Keilte could be that ally. So far, he'd been nothing but kind and helpful. If she confirmed what he already seemed to know, she could earn his trust instead of his suspicion. Trying to fly solo wasn't working. Pushing through the anxiety and trusting him was just something she had to do. Was this what adulting felt like?

"Okay, you're right. I can run Jin tech. They created my people, so maybe that's why." The Jin hadn't actually told her that they'd created humans, but the flinch was pretty clear.

"Whoa!" His voice dropped to a whisper. "The Jin are forbidden from creating life without the Council's permission. It was their big concession in the Treaty of the Twelve. You could be an illegal entity!"

"What happens to illegal entities?"

"They get shipped off to the fringe colonies."

The way he said it made the back of her neck prickle. Was that why the Jin wanted to keep her locked up in their infirmary? But she couldn't be an illegal; the science fair in the flinch was as well attended as a grad party. Why would the Jin hide a species that everyone already knew about? She had to nix this rumour before it even started.

"The Jin didn't make my people in secret. I know that for sure."

"Whatever the reason you can run Jin tech, your secret is safe with me. Best not to tell anyone else, though. If Kyrrha finds out, she will use it against you. And watch out for Rama. His questions are hard to dodge."

"Thanks. This is a lot to unpack. Until a few days ago, I didn't even know there were other people in the galaxy. The people in charge of my planet claim that we're the only intelligent life in the universe."

"Seriously? What systems have they visited?"

"They're still trying to build a base on the next planet over."

"Whoa! Your people are primitives? Messing with a primitive colony is against the rules. The Jin must have had special permission to bring you here. Look, you can do what you want, but I would keep this a secret, too." His warning was meant to protect her, but it made her feel like she was somehow less than the rest of them.

"I'm going to hate myself for asking, but is there anything worse than being a primitive?"

"There is nothing wrong with being a primitive. It just means you still have much to learn. But if Kyrrha finds out, she will have you expelled. Primitives are not evolved enough to join the Guardian program."

"But you're not going to turn me in?"

"Normally I would. It is against the rules." He thought quietly for a long moment. "I will have to pretend that I am unaware of this detail. Your people are on the verge of becoming interstellar, you just arrived at the Crystal Academy a little early. I mean, it would be an entirely different bag of brackle if you came from Terra." The lilt in his tone said he was half joking, but the hairs on the back of Olivia's neck bristled to attention. AmmaNa had called her a Terran child.

"What's the deal with Terra?"

"In ages past, when Terra was discovered, the Council claimed it as a protected refuge. Then something happened... I do not remember what, but it was serious enough that Terra became a forbidden planet. The Council erased it from the star maps to stop anyone from finding it. As kids, we told ghost stories about Terra."

That had to be why the Jin wanted to keep her hidden. But what could possibly have happened on Earth to make them want to hide it from the universe? Until she knew why, she wasn't telling anyone where she came from. She needed to redirect. She reached over to put her hand on the panel. "Archive, where are we right now?"

The hologram spun around Olivia's head, bringing a large, bright blue star to the centre of the room. Seven planets orbited Maia. As the third planet out, Bodie seemed like it was a good distance from its parent, but it was still completely dwarfed by the star. The hologram brought one of Bodie's nine moons to the forefront. It was currently on the bright side of the planet, heading towards Maia. It would be a while before they spun back into Bodie's shadow. No wonder everyone hid underground. Maia was both shocking and beautiful.

A cloud of blue surrounded the star in a haphazard way, like it was trying to escape, and Olivia reached into the hologram, pulling her fingers through the halo. She was shocked to find that the entire hologram was interactive, her hand leading its movement. She grabbed for other stars, pulling them in only to throw them away again. As she did, the entire map moved, each star, each planet fixed in relation to all others. She grabbed for Maia again and pirouetted around the room, pulling Maia with her, the entire Pleiades spinning at her whim. Keilte could only stare, entranced as she danced with the star cluster as her partner.

"This technology is so beyond!"

It wasn't until she stopped dancing that she noticed Keilte staring, like he'd never seen anyone dance before. Weird. Something to ask him about. But not now. Now, she had research to do, and she wasn't going to be able to ask her most pressing questions with him listening. It was time to drop the fun and put on the mask of a dutiful student.

"Archive, display details of the eleven interstellar tribes of the Pleiades." The hologram zoomed back out to show the entire cluster of 113 stars. Rings of light appeared, highlighting ten of them. Across the wall, the archive projected the names of the tribes, colour-coded to the highlights. "It's time to hunker down and study. Thanks for being super helpful."

"Just remember to use the panel...in case someone's watching."

Olivia went through the tribes in the order they appeared on the wall. She didn't understand the writing, but once she figured out that the archive could read everything aloud, her ear worms translated the information wonderfully. She repeated the details of each tribe out loud as she circled their planets in the hologram, trying to learn the place of each one in relation to the others instead of just memorizing a list of strange-sounding words. When she reached the last tribe, the Maya, also known as the Hopi, she couldn't help but dig deeper. She sat at the bench and placed her hand on the panel, heeding Keilte's warning. As the new girl, it was likely that others would be curious about her. She had to guard her secrets.

"Archive, display images of the Hopi, native to the Maia system."

A hologram appeared above the panel. Olivia almost choked on her own tongue. The names this tribe used weren't the only familiar things about them. They looked exactly like images she'd seen of the indigenous people of Arizona; the women even wore their long hair twisted up on the sides of their heads like satellites. This couldn't be a coincidence.

"Archive, have the Hopi ever sent colonies to other star systems?"

"There are fifteen Hopi colonies in the galaxy." A list appeared of planets orbiting stars she'd never heard of.

"Archive, display the list visually, using the Pleiades as a central point."

The Pleiades hologram shrank to the centre of the room, making space to include many other star systems. The Hopi colonies spread away from Maia in all directions, highlighted with a halo corresponding to the same colour in the list. But strangely, the fifteenth colony in the list didn't get a colour. It also didn't have a planet or star system listed in its details.

"Archive, highlight the location of this fifteenth colony in the holographic map." A dot lit up, in the far corner of the room near the floor, the furthest of all of the colonies. With a swipe of her other hand, Olivia pulled the colony towards her. It wasn't in any star system at all; it was just hanging there in empty space. What was a colony doing in empty space?

"Archive, what is the name of the star where this colony is located?"

Something bit her finger, and she instinctively yanked her hand away from the panel. Her fingertip was bleeding. "Archive, what did you do? Why am I bleeding?"

"You requested information that is restricted. We took a sample of your genetic code and compared it to those who are allowed to access this information. You do not have the required clearance. Your access is denied."

It would have been nice to get a warning that she'd need to give a blood sample for that question, but it wasn't a dead end. When a door slams in your face, find a window and pry it open. "Archive, what is the closest known star system to this colony?"

"The closest known star system to this colony is the Centauri system."

She'd heard of Alpha Centauri. It was the closest star to Earth. Terra might have been erased from the star charts, but the Hopi colony was still listed, sitting in a void, a treasure map waiting for anyone who knew where to look. With that question answered, it was time to learn about primitives, something Keilte had called her because her people didn't have interstellar travel.

"Archive, how many primitive tribes are there in the galaxy?"

"This archive only contains information on primitive tribes within this galactic quadrant. There are currently 458,322 primitive tribes in this galactic quadrant. Some have recently harnessed fire. Some have advanced to the Stone Age. Others have evolved to smith tools from metals available in their environments. Four tribes are on the cusp of developing technology that will enable them to harness interstellar travel."

Not wanting another jab to the finger, Olivia peeked over her shoulder to make sure that nobody was watching before asking a question without touching the panel.

"Archive, display information on Project Human."

"Nothing exists in the archive under that heading."

"Archive, display information on humans."

"Humanoids are a supra species of the Milky Way. The humanoid umbrella comprises over one hundred thousand different species in this quadrant and is considered one of the major root tribes of this galaxy. Would you like information on all humanoids, or a specific subset?"

What else could she ask that would help her understand her

origins? So many questions swam around her mind. But as she was considering the next one to ask, she heard heavy footfalls coupled with giggling. Someone was coming.

"Archive, display the eleven interstellar tribes of the Pleiades, just as before."

The display shifted back to her study notes just in time. Tuatha flitted into the room with Keilte close behind. "Are you still working on this? I figured you'd have it memorized by now."

"I can't read whatever language this is, so I had to get the computer to repeat everything for me over and over while I memorized the details by ear. I'm exhausted. I need sleep."

"Aw, come on, Carpenter, you can't tap out yet. Everyone's waiting to meet you."

10 THE SEER

"COME ON, CARPENTER. If you want to be one of us, you have to show up. Everyone's curious about the new girl." Tuatha couldn't help but add a wink. "Me included."

Being invited to attend social gatherings was new territory. The only party she'd been invited to in Swift Current was Miley's sixth birthday in grade one. Olivia had begun the day excited at the prospect of making new friends but quickly learned that her only purpose was to be a stooge for Miley to humiliate. This invite felt different, but it still meant that all eyes would be on her, and that sounded like a lot of work.

"How long do we have to stay underground?" Olivia tried to sound lighthearted.

"Daylight lasts for twenty hours, and then we spin away from Maia. Twilight lasts another four hours, and then we orbit back to the dark side of Bodie. The dark side is the best side, because you can see out to the rest of the Pleiades. Right now, we are four hours in."

"It seems like a really dangerous place to build a school."

"Being this close to Maia deters intruders because you can only approach at specific times. It helps with security, but our proximity to Maia is also functional. The organisms in the crystal absorb light and store it to power the city. Look around."

As on the Jin ship, light radiated from the walls themselves.

Keilte and Tuatha easily navigated the tunnels back to the teal dorms and then beyond into a large common area offering six distinct places to socialize and play. Two other hallways, one decorated in coral and the other done in buttercup, also fed into this lounge. On either side of the massive social space, a large archway led into another common lounge, and beyond it, another.

"Our dorms wrap all the way around the falls and the common rooms wrap around the dorms. Each one has its own vibe. One of them is even full of books."

"Oooh! Is Carpenter a bookworm?"

"I enjoy a good read. Even brought a few with me." She patted her backpack, relaxing a little. As they entered the large room, she eyed a spread of delicious-looking fruit set out on a table against the wall. Would it taste anything like the honeycomb?

Tuatha grabbed a bunch of yellow pancake-shaped fruit on a vine and began munching.

Keilte stopped. "Are you hungry?"

"Yes. How do I pay? What do you use for money?"

"What is money?"

"You know, whoever worked to grow and harvest the food has to get paid so they can buy other things that they need."

"The Jin grew this food. They have everything they need. Why would they need a…money?"

"So they can go on vacation, or buy a bigger house, or nicer clothes."

"You're a strange bird, Carpenter. Everyone has plenty. Nobody needs bigger or nicer."

"Here." Keilte picked up a large piece of burgundy fruit for himself and one for Olivia. He popped the top off and showed her how to peel back the skin to get at the flesh. Her taste buds did pirouettes, and her belly responded with a happy gurgle.

"The Jin eat delicious fruit!"

"This is not Jin food. They grow this for us."

"What do they eat?"

"Queen Tara eats honey made by the bees on this moon, and the rest of the Jin feed on her energy through the crystal. They absorb it through their hands."

"What, like they touch the wall and power up?"

"That is an interesting way to describe it, but yes. They power up quite often."

"I thought the power in the crystal came from Maia."

"As with all life systems, theirs has many parts that all work together. We will be learning the details this semester in Master Eldrin's life studies class."

So the honeycomb in the infirmary was reserved for the Queen? Whoops. Olivia followed as they wove through a maze of vibrantly clad bodies—around a group in emerald playing a three-dimensional card game, past a mix of violet and peach animatedly bouncing a ball around a grid on the floor. When they reached the far end of the lounge, close enough to see the activities in the next lounge over, they joined the familiar faces of the teal pod in a corner full of comfy chairs with fluffy pillows. Rama pounced before Keilte even had a chance to say hello.

"Everyone wants to know where you're from."

"Whoa, Rama. She was almost melted on her very first day. Give her room to breathe, okay? Everyone, this is Olivia. Let us all be mindful of how hard it is to be the new kid."

Olivia sat, dozens of eyes assessing her. Even Tuatha's gaze was steady and full of curiosity. "Hey, everyone." She added a weak-ass wave and immediately regretted it. She was more than a little grateful when Rama's questions resumed.

"We've never seen anyone like you at the academy. You look kind of like the Hopi, but your hair looks like a Teuton's. Where are you from?"

It was the same question he'd asked in front of the pyramid, but this time he'd included observations about how she looked, making the question even harder to dodge. Clever. Very clever.

"My planet is hundreds of light-years from here. We're probably so far away you've never heard of us."

"I doubt that. Vegans have colonies all over the galaxy. We know everyone. Back in the Vega system, we have a saying: If we don't know you, you don't exist."

Olivia looked at her hands to make sure she was real. "Well, obviously, I exist. You'll have to let them know their saying is wrong."

"So, what do you call your planet?"

She knew what they probably called it, which meant it was unlikely they knew her home by the human name. "We call it Earth."

"You named your planet after dirt?"

"Technically, earth is more than just dirt. It's full of organic matter."

"Okay, so you named your planet after compost? Not much better."

"I didn't name the planet. But apparently you haven't heard of it. Like I said."

Rama was confused. "Well, what star does your planet orbit?"

"We call it the sun."

"But every star is a sun. You named your star, star?"

"Soooo basic." Kyrrha couldn't pass up an opportunity to pull focus. "So, if you came from hundreds of light-years away, how did you get here?"

She was baiting, trying to cast doubt on Olivia's story to trap her in a lie. But her question told Olivia that not everyone arrived here the way she had. Kyrrha had unwittingly given Olivia the opportunity to pull focus right back.

"The Jin brought me through their quantagate."

Rama's lungs squealed as he sucked in a breath. He was the loudest, but he was not the only one who inhaled a tone of surprise. He no longer cared that Vegans might not have heard of her; she was suddenly the most interesting thing about being at the academy. Kyrrha crossed her arms, pouting. Her plan had backfired.

"You got to travel through a quantagate? Colour me jealous!" Rama's skin turned green, and Tuatha backed away from him using two fellow students as a shield. "What was it like?"

"It was like being squished through a blob of goo. It didn't hurt at all, but when I popped out the other side, my head was spinning like I'd been on the Tilt-A-Whirl."

Rama's eyes glossed over as he imagined himself moving through a squishy quantagate, and Olivia saw her opportunity to take control of the conversation. "You ask a lot of questions, so you must know a lot of stuff. Tell me something interesting about the Jin."

"The Jin have a sacred tree. Anyone who eats the fruit is supposed to connect to their hivemind, where they keep everything they know, but it only lasts five minutes. I don't think you can learn much in five minutes."

"Where's the tree?"

"Up on the surface, on an island in the middle of the lake."

She hadn't noticed a tree or an island, but that was an easy thing to miss when surrounded by a garden full of crystal pyramids. If she could get a piece of this fruit, maybe she could learn more about the twelve pools, about where humans came from.

"What's your special talent?" Rama's eyes sparkled. The shadow that passed over Keilte's face was a warning, but Olivia already knew from her short exchange with Rama that she had to give him something. If he wasn't satisfied, he'd just find another way to ask the same thing again.

"I'm really good at fixing machines. I grew up on a farm, and I fix all of the tractors when they break down." Thinking of home made Olivia miss the fields, the graveyard of tractor parts, and of course, her private loft hideaway. She gulped back a swell of homesickness and pushed it deep down, along with thoughts of Retchen's creepy hair and eyeliner eyebrows. "Sorry, Tuatha. That question reminded me of things."

Tuatha nodded, still studying Olivia with intense curiosity.

"Back in the Vega system, we have a saying: Anyone can learn to be a mechanic. But can you do this?" He smiled, winked, and then vanished. One moment he was there, and the next, he was gone. Olivia heard a chuckle coming from the exact place he had been sitting. Moments later, Tuatha appeared.

"Hey, hey, no way! Stop pretending to be me." Tuatha zipped in from Olivia's left, outraged. The copy of Tuatha blinked, and Rama reappeared.

"I can get inside your head, make you think you see me differently, or not at all. Every tribe at the academy has a special talent. Are you one of us, or not?"

And there it was. He had thrown down the gauntlet. Without some kind of special ability, she didn't belong. She couldn't reveal her Jin ability until she understood what it all meant. Migitju had warned her to keep the flinching a secret, but her grandmother had never visited another planet full of interstellar beings. They all had special powers. She had to prove that she belonged here.

"Do you have something personal? Something you've owned for a while?"

From the pouch at his waist, Rama produced a small object that resembled the bottom half of Aladdin's lamp, cut off at the middle, with a pickle sitting upright in the centre.

"I'll be careful, I promise." Olivia took the object into her hands and closed her eyes. She inhaled to the bottom of her lungs, filling her belly, and let it out slowly.

What is your attachment to Rama?

They all watched expectantly, and she could feel their eyes, like the Jin, judging, deciding her worth.

"What is she doing? Nothing's happening."

Olivia's heart drummed in her throat. She tried taking in more breaths, but the flinch wouldn't come. Great. Ever since she'd first learned to flinch, she'd been worried about doing it on autopilot. She'd flinched with Dr. Retchen and AmmaNa by mistake. And now that she needed to, she couldn't do it on purpose? What the heck was the good of having a special ability if she couldn't even use it?

Rama reclaimed the shiveling. "What were you trying to do?"

"I was trying to listen to its story. My grandmother taught me how, but I'm not very good at it, I guess."

"What, like seeing into the past?"

"It's hard to do with everyone staring at me."

"Ha! The girl with two names thinks she's a seer. I told you, Rama. I told you she's an impostor." Of course the galactic version of Miley had to jump on the hate-train.

"I can totally do it without all the pressure."

"Right. Sure. And I suppose they're recruiting a Yanisma Master to help train you. Mmm hmm." Kyrrha burst into laughter. Olivia was done with being social. Tuatha wanted her to come meet everyone, and she'd met that obligation. Being their stooge wasn't part of the deal. She abandoned the pod and headed for the food table, leaving Kyrrha to laugh at dead air.

Keilte joined her. He took his time selecting another piece of fruit, choosing his words just as carefully.

"You held back this information. Did you not feel like you could trust me?"

"I wasn't supposed to tell anyone, but Rama said everyone here has, and I just… I wanted to belong."

He peeled the yellow rind off a pancake-shaped fruit before handing it to her. "Try this one."

She was expecting something tart, like a lemon, but instead, it was sweet and salty at the same time, without being too much of either. Why didn't they have fruit like this back on Earth?

"Keilte, are we friends? I mean, you haven't known me long, but…"

"I barely know you at all."

She chewed uncomfortably, looking at the table, then the floor, then for an exit.

He waved his hand to pull back her attention. "Hey! Of course we are friends, unless you give me a reason to change my mind."

"Why is it such a big deal that I'm a seer?"

He dropped his voice, aware that a few emerald-clad students were perusing the far end of the banquet table, close enough to eavesdrop. "If you really can see the past, it is a big deal because you are not Yanisma. The Yanisma do not teach their abilities to anyone. Kind of like the Jin. That is two for two."

Their conversation was cut short as a trio of Jin appeared at the entrance to the common room.

We seek one named Olivia.

Is she among the Guardians?

Everyone looked around, wondering who would claim the name. If she didn't step forward, Kyrrha would likely tattle anyway.

"I'm Olivia."

We wish to introduce ourselves.

A royal visit is prepared.

Our guards will guide your way.

The message sounded like an invitation, but Olivia knew this was much more like a peaceful arrest than a welcome wagon. What choice did she have? The Jin were waiting. Everyone was staring. She gave Keilte and Tuatha a determined nod and followed the Jin to her doom.

Anxiety bubbled in her veins as the guards led her up a few dozen levels and along a hallway, closing multiple doors as they went. They moved in unison, just as AmmaNa's crew had, but their vibe was anything but welcoming. They brought her to a massive door that opened into the inside of a light bulb. Everything glowed with such intensity that she felt her head begin to pound.

Dim the light, please.

The room complied with Olivia's order, muting the light to a more suitable intensity.

How is it you command our world?

Who taught you how to do such things?

The Queen of the Jin glared down at the disobedient newcomer.

"Nobody taught me. I just think, and stuff obeys."

She was easily ten feet tall, occupying every inch of a massive throne, but aside from her size and her opulent garb, she was identical to AmmaNa. Multicoloured robes flowed from her shoulders like water, concealing some form of armour underneath. Her head sparkled, adorned with a golden crown that reminded Olivia of a pine cone. A swarm of attendants buzzed around her, adjusting her robes, filing her toenails, feeding her. She gulped down chunks of honeycomb like she hadn't eaten in weeks, despite being the most well-fed Jin in the hive. Each time she ate, her throne glowed, the glow eventually fading into the crystal until she helped herself to another gulp. Olivia remembered how the wall had reacted to her own touch after she'd eaten the honeycomb.

You stand before us as a guest.

We are in charge of all you see.

We are not happy that you left

the pod in the infirmary.

You do not understand our ways.
As such, you are not free to roam.
From now on, you will ask us first
and will not venture on your own.

The door to the throne room skittered shut. This queen was nothing like the Jin who had saved Olivia's life. She didn't have a shred of compassion in her bloated body. How could they be so different if they were part of the same collective? Why hadn't AmmaNa told her queen why they'd come here? Olivia searched the golden faces one by one, but if AmmaNa was in the room, she didn't make herself known. It was impossible to tell. They all looked like twins, or triplets, or whatever you were supposed to call thousands of identical siblings.

We do not recognize your kind.
What is the planet you call home?

Suddenly, Olivia thought of the endless fields of gold behind her big, cozy farmhouse. She missed the swishing of the cornstalks as they nudged each other under the full moon. She missed the bright blue orb she had seen from the deck of AmmaNa's ship.

A Terran child? This cannot be.
We vowed we would not interfere.
Why has our captain brought you here?

"For protection." Olivia was about to explain, but Queen Tara had already seen the images.

How did you come under attack?
What happened to provoke this act?

Olivia's mind jolted forward, spinning through the memories of the Greys demanding that the Jin hand over Olivia, her frantic need to escape, and the Jin ship dodging and diving around boulders the size of small islands.

How did you give our ship commands?
Who taught your genes to work this way?

"I don't know the answer."

But Queen Tara wasn't interested in what Olivia had to say. Olivia's mind spun backwards, rewinding at lightning speed back to the moment before AmmaNa beamed her up. The memories came to a lurching halt, then began flipping through each moment like a picture book on fast-forward. The Queen was rummaging through her mind, searching her memories without permission, making her head spin so fast that she couldn't tell up from down.

She felt sick. This needed to stop.

She tried to focus on her loft, or the farmhouse, but the Queen kept moving through her memories back to the ship. So Olivia focused on the only thing she could hold. She focused on AmmaNa, on her large ebony eyes full of compassion. That was what made these Jin different. Their eyes held no compassion, only contempt. Olivia locked onto the memory of AmmaNa's compassion and pushed everything else away. She held tight, and miraculously, it worked. The spinning stopped.

She took a deep breath, trying to calm her churning guts.

What trickery is this you use
to stop our mind from seeing truth?

"You don't have permission to invade my brain. If you want to know something, you can ask me, but you can't just rummage around."

The bloated blob of gold glared down at her.

This is our way. We see the truth.
We do not hear the lie of words.

Once again, the Queen pushed into her memories like a tornado, grabbing everything in its path and churning it up into a dizzying frenzy. Before Olivia could reclaim control, she was reliving the flinch with AmmaNa. She saw the twelve pools where twelve children were born. She saw the Jin bring the children out of their ships. She saw them teach the children to write, to build, to watch the sky.

Olivia's stomach churned as fast as her thoughts. "Stop it!" she cried. "Get out of my head!" Unable to hold back against the vertigo, she sprayed vomit everywhere.

Startled, the Queen let go of her grip on Olivia's mind. A small army of attendants moved in to clean up the mess. Olivia dropped to her knees. The worms in her ears twisted and stretched, intensifying her vertigo. But Queen Tara was not finished.

You saw The Twelve creating life.

How were you able to connect

with memories that are not yours?

Once again, the Queen's probe drilled into her brain, crashing into tender memories and chewing holes through her sanity. This time, before the nausea overwhelmed her, Olivia scrambled up to the throne and grabbed the Queen's ankle.

What project are you running on my home planet?

The throne room exploded into shards of light, and Olivia was sucked through the blackness. She hurtled towards a blue planet, lit by two large, pale-blue stars, each with a smaller reddish companion. She plummeted towards an ocean, where a magnificent city floated on the water. At the top of the tallest tower, twelve beings were gathered around a table. They were the same people present at the science fair.

The Atlantian emissary addressed the group. "The Jin believe they can create what we need. Are there any objections?"

The room was silent.

"Then we are all agreed?"

All around the table nodded.

"Let the record show that all members of The Twelve support the creation of Project Human."

DR. RETCHEN STRAIGHTENED the arms of his cashmere sweater, pulling the sleeves taut from the wrists. Pins all over his map vied for his attention, but he was focused on a pin in eastern New Brunswick. His moment of contemplation was interrupted as his computer beeped and Keelo appeared on-screen, clad in silk and dripping in jewels. Her skin was grey and scaly, her eyes yellow with black slits for pupils. Her smile was both happy to see him and a condescending rebuke.

"So now you're parading around in human-face all the time? Seriously, Yekchen, this is why we don't take you seriously. We only wear human-face when we absolutely have to."

"Did you call to give me fashion advice, or is there an actual reason?"

"Trinity's logs show you performed an extraction. Tell me about the child."

"Jasmine and cloves. What does that mean?"

"Jasmine and cloves? Where?"

"Saskatchewan, Canada."

"You're sure of this? And you have the child?"

"I was too late, but I have her DNA. I can grow a copy."

"Disgusting. I will not eat food grown in a lab."

"What does that smell mean?

"It means that either she's dead or you're still hunting."

"Locals saw a flying saucer. The girl is gone." Retchen tried hard to dampen the impatience in his tone, but he hated having to ask a question more than once. He wanted answers. "What is the significance of jasmine and cloves?"

"It's the smell of a powerful ability from someone who must not be allowed to interfere in this colony. We disabled the star gates for a reason, correct? And all of that work is pointless if jumpers can find another way to get off-planet, yes? Seriously, Yekchen, this is why you aren't awarded real privilege. You can't even handle a simple extraction."

Keelo did not enjoy her duties as a liaison between the court and its staff. She detested speaking to subordinates, answering their questions. She disconnected the call before he could press further, before she could ask whose saucer had taken the girl.

"It's not a simple extraction when the Jin intercept. They would only interfere if the girl had proven to be precious cargo. Trinity, bring up any information you have on the combination of jasmine and cloves."

Without hesitation, Trinity replied. "The combination of jasmine and cloves indicates a seer, such as the lethal and elusive Yanisma."

11 MINDSHIELD

BACK IN THE privacy of her room, Olivia lay on her bed, staring at the ceiling, trying to make sense of what had just happened. She had been violated. She hadn't given anyone permission to probe her mind; the Queen had invaded her private thoughts without her consent. And of course she'd reacted without thinking. Touching the Queen of the Jin without permission was probably going to get her shipped off to the fringe colonies, whatever that meant, but she wasn't sorry. That bloated bitch deserved to swallow some of her own brew. It was just that…she wanted to stay.

Sita was the answer to a wish. Olivia was closer to having friends here than she'd ever been in Swift Current. And she'd gone and screwed it all up. She considered making a run for the quantagate. But what would that do? Even if she could fly the ship back to Earth, the Greys would get her. And if she brought the quantagate to them, she'd be giving them access to Sita. She couldn't put everyone's safety at risk. Who knew what Retchen would do if he had the chance to invade this moon? She tried to ignore the dark and twisty knot in her stomach, focusing instead on what she had just learned. Twelve alien tribes had created something called Project Human. But why didn't they stay? Why create a whole species and then abandon it? Why didn't humans know anything about them?

"Olivia? You there?"

Open.

Keilte lumbered in, followed by Tuatha. Olivia chewed on her lip.

"The new girl is in here building a ginormous castle of despair. Meanwhile, the entire hive is buzzing with anxiety. What did you do, Carpenter, poop in their honey?"

"Queen Tara only summoned me to steal my memories."

"Is this because of…?" Keilte checked himself, realizing Tuatha was in the room.

"I don't know. And I don't care if they made me. I'm not their toy."

"I thought you were keeping that to yourself."

Tuatha wheeled around on him. "Did you seriously tell the new girl to keep secrets from me? Trying to keep her all to yourself, are you?"

"Migitju says the best way to keep a secret is not to talk about it."

"Oh, look at you with your cute little sayings. I like you." Tuatha got right up in Olivia's face. "We're going to be best of friends, I just know it. I've already decided I'm calling you Carpenter. I hope that's okay. Since you have two names, I should be able to choose which one I like best. And since we're friends, what's all this about the Jin making you? The Jin aren't allowed to make anyone anymore."

"I saw it in a memory. I saw them make my people."

Tuatha let out a long whistle. "Wait, what? That whole 'seeing memories' is really your deal? Like Yanisma-style? That's gotta be why they're on edge."

"Not exactly."

"Uh oh." Keilte sat on the floor next to the bed, but he was so tall his eyes looked directly into Olivia's. "What happened?"

"She was invading my head, rummaging around. It made me sick, and she wouldn't stop, so I…I grabbed her."

"You touched the Queen? Without permission? Touching anyone without permission is forbidden. Seers can use touch to dig into the past and the future, and doing that without consent is not okay."

"She was rifling through my head without consent. How is that any different? She can do it without touch, but it's the same thing. She violated me, so I gave her a taste of her own medicine."

"Our new classmate has guts!" Tuatha did a spin in the air. "And you're going to need them. Pissing off Queen Tara is a big deal. Have you seen how many Jin live here?"

Well, shit. Plenty of Indigenous women and children had

disappeared over the last century just for existing. Finding them had proven impossible. Soon, Olivia would be part of that statistic. It made her wonder how many of those lost sisters had been picked up by flying saucers piloted by the grey menace. She shuddered.

"I understand how this feels," Keilte offered.

"Oh, get over yourself. You can't possibly imagine how she feels. The Jin can't walk around in your head like they can with the rest of us."

"That isn't fair, Tuatha. We remember. It's part of our culture. It's a wound felt by our entire tribe." A shadow clouded his eyes.

"Wait, you can block their telepathy? You have to tell me how to keep them out."

"You must have heard of Mindshield. Teutons practice it to block Jin telepathy."

"Tuatha! It's not for you to tell our secrets!"

"It's hardly a secret! The whole galaxy knows. Everyone knows except Carpenter. Why is that, anyway? Why is it that you don't know the most basic things about our galaxy?"

To Olivia's relief, Keilte deflected Tuatha's questions with the story of his ancestors.

"Long ago, before The Twelve came together to create the Galactic Council, the Jin convinced my people that their thought-sharing would make our world a better place. Innocent people wouldn't be mistakenly punished. Criminals would always be apprehended because the truth would always be known. We trusted them. But once we opened our minds, another species interfered. They invaded our thoughts. They implanted fake memories that built walls of suspicion between us. A civil war broke out on Teutonia that almost wiped us out. To save us, the Jin taught us how to Mindshield, to block telepathic signals. Now, all Teuton children are taught to Mindshield as soon as we can speak. It's not something they like to teach. They much prefer having the power to see whatever they want to, but because of our discipline, we will never be that vulnerable again."

"Can you teach me?"

"No."

"But surely I can learn something that you learned as a child."

"He wants to. He likes you so much that he's actually considering it. But he can't."

"Why not?"

"Because if he does, Queen Tara will kick him out of the academy."

Right. The academy was part of the Jin hive. Queen Tara controlled all of it. Of course that's how things worked—whoever held the power made the decisions, fair or not. The Jin would do whatever they wanted to do. Olivia was just a speed bump. She couldn't get Keilte expelled. This was her problem, not his. She had already figured out how to interfere with the Queen's mind probe. Maybe if she practised focusing on AmmaNa, she could use it to protect herself.

"I can't ask you to do something that gets you kicked out. If they send me back to the little grey monsters, I'll figure something out."

Keilte's mane fluffed to attention, like an animal in danger. "Back up a minute. Did you say little grey monsters?"

"That's why the Jin brought me here. To protect me."

"Describe them."

Olivia dug her journal out of her backpack. On a fresh page, she drew the aliens who had chased her out of the solar system.

Keilte ground his teeth against each other, Tuatha wincing at the sound. "Those are the monsters who started our civil war."

"Great, Carpenter, now you've done it. You've woken up the warrior in him. Did you know that the Teutons are some of the fiercest warriors in the galaxy? Probably not, since you didn't know about the Mindshield. Seriously. How come you don't know this stuff?"

Keilte punched the wall, cracking it. Within moments, the crack had repaired itself. He rubbed his fist, shaking his head.

"What's the story with these grey monsters?"

"The rumour is that the Greys used to be a Jin hive until something damaged and warped them. But the Jin refuse to talk about it. Kind of like how you clam up every time I ask you why you don't know things everyone else knows."

"You can't go back to them. They will turn your brain to sludge."

Keilte was adamant.

"If Queen Tara kicks me out, I won't have a choice."

"If you touched Queen Tara without permission, the Jin will demand a tribunal."

"Great. If that's anything like the justice system where I come from, I'm doomed."

"How does your justice work?" Tuatha was not passing up the opportunity to learn something about the new girl's home culture.

"It doesn't work. The guy with the most money hires the best lawyer and always wins, even if he's the biggest scumbag alive."

"Wow." Keilte was disgusted. "That is not justice."

"What is money? Is it a superpower?" Tuatha pressed.

"It's paper that's supposed to be worth gold, but it's not even really worth gold anymore."

"I don't get it." Tuatha's head tilted sideways, confused.

"Neither do I," Keilte admitted. "She thought she needed to give us this money stuff for food. Like if she didn't have any, we'd let her starve."

"Your people need to evolve beyond this money thing."

"Not likely. Not in my lifetime. The people with the money control everything. And they like being in control, so they aren't going to change unless it's a matter of survival."

"Wow. I wouldn't want to go back there, either."

But it wasn't that simple. Migitju was back on Earth. If Olivia never went home, she'd never see Migitju again. Her heart tore into thousands of little shreds at the thought.

Tuatha sensed it and tried to change the subject. "On Sita, we use the Jin tribunal. The Jin show memories of the event on a screen so the judges can see what happened. That way, nobody can lie."

"So the only way to prove I'm innocent is to let the Jin probe my memories again?"

"If you refuse to participate, everyone will assume your guilt."

"I don't care. This whole thing happened because the Jin think they have the right to invade my brain. I don't want them digging around in my head."

Keilte thought for a long moment.

"Okay, it's super duper cute that you're all smitten with the new girl, but you can't seriously be considering this. Your ancestors made an agreement with the Jin not to share the Mindshield with anyone. This could cause a war among The Twelve."

"If the Jin send her back, Mindshield is the only way she can defend herself against the Greys. Besides, Olivia rescued us from Maia. The Jin were nowhere to be found. You said so yourself. If I have to pick sides, I choose the girl who saved my life."

Keilte had been welcoming from the moment they'd met, and now he was willing to risk getting kicked out of the academy to help her.

"I can't believe… You never break the rules. What will your parents think? What will Teutonia think?"

"Teutonia will understand that I was protecting someone from telepathic assault."

"And Lord Harvarder?"

"Why? Are you going to fly away and tattle on me?"

"What? Are you kidding? I've been trying to cultivate the rebel in you since we got here! Carpenter for the win!"

"Okay then, Olivia. Make yourself comfortable."

Olivia filled her lungs and exhaled slowly, fully. Keilte's voice was deep and soothing.

"Picture a field or a grotto, somewhere outside. It can be real or imaginary, but it needs to be vivid and familiar. A place you can recall automatically, without thinking."

Olivia's mind went directly to the path behind Migitju's house that led through a stand of massive oaks and maples to a clearing.

"Feel every detail of this place. Touch the ground. Smell the smells."

A brook babbled through the clearing. On either side of the brook, wildflowers stretched out to the forest, butterflies flitting from flower to flower. She ran her fingers over the cracked bark of a giant maple. Her toes played among the cold, velvety carpet of bugleweed and clover. She took a deep breath, filling her nostrils with the pungent smells of pine and cedar.

"Absorb this place into you. This place is safe. This place will come to you when you need it."

She wandered along the brook, her hands playing through the butterflies.

"There is a memory you want to hide from Queen Tara. Next to your feet, you will see an object that represents this memory."

Olivia looked down, and beside her feet was a small toy UFO made of white plastic. Three small, golden faces looked at her from the toy's windows.

"I want you to pick up this object and carry it with you, walking until a big square stone appears in your path. The stone is solid. The stone is too heavy to move. The stone feels safe. Another stone appears next to it, and another, and another. They form a wall. This wall will protect you. Feel the strength of this wall."

She ran her hand along the cold stone. It felt rough and uneven in places. She pushed against it, but it did not budge. The wall was solid. She looked up. It reached into the sky.

"Find the crack in the wall. It is a door."

She walked the length of the wall until a crack appeared. The stone parted just enough to reveal a door.

"Go inside, but just for a moment. Take the object inside and leave it there, but make sure you don't stay too long. I'll be waiting for you. Remember to come back."

She pushed through the door and closed it with a thud behind her. A staircase spiralled upwards, hugging the inside of the stone wall, lit by candles casting a warm orange glow on the grey rock. She passed five empty levels, but as she climbed higher, empty bookshelves began to decorate the walls. The further up she went, the more the shelves were full of books. They called to her, compelling her to stop, to give them the attention and love they deserved, but something pushed her to resist their call—to keep climbing.

At the top, two comfortable recliners waited, surrounded by stacks of books. Everything she needed was here. A telescope pointed skyward, disappearing into the rock overhead. She put the toy UFO on a shelf, enthralled by the aromas of old paper and leather. She was surrounded by the things she loved: shelves full of adventure, science, math, and astronomy. She ran her index finger along the spines of her favourites and chose a story about a journey into the underworld. It had been ages since she'd read this one. Or was it yesterday? No matter. She'd read it again.

The recliner was comfortable, welcoming, but it was strange that it had a twin. Was she expecting company? She headed back downstairs to check the door—her guest would never find the secret door if she wasn't there to hold it open. The books and the recliner called out, pleading for her to come back and give them the attention that they craved, but she couldn't shake a nagging feeling that someone was waiting for her. At the bottom of the stairs, she poked her head outside.

"Olivia, please. You have to hear me. You have to come back."

Olivia opened her eyes. The wooded clearing disappeared, and once again, she was surrounded by crystal.

"Thank the stars! I thought you were lost." Keilte was a sickly pale orange.

"My tower was wonderful. I almost forgot to come back."

"You could sleep for aeons like that. It is called the sleep of the dead."

"Why the sleep of the dead?"

"Because nobody can wake you. Once you enter your sanctuary, you cannot be woken until you decide to return. Did you feel the pull to stay?"

"It was really strong. It was like my castle was having a fit at the mere idea that I would step outside."

"It is not somewhere to stay. It is a place to hide the things you need to hide. It is dangerous to remain inside for too long. The more you practise using the book to come back, the easier it gets."

"Practise using what book?"

"The book you picked up before you found the wall."

"You didn't say anything about a book. I picked up the memory I wanted to hide."

"She's right," Tuatha chimed in. "There was no book."

“Oh, stars. We could have lost you for good and it would have been all my fault. This is why Mindshield coaches get special training. I was supposed to lead you to a book. You bring it into your tower, and it reminds you to come back.”

“But my tower was full of books. It was a library.”

“That is problematic. Losing a book in a library is an easy mistake to make. This book is special, so it has to be unique. Close your eyes. Go back to your safe place.”

“Are you sure Carpenter should do this again so soon? After being lost in there for a whole hour?”

“I was gone for an hour?”

“Yes. And you have to go back in. We need to finish setting up the Mindshield properly so that if you ever use it, you have the tools to remind you to return.”

Determined to get this right, Olivia took a deep breath and closed her eyes. But the meadow with the butterflies didn’t come. Instead, Queen Tara leered down at her, thousands of Jin minions closing in.

“I can’t do it. I can’t find the place.”

“Take a deep breath. Think about the smells. Think of how this place feels.”

She closed her eyes and thought of smells of pine and cedar, of petrichor from fresh rain, of the sound of the burbling brook. Suddenly, she was there again, pulled into the meadow by these senses. She took in a deep breath again, using the smells to hold onto the vision.

“Good. You walk through this place, but you stub your toe. A large book sits at your feet, blocking your path. It is heavy and unlike any other book you have ever seen. Pick up the book.”

It was as heavy as a load of firewood. The cover smelled of freshly tanned leather, its surface recently oiled.

“The book is called Someone Waits Outside.” As she heard this, the title appeared letter by letter, branded into the leather. “Go back into your tower, and find somewhere to put this book where it will always be close, where it will always be seen. Find a special place, a place of honour in your library. And remember to read the cover.”

She found the crack in the wall and climbed to the top of the tower. A glass display case on a pedestal now faced the two comfy recliners. She felt compelled to put the new book in the case, but she wasn't sure why. It seemed strange to give a place of distinction to a book she'd never read. She sat in one of the recliners, admiring her library. Why did she have a second chair? Was she expecting someone? Was someone waiting for her?

Keilte. She raced downstairs, saying his name over and over until she reached the meadow. She opened her eyes.

"I almost forgot again."

"Fighting the urge to stay inside takes practice. That is why Teutons learn this skill as infants. The instinctive need for our parents ensures that we return."

This made perfect sense. But before Olivia could request that they keep practising, the door skittered open, and seven Jin sporting official badges entered.

We come to claim Olivia,
who must now face the consequence.
You had no right to grab our leg.
You will now pay for your assault.

"I was defending myself!"

"We believe you, Liv. So let's go prove your case." Keilte's baritone voice rumbled as he stood, and all seven guards backed up a pace, intimidated by his height. It was clear that Queen Tara was not queen of the Teutons.

"Wheeee! Carpenter stirs the soup, and we get front-row seats for whatever floats to the surface. Let's go watch a tribunal!"

12 THE TRIBUNAL

OLIVIA ENTERED THE tribunal room to find Queen Tara perched high above her, glaring down. Joining her were a Teuton, an Atlantian, and a clan Olivia had not yet met.

"The Teuton judge is Lord Harvarder," Keilte explained. Despite being high above her, Olivia could tell that he was much larger and more muscular than Keilte. "Next to him is Lord Tamiel."

This one leaned forward to get a closer look at Olivia. The sharp angles of his nose, eyebrows, and hairline made him even more severe than Master Eldrin.

"And finally, Duchess Damia, a Polarian." The Duchess's boulder-shaped head sat atop her torso the way a snowman's head sits on its body. She easily dwarfed her peers, including Lord Harvarder. Her nose and mouth occupied most of her symmetrical face, stretching as wide as her eyes. As she caught Olivia's gaze, her pouty lips curled into a smile that touched her ears.

Keilte and Tuatha nodded in support and headed for a gallery on the left. It was roomy enough for hundreds of spectators, but only a half-dozen of the seats were occupied, with Master Eldrin in the front row.

A chair in the middle of the pit waited for Olivia, putting her on full display. She clutched at handfuls of her tunic to dry her clammy hands and chewed some cheek. Hopefully, the judges would be fair once they saw how the Queen's mind probe had made her violently ill.

"A tribunal has been called." Lord Harvarder boomed. "What is the complaint?"

The one that sits before you

is accused of bodily attack;
she rushed our throne and grabbed our leg
and meant to cause us harm.

That was a lie! Olivia clenched her jaw, and her hand shot up to get Harvarder's attention.

Lord Harvarder put his hand up in response, halting Olivia before she could plead her case. "It is not customary for the accused to speak before evidence is shown. You will have your say in due course."

Olivia put her hand back down. She had to be patient. She had to show restraint.

"The complaint has been made. Let us see the evidence."

Knowing what was coming, Olivia closed her eyes and took a deep breath, imagining pine and cedar. The meadow appeared, but there was also a crawly thing, wriggling into the periphery of her senses, pulling at her. She fought back, listening for the brook, swimming through a cloud of butterflies, but the thing kept up, waiting for her to falter. She wasn't good at focusing on one thing. Not like the maples that only had one view to look at for hundreds of years. Migitju had taught her to be like the maple, to grow roots from the soles of her feet down into the ground. The cold rose to meet her request, and suddenly, she was everywhere, a tangle of roots.

"What kind of evidence is this? This is not an attack!"

Olivia opened her eyes. The roots of a massive maple tree filled the screen to her right. It was magnificent.

We need to probe her mind so we can show you the event.
She disrespects the court today by blocking our attempt.

"Harvarder, could this be Mindshield?" Lord Tamiel asked his query loud enough for the entire gallery to hear. "Surely the Teutons don't have anything to do with this?"

"The Jin brought her to this place, Tamiel," Harvarder rebuked. "Mindshield is their trick. Be careful of your accusations, especially in such a public forum. Our mission as Councillors is to cooperate, not to fuel new grievances." He threw a glance in Keilte's direction before turning back to Olivia. "What do you say to this? Are you blocking the probe?"

"I am doing my best, yes."

"You dare interfere with a tribunal proceeding? Who are you to show such disrespect?"

"I mean no disrespect, but I do not give my consent to let the Jin invade my mind. Since Queen Tara has made this accusation, it should be on her to present evidence from her own memories."

Seconds felt like hours as the three judges conferred quietly. Duchess Damia stole several glances at the Jin queen, while Lord Tamiel threw a few at Olivia, amused with this curve ball. Lord Harvarder was not amused in the least. This was his tribunal, and his rules were being subverted. Nonetheless, they arrived at the logical conclusion.

"Since Queen Tara is a witness, she can present her own memory. Proceed."

The Queen's golden face deepened to a copper hue. The screen lit up, showing the Jin cleaning barf off the floor. Olivia rushed up the steps and grabbed the Queen's ankle. The playback stopped.

That was it? But of course that was all she was going to show. So much for the telepathic version of justice. This was Queen Tara's city. She going to get the outcome she wanted even if it meant lying in court.

A fire welled up in Olivia's gut that was two parts anger and three parts fear. She had to defend herself. Nobody else was going to do it for her. "I object."

"State your objection." Lord Tamiel's blue lips curled into the hint of a smile.

"She didn't show what caused me to grab her ankle. What I did was self-defence. I would like the court to see the memory from the moment I entered the room."

The purpose of your summoning is solely our concern.

The judges conferred again. This time, Harvarder and Tamiel turned toward the Duchess for a brief exchange. By the look on her face, Olivia suspected that the Queen was listening, even though whispering was a clear sign of a private discussion. They all nodded.

"Your objection is denied. You have been difficult, and we have no reason to grant your request."

"So the truth isn't a good enough reason?"

"You have a smart mouth, young one. You would do well to learn some control."

Control was exactly what Olivia needed, but not of her mouth. She wasn't going to be denied the chance to show her side of these events. She focused on the screen, willing it to obey.

Show the moment I entered Queen Tara's chamber.

The screen flickered to Olivia's memory, walking in to face the Jin queen.

Play.

The Queen's black eyes went wide with shock as the courtroom watched Olivia asking Queen Tara to stop invading her mind twice. On both occasions, the Queen ignored her pleas. Olivia got sick and finally lunged at her ankle. Olivia felt Queen Tara struggling to take control of the screen. When the playback showed Olivia grabbing Queen Tara's ankle, the image froze and the screen went blank. Queen Tara's cheeks were bronze, whether from effort or from emotion was anyone's guess. What was clear to Olivia, however, was that she didn't want the judges to see the flinch.

Our evidence is now complete.

Lord Harvarder contemplated in silence, unsure of what had just transpired. Hadn't Queen Tara refused to show the entire episode? Finally, he broke the silence that had settled over the tribunal room like a deep January snow.

"Olivia Carpenter. Do you have any evidence to present?"

Was she actually being given the chance to speak? The whole tribunal had seemed like it was rigged to railroad her. From the moment Lord Harvarder had refused to let her speak, she'd gone on the defensive. She'd already shown the court what she needed them to see, and commandeering the screen out of turn had given her the element of surprise she'd needed to use Queen Tara's technology. She was good.

"You've seen the entire event. Queen Tara's mind probing made me physically sick. Her actions caused my reaction."

Lord Harvarder nodded. "Please wait in the anteroom while we discuss the evidence."

Keilte and Tuatha joined her in a small room along with three Jin guards. The effort of running the screen against Queen Tara's will had left her depleted and sleepy. She crumpled into the corner to rest.

"Wow! You're a total rebel!" Tuatha gushed. "Never would have guessed it. That red hair makes you seem like a Teuton, but you're nothing like Mister Straight-as-a-Dagger over here." Tuatha patted Keilte on the shoulder. "It's okay that the new girl has more guts than you. You'll learn to live with it."

"She stood up for truth and justice, which is exactly what I would have done, thank you very much. I am proud of you, Liv."

"You two are so cute," Tuatha snickered, obviously trying to ship them together.

Olivia was dazed. It was the second time Keilte had called her Liv. And Tuatha thought she had guts. She liked being here. She wanted to stay. She needed to make peace with the Jin. But the Queen was angry and had other plans.

You pull your stunt to use our screen,
and think that we'll repay that deed
by making a concession that will keep you here for good?
Assaulting us has no defence.
Your reasons hold no consequence.
We will make sure you pay for this by making sure you leave.

The message was clear—no deal would be made. Olivia only had one option. Her heart thumped so quickly in her chest that her ribcage ached. She took a deep breath and turned to the guards. Just like chopping off Miley's bangs, Olivia did what had to be done.

"I propose a truce. You withdraw your complaint and agree to let me stay. In return, I won't tell the tribunal what I know about Project Human." Threatening royalty was not an easy play, but she was out of moves and determined to stay on Sita.

Immediately, the Queen's thick voice filled her mind.

We will agree to your demands.
We are withdrawing our complaint.

"What just happened?" Keilte was dumbstruck.

"I did what I had to do."

"Really? To me, it sounded like blackmail."

"Blackmail isn't cool, Carpenter."

Olivia looked at the floor, unsure how to respond. She just wanted the chance to stay, to belong.

"Why did you blackmail Queen Tara with Project Human?" Keilte was a bulldog with a bone. He was not going to let this go.

"It's something I heard when I flinched with her earlier. I don't understand it. I just knew she didn't want anyone else to see it. She stopped the playback right before the flinch. Twice. I made an educated guess."

"You're hiding something, Carpenter. I can smell it."

"Tuatha's nose knows."

She had to give Tuatha something believable. "Sure, I'm hiding something. I mean, he already knows, but I can run Jin tech. I can open their prisons, their doors. I can get away from Maia if they leave me on the surface."

"Whoa! You can run their tech?" Tuatha looked to Keilte, who nodded to confirm. "And you think they stranded all of us because of you? That's harsh."

"It's really starting to feel like I'm the reason they didn't show up."

Tuatha was tuned in to Olivia with intensity. "For some reason, I'm way more sensitive to your emotions, and I can say with one hundred percent certainty that you're still hiding something monumental."

"Maybe your extra sensitivity to me also means you're seeing things that don't exist."

Tuatha bristled at the rebuke. Keilte didn't like it, either; Tuatha was his bestie, and he wasn't about to let Olivia become a wedge.

"So I put my future at risk by teaching you to Mindshield, and this is how you thank me?"

"You taught me how to Mindshield because of the Greys. To protect me. And I'm so grateful. They're involved in all of this somehow, too, and now that I know there's a connection between them and the Jin, well…you said it yourselves. Look at how many Jin there are here. I'm just trying to survive."

Keilte wasn't swayed. "I was foolish to waste my time on you. The Jin are suspicious for good reason. Keep your secrets. Good luck with everything." He wheeled his hulking body around, and the door to the anteroom slid open. Tuatha gave her a disappointed shake of the head and fluttered out after him, wings drooping.

The guards led Olivia back into the tribunal room, where Lord Harvarder shook his head, confused. "The complaint against you has been withdrawn. Queen Tara would like to explain."

We do not wish to do you harm;
we did not mean to make you sick.
Your presence here has caused alarm.
We only sought to find the truth.
We will not probe your mind again
unless you give us your consent.
We hope that you will work with us
to find the answers that we seek.

"Queen Tara, for my part, I am sorry that I lunged at you and grabbed you. It won't happen again."

Lord Harvarder's expression was a mixture of questions and confusion. The judges likely saw few tribunals end in a double apology, but they had never met Olivia Carpenter. She'd been trained to apologize, even when she wasn't wrong, but beyond that, she saw the value in reconciliation. Without it, there would only be continued animosity.

"This is…unexpected, but since the matter is resolved, this tribunal is adjourned."

As Olivia made her way back to the lift, a trio of Jin blocked her path to deliver a chilling warning.

If you divulge your origin,
you will be hunted by The Twelve.
We weren't allowed to interfere.
It was a crime to bring you here.

If Project Human was created by The Twelve, why would they

hunt her down? Was it the same reason the Greys had come after her? And where was AmmaNa in all of this? She had a good reason to bring Olivia here. Why hadn't she explained it to her queen?

Suddenly, Olivia couldn't breathe, like someone had crushed her ribcage. She had no clue where to turn for help, and she had just lost her only allies. She was hundreds of light-years from home, from anyone who cared about her safety. She made it back to her room just in time for the hot tears to gush down her cheeks.

IN A FULLY stocked lab, deep underground in the bunker he called home, Dr. Retchen briefed a group of five Greys dressed in black lab coats. He gave them the blood recovered from Olivia's bike chain.

"Analyze this. Find sequences foreign to Earth."

He smoothed his hair back, making sure every strand was in place as the elevator carried him back to his office. A small suitcase full of neatly folded dress pants and black cashmere sweaters matching the one he now wore sat next to a large duffle bag. Into the duffle, he packed three pairs of black leather gloves, three rolls of duct tape, a box of garbage bags, two coils of heavy rope, a plastic bottle of ether, a brand-new package of hand towels, a bottle of bleach, a monkey wrench, a bag of extra-large zip ties, and a large flashlight.

His incidentals gathered, he brought them to his SUV and hoisted them into the back next to a kennel large enough to transport a Great Dane. But he had no interest in Great Danes. He double-checked a multi-tiered toolbox for power tools and spy cameras, lifting out a fake bottom to count his ammunition. As the engine of the SUV roared to life, he grinned, baring his pointy teeth. The pecking order on this planet was going to change drastically once he fully realized his plan.

13 THE DOGGOS

AS SOON AS Maia ducked below the horizon and the distant burn of Celaeno and Electra bathed the moon in a blue twilight, hundreds of well-rested students assembled in the commons to catch the lifts back to the surface. Keilte shoved his way to the far side of the platform, putting as much distance as he could between himself and Olivia. Tuatha remained at his side, clearly still disappointed.

So many questions churned in Olivia's head. Why was Queen Tara so determined to keep Olivia's origin story a secret? Was Terra a fringe colony? AmmaNa and Queen Tara had both said they weren't supposed to interfere. What had gone wrong between the science fair and now? Why would The Twelve hunt her down just for being from Terra? She wasn't going to find her answers without help, and her only allies had just abandoned her. She could either give up or try to make another friend.

Forcing herself to smile, she struck up some small talk with Rama, trying to keep it light. "Do you know why we do our lessons in a pyramid?"

"The structure focuses power, making it easier for us to practice our skills." He squinted like he was trying to see into her. "How can you not know that? Pyramid power is basic knowledge."

"Soooo basic!" Kyrrha had planted herself right next to them. "Hey, refugee, tell me what you know about our lost city."

"All I know is it was lost thousands of years ago."

"That tells me nothing. You're useless."

Olivia bit the inside of her cheek. Starting a war with Kyrrha mere hours after surviving a tribunal was the last thing she needed. "Yup, I'm useless. Not worth any more of your time."

“A year is based on the time a planet takes to orbit its star,” Rama said. “The fact that you talk about years without a planetary qualifier is very strange.”

“VERY strange,” Kyrrha stressed.

“I know very little about the cosmos. My parents sheltered me from that stuff. They didn’t want me going off-world. You seem to know a lot, so I thought maybe you could help me fill in the blanks.”

“It is true. I do have a vast knowledge of the cosmos.”

They hopped off the lift and made their way around the lake toward a river on the far side.

“What do you know about Terra?”

“That’s quite a jump from pyramids. Why the interest in Terra?”

She was running out of time. She wouldn’t get a second chance without being totally obvious. “It’s okay if you don’t know anything about it, I just heard it was interesting.” Challenging his ego was a risk, but she had to go all in.

“Don’t know anything about it? I know all about Terra—secret things most don’t know!”

“You know secret things? Come on, Rama. Spill.”

“Terra is forbidden. A long time ago, the Council built a base there to make a weapon.”

“What kind of weapon?”

“Something to destroy the Draconians and end their enslavement of our galaxy. It was top secret. The Twelve went together to set everything up, and then they erased it from the star maps to protect it. But the Atlantians wanted control, like they always do, so they broke the pact and went there secretly. When we found out, we went there, too. They accused us of spying and tried to wipe us out of the sky. They lost, obviously.”

“Did I just hear you talking about my people?”

“Mind your own business, Kyrrha.”

“Everything is my business, Vegan.”

“You see? She thinks being Atlantian makes her better than everyone.” Rama blinked, transforming into an exact replica of Kyrrha. “Look at me, I can bend a stick with my mind.” He blinked back before she could tattle. “Of course, they don’t teach the history of the Terran conflict at the academy because it’s an embarrassment to some of our paler students.”

Olivia absorbed this revelation as she followed Rama. The pyramid for their next lesson was set well back from the others next to a deep part of the river that fed the lake. The inside of this pyramid was arranged like a bullseye, with a ring of drums surrounding a larger one in the centre. Each one had a large horn pointing directly at its underbelly. Was this a music class? Great. Maybe she could ask to sit this one out.

Kyrrha took the drum on Rama’s other side, still working on him. “You’re so gullible. Don’t you see her game? She was all cozy with the Teuton and the Deyonn, but now suddenly they don’t want anything to do with her. You’re her next target. What do you even know about her? Do you know where she’s from? Has anyone actually witnessed her special ability?” Kyrrha was playing dirty, reminding Rama of a question Olivia had avoided, but before he could begin his interrogation anew, Tuatha squeezed in between them, forcing Rama to shuffle over.

“Carpenter, as fun as it is to have a front-row seat in your little lover’s quarrel, enough already. Fix this.”

“He won’t even look at me. How am I supposed to talk to him?”

“He doesn’t like secrets. Come clean, and then we can get back to normal.”

“He wants me to explain something I don’t understand,” Olivia whispered, knowing that Kyrrha and Rama were eavesdropping. “Have you ever tried to explain a dream?”

“My dreams fly away faster than I do.”

“That’s what this is like. I think I understand, then I wake up, and it’s gone.”

Tuatha’s voice dropped to a whisper. “I love the craziness of how you move, but you can’t just drop a steamer like that and then shrug and pretend it didn’t happen.”

The conversation ended as the Master entered the room. She was a stunning cross between a fish and a kangaroo, her body covered in black scales with an iridescent sheen that glinted in a rainbow of colours as she glided across the space. When she stopped in the middle of the room, she sat on her thick tail, using her slight legs for balance. It was not how Olivia would have described a mermaid, though she had never imagined she'd ever meet a humanoid sea creature, so this was the closest to a mermaid she had ever been.

She turned to address Olivia. "Welcome. I am Master Yamma of the Doggos. In my lessons, you will learn the power of sound. Observe."

She emptied a pouch of black sand onto the skin of the central drum. Slits along her slender throat opened to inhale a giant breath and fluttered closed again, leaving no trace of their existence. She put her full lips to the horn and sang a rich note into its mouthpiece. The sand danced across the surface of the drum and, to Olivia's astonishment, formed itself into a four-leaf clover. Master Yamma's gills opened as she inhaled to sing another note, this time in a much higher pitch. The sand danced around once again, reforming into a ring of eight heads pointing toward a central circle.

"A pure frequency creates a harmonious pattern. An impure frequency creates discord. Using the sand beside your drum, sing into the horn, find a pattern, and hold for a count of ten. Begin."

Olivia dumped her bag of sand onto the drum and sang a note into the horn. The sand scattered across the skin, but no pattern appeared. She took a deep breath and picked another note. Once again, the sand bounced around haphazardly. Around the room, the other students produced beautiful patterns, some more intricate than others, all with ease.

Olivia tried a third time, taking the deepest breath her lungs could hold. She started with a medium note and slowly bent it up through the scale, watching for a pattern to form. If she could just find a note that worked, maybe she could hold it. She went through an entire octave and ran out of breath without making any kind of harmonious pattern on the skin of her drum.

"There's nothing pure about your frequency," Kyrrha quipped.

"You are having troubles," Master Yamma noted.

"I've never been good in music class."

"Any skill can be learned with practice. Sing me the note at 432 hertz."

"I don't know what that is."

Master Yamma sang a note in the middle of the scale. Olivia copied it, then leaned over and sang into the horn. A pattern began forming but stopped as Olivia's note went flat.

"Don't watch the sand. Close your eyes and hear the tone."

Again, Master Yamma helped Olivia find the tone and continued singing with her as Olivia pushed the note into the drum. The pattern appeared, but as soon as Master Yamma stopped singing along with her, the sand scattered. Master Yamma produced two tuning forks. She struck them on the wall of the pyramid and held them on either side of Olivia's head. She bent in, listening to the top of Olivia's skull.

"Your head is out of tune."

Kyrrha sniggered. "Her head is definitely missing something."

"That is enough, Kyrrha. When you first arrived on Sita, you couldn't even master your own ability. Learning is a process. There is nothing shameful about starting at the beginning."

Kyrrha's cheeks went blue, and she looked down at her drum, rebuked.

"Take these." Master Yamma handed Olivia the tuning forks. "You will tap them to make them resonate and hold one at each ear to let the sound pass through you. You will practise this until the sound meets in the middle and re-tunes you to the correct frequency. Until the end of the lesson, you may sit in the centre where the pyramid amplifies the effect. Kyrrha, please move my drum."

Kyrrha's hand went up, and the drum, suddenly weightless, floated like a dandelion seed on the wind. Without touching it, she moved it to the only empty space in the circle. How was that even possible? Master Yamma cleared her gills with a puffing noise, bringing Olivia's attention back to the task at hand.

"How will I know when I'm in tune?"

"Your body will begin to feel the frequencies around you."

"How long will that take?"

"Every being is unique. It will take as long as it takes."

Being singled out sucked, but at least Master Yamma was nice about it. While everyone else made beautiful patterns with beautiful sounds, Olivia spent the rest of the class cultivating a mild headache. She hoped that her diligence would earn her a one-on-one conversation with her new teacher, but Master Yamma was the first to leave at the end of the lesson. Olivia raced to follow, but the pink river swallowed her hopes as the scaly black tail of the Doggo Master vanished below the surface. Learning more about why she was out of tune would have to wait.

With nobody to talk to, Olivia watched the other students file out of the pyramid and for the first time, she noticed that Kyrrha was a solo act. She'd been so focused on the ways that Kyrrha reminded her of Miley that she hadn't noticed the differences. Kyrrha didn't have a wolf pack. It couldn't be easy, leaving home and coming to an academy where everyone disliked her just because she was an Atlantian. Maybe being frosty was a coping strategy. Maybe Olivia could melt through that frost. It couldn't hurt to try.

She pushed down the knot in her stomach and approached the ice princess. "That was pretty cool, how you moved the drum across the room."

"Oh. Well, thanks."

"And I really don't know anything about your lost city. I wasn't trying to be a jerk. Losing a whole city is a lot. If I knew something, I'd tell you."

"Well, if you're really a seer, why can't you just look and see where our city went?"

"I can only flinch with an object if I'm touching it. And I just started flinching before I arrived. I'm not very good."

"Seeing the past and the future is something only the Yanisma can do. They don't teach it at the academy. They don't teach it to anyone. So you'll have to excuse me if I don't believe you."

Had the Yanisma broken the pact and visited her ancestors on Terra? Olivia needed to know more about the people who had given her this ability. "What are they like? The Yanisma, I mean."

"I've never met them. Facing the Yanisma is the final trial before we become actual Guardians. They see deep into your soul. They force you to face the truth about yourself by showing you who you really are."

"Where do they come from?"

"You should know. You're the one claiming to have their powers. Do the Masters know?"

"Of course," Olivia lied. "That's why the Jin brought me here. They want me to learn to control it so I don't go flinching all over the galaxy."

Kyrrha seemed satisfied with this answer, despite the obvious lack of Yanisma Masters at the academy. "Since you were nice to me, you get one piece of advice. Don't be late for Master Eldrin's class. He despises tardiness."

Kyrrha scowled and her pointy nose shot in the air as Keilte and Tuatha emerged from the pyramid. She vanished along the path as they approached.

"You weren't making nice with Miss Frosty-Face, were you?" asked Tuatha, offended.

"You ditched me. You don't get a say in who I talk to."

"You keep secrets," Keilte huffed. "Friends have no need for secrets."

"Keilte, I don't know what Project Human is. I heard the words when I flinched with Queen Tara."

"You knew enough to use it as blackmail."

"Like I already told you, Queen Tara stopped the playback right before the judges could see the flinch. Twice. I made an educated guess that she didn't want them to hear about Project Human. It doesn't mean I can explain what it is."

"You really don't know anything, do you, Carpenter?"

"How could she? She comes from a planet of primitives."

"Keilte, you told me to keep that to myself!"

"Yes, I did. Encouraging you to keep secrets was my mistake. Showing you how freeing it is to reveal them seems like an appropriate correction."

"Okay, but if Carpenter's a primitive, she wouldn't know what Project Human is, would she? Stars, Keilte, you withheld crucial information! This all makes perfect sense now." Tuatha dropped serious and turned to Olivia. "Listen, kid. Here's some Galactic History 101 to get you caught up. Project Human is a code name for a super-weapon. No wonder Queen Tara is pissed. You blackmailed her with one of the most sensitive projects in the galaxy."

Olivia digested this, becoming keenly aware that Keilte may have just taught Mindshield to someone who could destroy his whole planet. She wanted to tell him that she wasn't a threat, but that would involve revealing the whole truth, something she couldn't give him until she understood it herself. Every time she learned something new about her origins, the truth got darker and even more twisty. If Project Human was supposed to create a super-weapon, was that why Retchen was after her? Was that why Migitju had told her to keep her ability a secret? But how could she be a super-weapon? She was only fourteen.

Unfortunately, their catch-up made them late for Master Eldrin's lesson. His icy stare followed them as they slid into the seats closest to the door. Kyrrha shook her head and rolled her eyes.

"All three of you. Stand." They obeyed like soldiers. "I do not tolerate tardiness. Explain."

"I'm sorry, Master Eldrin. I'm sure Keilte and Tuatha have never been late for your class before. It was my fault."

"I assumed as much. You've been on Sita for less than one solar cycle and you've already caused a tribunal. My question is not who. My question is what. What is so important that it is worth disrupting my class with your tardiness?"

"I don't have a good reason, Master Eldrin."

"Stop telling me things I already know, and tell me WHAT made you late."

"Keilte was upset with me, and I wanted to talk about it."

"Interesting. You prioritize friendships over the knowledge I have to convey. And despite this, you seem to be as bad at maintaining friendships as you are at listing the interstellar tribes of the Pleiades. All three of you will spend the next meal break in detention. The

Teuton and the Deyonn will go to the island and water the Tree of Life. You, Girl With Two Names, will serve detention with me. Separated from your friends. Now sit."

Great. Detention with Master Eldrin was the last thing she wanted.

"Today, you will practise your elemental skills. I have placed a marble in front of each of you. You will focus on the marble, feel its atoms, find the invisible string that connects your atoms to the marble's atoms, and use that connection to roll the marble off the table."

The students placed their marbles on the pedestals in front of them.

"And you. Since you can afford to be late, you will demonstrate this skill." He placed a marble on the pedestal in the centre of the room. "Come, Girl With Two Names. Show us how talented you are."

Olivia had no idea how to move a marble with her mind, but like Master Yamma had said to Kyrrha, everyone starts at the beginning. She had to suck it up and try. She took a deep breath and let it out slowly, emptying her mind like she was preparing to flinch. She closed her eyes and visualized the marble, making it her sole focus. She imagined it trembling, then shifting, then rolling off the pedestal. But when she opened her eyes, the marble hadn't moved a millimetre.

"What are we waiting for?" Master Eldrin asked. Contempt dripped from his smile. He was expecting her to perform a magic trick without being shown how the trick works. At least Master Yamma had helped her find a note. She deserved the detention for being late, but she didn't deserve his ridicule. Disliking her just because she had a second name was bullshit. Like it often did in stressful situations, Olivia's mouth took over.

"I shouldn't have been late, and I'm truly sorry for that, but I'm here to learn. So instead of assuming I know how to do something when clearly I don't, how about you be a teacher and teach me how it's done."

His eyes narrowed at her rebuke, but he raised his hand toward the marble. "You create a connection, an invisible string of energy between your fingers and the marble. And once that connection is made…" He swiped his hand to the left, and the marble rolled left. He swiped his hand back to the right, and the marble returned to its starting point. He made it look so simple.

Olivia raised her hand as he had done. This time, she kept her eyes open, making it much harder to focus. Taunts and whispers floated around the class, adding to the doubt in her mind.

“She can’t do it.”

“She has some nerve, disrupting our classes.”

“She’s holding everyone back.”

Olivia couldn’t concentrate. Master Eldrin, whose rules forbade anyone from speaking out of turn, allowed the taunts to continue, amused by her struggle.

“If she can’t do the work, why is she here?”

“She doesn’t belong at the Crystal Academy.”

As the frustration swelled like a balloon pushing against her lungs, Migitju’s advice echoed in her mind. *You can't force it. Put it up. Try later.* Olivia missed her grandmother. She missed the gentle way Migitju taught her how to do things. She didn’t want to cry in front of everyone, but the tears burst from her eyes anyway, and they refused to stop. She fled from the pyramid and crumpled to the ground in the twilight, hugging her knees and sobbing alone under an unfamiliar sky. She could no longer look up and see the same moon as Migitju. The disconnect ripped at Olivia’s heart.

Kyrrha appeared in the doorway. “Master Eldrin sent me to check on you.”

“Go away.”

“So what if you couldn’t move the marble? That’s no reason to get all blubbery-faced.”

“It’s not about the marble.”

“Really? Because just now, you couldn’t move the marble, and—”

“It’s not the freaking marble!” Olivia bellowed, knocking the last part of Kyrrha’s sentence right out of her mouth. “It’s my grandmother, okay? She was so nice and so kind, and everyone here is so mean, and it just makes me miss her. I had to leave without saying goodbye, and I don’t know if I’ll ever see her again. It’s not about the freaking marble, so just leave me alone!”

Kyrrha sank to the ground and put an arm around Olivia's shoulder. Olivia sobbed, too defeated to push her away.

"I know what that's like to lose your grandmother." Kyrrha choked on the words. "Mine was an amazing teacher, spreading our technology and our culture across the galaxy, kind of like Master Eldrin. Then one day, she boarded the City of Atlantis and never came back."

"What do you mean? How do you board a city?"

"The City of Atlantis was a civilization ship, spreading our wisdom to developing worlds." Kyrrha looked at the sky full of twinkling stars. "That's why I'm so sensitive about it. You were acting all weird, like you knew something. And I thought if you knew where she was…" Kyrrha took Olivia's hand and squeezed it for support. Olivia took a deep breath, trying to calm her sobs and regain her composure.

"Where did she go?"

Olivia didn't mean to flinch, but it happened anyway. A jolt passed through her body, zapping all of her cells at once, and her world shattered into blackness.

Specks of light rained down, creating a bedroom. A beautiful Atlantian woman with eyes like the ocean pulled the covers up to the chin of a toddler, a small girl with frosty hair. The woman read to her from a picture book.

"Once upon a time, the people of Atlantia travelled out into the desert of space, to a star light-years away from any other, a star that was impossible to find. It was an amazing treasure, a hidden escape, far away from the wars that plague our galaxy. In this system, we seeded a nexus. The nexus attracted matter from all around, giving birth to a planet. It was beautiful—its oceans full of life—just like Atlantia. Eventually, the planet gave birth to its own children. The Atlantians cared for them and taught them about the stars, medicine, and technology. The planet was so happy to see its children loved that its crystal heart sprouted and grew a majestic tree."

"Is that where you're going, Nanna?" the little girl asked, her eyes wide like moons.

"Yes, little one. We must protect the children of this tree, for they will bring peace to the galaxy."

Olivia blinked. She was leaning against the pyramid once again, Kyrrha still squeezing her hand, unaware that Olivia had peeked in on one of her childhood memories.

"My grandmother went to a triple star system called the Triad, to a planet orbiting Alpha Centauri. Our people launched a cultural mission to help a primitive tribe develop, but the ship disappeared. Our people sent out so many rescue missions, but the galaxy is a big place. We have no idea where to look."

14 THE NEXUS

AS THE SOLE target of Miley Brewster's nine-year campaign of torture, Olivia had earned many detentions, mostly for crimes she hadn't committed. Detention was a waste of time. At least in class there was a chance to learn something, but there was no chance of learning anything in detention. To cope with the boredom, she'd brought books with her, and her love of reading had transformed those detentions into page-turning adventures. But now, as she climbed past the archives and continued to the level reserved for the Masters, doing time with Master Eldrin felt nothing like an adventure.

Master Eldrin greeted her in the hall with a feather duster and ushered her into his office, a large room with a desk, bookshelves, and comfortable furniture. She was relieved to be in a formal office and not his personal quarters. The room was decorated in a swirl of whites, blues, and cerulean. He directed her to a wall of alcoves, where his most prized artefacts were on display. "You can start here and work your way across the collection."

She could think of a thousand better uses of her time. She could be investigating Project Human, for one. Instead, she got to dust the crusty old knickknacks of a teacher who seemed to enjoy finding reasons to despise her.

"Oh, good. The entertainment has arrived." Another Atlantian was sprawled across a sofa next to Master Eldrin's large desk. His blue robes blended so perfectly with the curtains that Olivia didn't notice him until he spoke. Fantastic. Detention with an audience.

"Lord Tamiel is our Atlantian representative on the Council of Twelve. He was surprised by the outcome of your tribunal."

"I am rarely surprised."

“He made me promise to introduce him at my first opportunity. Luckily, you presented that opportunity without delay. Lord Tamiel, Olivia Carpenter. She comes with two names.”

“The pleasure is mine.”

Olivia didn’t know how she was supposed to act around a Councillor, but being polite couldn’t hurt. “The tribunal is lucky to have fair judges.”

“It was a tribunal unlike any I have adjudicated. Not that my adjudication was required.” Olivia’s truce with Queen Tara had stolen his opportunity to pass judgment, and he was being all butthurt about it.

“The whole proceeding was odd, Lord Tamiel. Especially Queen Tara’s flip-flop.” Olivia made herself small, fixing her attention on the artefacts. She picked up a stone circle with a large X cutting through it. She dusted all of its cracks and crevices, making sure to clean every surface.

“Indeed, the Queen’s behaviour was perplexing. One minute she refuses to show us the full event, but moments later, the screen restarts. The look on her face! Almost as if it were happening against her will. Do you have a theory, Olivia Carpenter?”

“Maybe the Queen realized there would be consequences for violating the Council’s authority.” She moved on to dust the next item. It was identical to the stone sculpture, but this one was made of wood.

“An interesting theory, but it doesn’t explain why Queen Tara withdrew her complaint and offered an apology.”

He was a cat with a mouse under his paw. Playing dumb was not going to work. She had to redirect how he interpreted the situation, give him a different angle to consider.

“Since you insist on involving me, let’s reason this out. What would happen to Queen Tara’s position on the Council if the Jin were found guilty of breaking the rules?”

“She would be permanently replaced.”

“Would you want to lose your seat on the Council?”

“Certainly not.”

“So it’s a question of survival. The Queen chose short-term pain for long-term gain."

"Indeed." His eyes glittered. "What about you? Are you playing the long game?"

"I don't even know what game we're playing." She put the wooden sculpture back. The next one was the same but made of glass.

"Careful, that one is fragile."

Wanting desperately to change the subject, Olivia latched on. "What is it?"

"It is called a nexus. Do you know the purpose of a nexus?" Olivia shook her head. She'd never seen sculptures like these. "The nexus acts like an anchor for the matter needed to grow a planet."

"You can grow planets? Wow."

"Moving a marble is child's play."

"Did she move a marble?" Tamiel sounded amused.

"No. She did not."

Olivia's instinct was to defend herself, but she swallowed her smart-ass retort and moved on to the next artefact, a curious gadget with dozens of interlocking copper gears. It was identical to the gadget AmmaNa had checked before stepping through the quantagate. Each gear was inscribed with a name. A large one bore the name Bodie, and the smaller one in front of it, Sita. The gadget ticked, and with each tick, the gears moved.

"Can you identify that object?" This time, Olivia did have a theory, but she shook her head anyway, deferring to Master Eldrin.

"She is able to represent herself in a tribunal but knows nothing of basic technology." Tamiel was a wolf sizing up its dinner. "She's virtually a blank slate. You could teach her anything."

"Those gears track the orbits of the planets and moons in this system. Can you guess why that is important?"

"It's important to know when Maia is rising, since her rays are deadly."

"Yes. That was a close brush with disaster. We're lucky Tuatha was able to find help, though I am still perplexed as to how that lift could have ended up on the surface without a Jin escort…"

Another dangerous topic. How did he keep landing on the

conversations she desperately wanted to avoid?

She grabbed the next item, an amethyst point much like the one in her backpack. "This is pretty. I have one just like it."

"You must be mistaken. Amethyst is incredibly rare. The closest amethyst deposit is over three hundred light-years away."

Tamiel sat up, suddenly interested. His voice was smooth and thick. Boiled icing. "Where did you get the amethyst, Olivia?"

"My grandmother gave it to me."

"And where did your grandmother get it?"

Something about him made her uneasy. Her answer was purposefully vague. "I don't know. You'd have to ask her."

"Excellent. When do I meet her?"

"She didn't come with me."

She took a deep breath and gripped the shelf, trying to hold back her longing for her grandmother. It rose inside her like a tidal wave, bringing visions of Migitju's acorn cheeks and smiling topaz eyes. If Migitju knew that Olivia was talking to such advanced people, she would tell Olivia to be respectful and learn all she could.

"Where did you get your amethyst?" She hadn't meant for the question to become a flinch. But everything went dark, and the darkness shattered into a vision.

Two men stood outside of a tall building, its metal spires reaching deep into a cloudless blue sky. One of the men was Master Eldrin. The other one looked strikingly similar, but his face was curled into an impish grin that her teacher would never wear. The man with the grin gave Master Eldrin a large chunk of amethyst. "A small sample of what we've created. You wouldn't believe it, brother. It's paradise! Using a crystal for the nexus was a fantastic idea. Are you sure you won't come with me?"

"I am needed in Atlantia."

"But think of the opportunity. We're building a civilization from nothing! Haven't you ever wondered what it would be like to start at zero?"

"You may yet convince me, but not this time." They shared a long hug before the brother boarded a spaceship the size of a metropolis.

Olivia blinked and was back in the office, clutching the amethyst. She dusted it quickly and put it back. Master Eldrin would be furious if he knew she'd flinched into his personal memories. But Lord Tamiel's snowball eyes had been fixed on her the whole time. He sniffed the air, his nose catching a scent of jasmine and cloves. He inhaled deeply.

"My, my, my, can you smell that, Eldrin? It's the strangest sensation, like the Yanisma just floated into your office."

She felt her knees tremble as Master Eldrin inhaled. "Hmm. The air does smell of Yanisma."

She leaned on the display shelf to steady herself. How could she be so careless?

"It's like they were right here moments ago." Tamiel's eyes hadn't left Olivia. "Just now, when you held that amethyst, what did you see?"

"I…I saw an amethyst. Covered in dust."

"Don't play coy with me, Olivia Carpenter. You arrive midterm at the Crystal Academy, yet you lack basic knowledge of the galaxy. Queen Tara charged you with a crime but withdrew the complaint midtribunal. What do the Jin know about you that we do not?"

"If you think they're hiding something, you'll have to ask them."

"You accused Queen Tara of rooting around in your mind without permission. What was she looking for?"

"She didn't say."

Lord Tamiel leaned in, a white-hot fire igniting inside him. He was determined to learn her secrets. Why else would he invite himself to her detention? "You are not being truthful. I demand to know what you are hiding."

He rose and stood directly behind Master Eldrin, dwarfing the tall Atlantian by at least a foot. "She was divining on your amethyst. Poking around in your private memories." He whispered the words in Eldrin's ear, his voice smooth and alluring, a song made of icing.

"You were divining on my amethyst."

"I didn't."

"How dare she intrude on your private memories!"

"How dare you!" Eldrin repeated.

"She took something precious from you. Take something from her.

Take her breath."

"Take her breath." Eldrin uttered the words like he was dreaming, but his eyes were wide open. His hand stretched out, his frostbitten thumb and index finger pushing towards each other. Olivia gasped for as much breath as she could, but it was no use. His invisible grip was too strong. Spots appeared in the periphery of her vision. She dropped to her knees, the blackness creeping in as the oxygen ran out.

She had to do something. She would not end like this.

In the spare moments before unconsciousness, she heard a noise, a very low hum vibrating through the room. She focused on the sound, and in the ensuing calm, she remembered Master Eldrin's lesson on moving a marble. She directed every last ounce of her focus at the stone nexus, and strings of energy appeared, growing from her fingertips. They wrapped around the nexus like a claw, gripping the crevices of the rough stone surface. She swiped her hand forcefully towards Master Eldrin.

The nexus flew off the shelf and shot across the room. It whizzed past its intended target, slamming instead into Lord Tamiel's forehead like a missile. He crumpled to the floor. Master Eldrin's hand dropped, and the pressure on Olivia's windpipe vanished. She gasped hard against the coughing spasms clutching her airway. Blackness came. She fought back. It tried once more. She clawed at her own arm, scratching blood from her skin, determined to remain conscious.

Dazed, Master Eldrin rubbed his temples. Noticing Olivia, he rushed to her side and spoke gently. "Are you okay?"

"Get away from me!" She winced from his reassurance, clambering across the room. He allowed her to retreat, giving her every bit of the space she made. "You tried…to kill me!" she gasped.

"What?" He was incredulous. "That can't be. I would never… I don't understand…"

Her lungs worked hard to return her breathing to normal. Behind Eldrin, Lord Tamiel lay in a heap, his face shrouded by the hood of his cloak.

"I am so sorry. I am not an easy teacher to please, but I would never hurt one of my students. That is not the Atlantian way." He cradled his head, shaking it. “I can’t remember. My mind is blank. Please believe that I have no desire to hurt you.”

If you divulge your origin,
you will be hunted by The Twelve

The warning delivered by the Jin guards echoed through her mind. Terrified and with blood dripping from her arm, Olivia bolted from the room.

15 THE MESMER

REELING FROM HER near brush with death, Olivia shut herself in her room, dug into her backpack for her first aid kit, and after cleaning and bandaging her forearm, set her tears free. First, the Greys had attacked her, then Queen Tara, and now Master Eldrin. How could he claim that he didn't remember trying to kill her? How could anyone almost take a life and not remember it? But he hadn't acted alone. Lord Tamiel had insisted that she was hiding something, goading Master Eldrin to act.

She wasn't safe. She needed to hide.

She grabbed her backpack, added a fresh tunic and pants, and took a last look at her crystal room, freezing it in her mind in case this was her last chance to remember it. Instead of making for the concourse, no doubt swarming with Jin, she headed in the other direction, towards the common rooms. She regretted this decision instantly. Two common rooms away, Lord Tamiel loomed over everyone except the Polarians, pushing his way through the crowd, heading right for her. She ducked down and pressed through the maze of bodies, putting as much distance as she could between them.

Her teal tunic gave her away, a neon sign beckoning to be seen. She darted down a burgundy hallway and chose the last door at the end of the hall, hoping it was vacant. Finding multiple sets of burgundy tunics in the dresser, she quickly pulled a burgundy outfit over her own. It was miles too big; Tamiel would never spot her under this mountain of fabric.

The burgundy hall was attached to the book room, where floor-to-ceiling crystal shelves held books of all sizes and colours. It was magnificent. Maybe one day, she'd have a chance to return and enjoy its comforts, but today, she couldn't afford that luxury. She rejoined the swarm of students, keeping her eyes down as much as she could, even while searching for him. She spotted him in the next room over, scanning every nearby face before moving on. She slipped through the crowd, tripping over her extra-large clothing a few times, and didn't look back. She'd only ever seen a few hundred students at a time, but today, as she searched for familiar faces, she was overwhelmed by how many other students wandered the halls.

Finally, she spotted Keilte and Tuatha in one of the cafeterias. Decadent trays of steaming-hot food tempted her with their delicious smells, but even though she hadn't eaten a hot meal since leaving home, she was not the least bit hungry. She spoke quietly, hoping Tuatha would hear her above the chaos of the crowd.

"Tuatha, Keilte, please help me."

Tuatha turned and was surprised to see Olivia in burgundy but was instantly overwhelmed. "What happened? You're terrified!"

"He's trying to kill me. I need to hide."

"Who wants to kill you?" As Keilte asked the question, Tamiel entered the common behind them.

Olivia scurried to a corner, out of sight. "We have to hide. He's looking for teal."

Tuatha led them up a stairway at the back of the cafeteria as a tone sounded the return to classes. The swarm made for the lifts, and the din followed, but even once they were alone, Olivia still couldn't muster any more than a whisper. She did her best to recount the trauma of her detention, including her flinch with the amethyst and her last-ditch effort to save herself. Keilte and Tuatha were dumbfounded.

"What do you mean when you talk about flinching?"

"That's my Yanisma thing where I can see the past. It makes a smell, and Tamiel knew it was a Yanisma smell."

"But you said it was Master Eldrin who was choking you. I'm on your side, Carpenter, but I'm confused."

"I don't know how to explain it, but maybe I can show you."

She wasn't keen on using the platforms again because any Jin near the waterfall would see her. This plan required discretion. Maybe the stairs could get them where they needed to go. Olivia climbed to the archives, and after checking around the corner for Tamiel, popped into the first room and placed her hand on the panel.

"Archive, how many levels can we go up by stairs from here?"

"From where you are, there are twenty levels that can be reached by stairs. However, the level above this one is restricted without an invitation from an Academy Master."

She pulled her hand away from the console and headed for the stairs. Keilte balked. "You heard the archive. This level is restricted."

"We're not stopping on the Masters' level. We're going up, so technically, we're not breaking any rules."

"Don't you love how Carpenter sees around the corners? Life with you at the academy is infinitely more interesting. Come on, Keilte. Are you a pussycat or a lion?"

He grumbled but followed nonetheless. Olivia was beginning to think that despite initial appearances, between the two of them, Tuatha was really in charge.

When they reached the next level, the stairway ended. The next one leading up started on the other side of a wide hallway.

Olivia hesitated. "How do we cross? What if we're spotted by the Jin? If one sees us, they all do."

"Tee hee! Why don't I just clear the way? Cover your eyes!"

Olivia covered hers just in time to avoid a blinding flash. Tuatha had vanished.

"What just happened?"

"Deyonns can shrink into teeny-tiny beings as bright as stars. Anyone in the way will be blinded long enough for us to slip by."

The stairs took them past three levels dedicated entirely to bees that Olivia hadn't noticed on the way down from her tribunal, but now, as the air became saturated with the sickly-sweet aroma of honey, it couldn't be ignored. At the top of the next staircase, Tuatha had returned to full size.

"That was amazing!"

"Thanks!" Tuatha giggled. "It feels great to let my light shine. I mostly have to keep it caged up on Sita. But then you arrived, and life got interesting!"

Olivia picked another staircase, and once again, Tuatha became pure light in case the way needed clearing. A third staircase that took them up another six levels finally brought them to their destination. Unfortunately, Olivia had been so focused on hiding from the Jin that she hadn't noticed Kyrrha following them. Kyrrha bounced up the stairs so quickly that she almost ran right into them.

"Why are you here?" Keilte was not happy to see her.

"Master Eldrin sent me to check on you. Again. But this time, he's really off. He's pacing around his office, ranting at the walls. He's really worried."

"Go tell him I'm fine."

"No. Keilte never skips lessons. Something's up with you lot, and I want in."

"This outing is by invite only." Keilte clenched his fists behind his back.

"Whatever you're planning to do is totally against the rules. Either you include me, or I'll tell on you."

"Wow." Tuatha was shocked. "They sure don't teach this side of Atlantian culture in galactic relations."

Clearly, Olivia's new friends didn't want Kyrrha's involvement, but despite their frosty beginnings, she and Kyrrha had shared a real moment outside of the pyramid. Besides, Olivia knew exactly how it felt to be excluded and wasn't cool with creating that kind of bad karma.

"We don't have time to argue. She's already come this far, so she's with us."

Olivia led them deep into the crystal to a familiar alcove.

Open.

Just as she had hoped, the door inside the alcove skittered away before Kyrrha could see it happen. But Keilte slammed on the brakes.

"I cannot participate. This is breaking in."

His obsession with rules was so frustrating. But she needed him. She had to convince him. "Has anyone ever told you this room is off-limits?"

"No."

"Is there a sign on the door telling us to stay out?"

"Again, no, but…"

"And we're not breaking in if the door isn't locked, right?" Keilte huffed, but he couldn't argue with her logic. She wasn't wrong. He pursed his lips but nodded and followed.

Without the pressure of the judges looming over her, the tribunal hall was truly majestic. The floor was made of white and pink marble cut and assembled into a pattern of overlapping hexagons. Twelve jewels were inlaid where the pattern touched an outer circle. To her left, a gallery for spectators rose up and away from the floor, thirty levels high. Facing her, a horseshoe-shaped staircase rose twelve tall stairs to a platform where twelve chairs, as ornate as they were unique, looked down on the marble floor. The place smelled clean, not like chemicals, but like it had been scrubbed with water.

"What is this place?" Kyrrha marvelled.

"The tribunal room." Olivia shut the door behind them.

"The Jin are coming! We have to hide!"

"Calm down, Frosty. Olivia can use Jin tech. She saved us all from Maia."

Kyrrha's eyebrows folded at the middle, making a tent over each eye.

"Ooh! An astonished Atlantian!" Tuatha teased, doing barrel rolls in midair. "You don't see one of those every day."

"You owe her your life," Keilte added, "so remember that before you go snitching to Master Eldrin."

Olivia focused on the screen.

Show me being choked by Master Eldrin.

The display sprang to life, showing Olivia as she dusted the artefacts in Master Eldrin's office. They all watched as Lord Tamiel moved in on Master Eldrin, whispering in his ear, urging him to choke Olivia. Master Eldrin obeyed without hesitation.

Tuatha interrupted the video. "Something's wrong with Master Eldrin."

"Well, obviously," Kyrrha protested.

"No, I mean there's something wrong with his aura. I assumed Carpenter brought me here to read auras?"

"I don't care about auras. Master Eldrin would never choke someone!"

"He is squeezing his fingers together. He is the one choking Liv. How do you not see that?" Keilte was redder than normal. He was containing himself, but Olivia could feel his outrage. A swell of gratitude flooded through her. And then she thought of how that would affect Tuatha.

"Sorry, I couldn't help it."

"No problem, Carpenter. Do that one again. That one felt great." Tuatha winked at her, so she took a deep breath and felt the gratitude again. She let it radiate out from her, imagining a ripple leaving her like the one she'd seen pass between AmmaNa and her crew. The focus calmed her, but it did nothing to calm Keilte or Kyrrha, who were both animatedly trying to argue over top of each other. Frustrated with how quickly this had disintegrated into chaos and keenly aware of her own inexperience at leading a group, Olivia did the only thing she could think of. She put her hand up. It worked. All eyes locked on her.

"Kyrrha, I know you want to defend Master Eldrin, but Tuatha is talking about reading auras, and I really need to hear that take. I need your take as well, but Tuatha goes first."

"Fine. I'll be quiet…for now."

"Like I said, something's wrong with Master Eldrin. Someone who's hurting someone else should have an aura full of anger, malice, contempt, possibly even disgust. But Master Eldrin has no aura at all. It's like he stepped out of his body and left the room."

"What about Tamiel?"

"Lord Tamiel's aura looks like a firestorm flower."

"Let's watch it through." Olivia started the playback again. It was a strange experience, to watch herself being choked. Just as everything began to fade, she whipped the nexus across the room, knocking Tamiel to the ground. Following a few moments of Olivia coughing and gagging, Master Eldrin was at her side, asking if she was okay.

"His aura is back. He's overwhelmed with concern."

When the Olivia on-screen told him what he had done, his eyebrows tented just as Kyrrha's had done moments earlier.

"He's shocked and confused. Shame is creeping in, but it's not the deep yellow I would see if he remembered doing this. He's overwhelmed by concern and confusion."

They reached the end of the memory, and Tuatha offered a hypothesis. "As soon as you knocked Lord Tamiel out with that nexus, the choking stopped. I think he was mesmerizing Master Eldrin. It's the only way I can explain Master Eldrin's lack of emotion."

"Can you mesmerize people, Kyrrha?" Olivia didn't mean to offend, but these magical abilities were a lot to process, and she needed to ask her questions just to maintain a whisper of sanity.

Kyrrha bristled, defending her bruised ego with deflection. "Ask Tuatha. The Deyonns are the Mesmers."

"We aren't born Mesmers. Eons ago, the Deyonns captured a Mesmer who tried to invade one of our clans on an outpost. They held him captive until they learned all of his secrets, including how to mesmerize. Now, all Deyonns learn the skill as protection, kind of like how Teutons learn to Mindshield. If you know your enemies' strengths, your knowledge becomes their weakness."

"Would your people have taught Lord Tamiel how to mesmerize?"

Tuatha shot a knowing look in Keilte's direction. "We're not supposed to. Anything's possible, but very unlikely. Deyonns and Atlantians aren't super cozy, if you get my vibe."

Kyrrha huffed through a scowl.

"And there's the vibe. Seriously, girl, if you're going to roll with us, you need to keep your nasty feels to yourself."

"Could he learn it here, at the academy?"

"Not officially. Guardians aren't trained to mesmerize. It's more likely that he learned it somewhere else. And if it came from the source, they may have taught him much darker things, too."

"But why would Lord Tamiel want you dead?" Kyrrha asked. "He barely knows you. None of us do."

Olivia didn't know anything about galactic politics, but the title of Councillor likely carried a lot of weight. Accusing Lord Tamiel of a crime was an uncomfortable place for Kyrrha. Her Atlantian pride ran deep. But it was pretty clear that he wanted Olivia dead. Maybe he'd figured out she was from Terra. Maybe it was just like the Jin claimed —being Terran put a bullseye on her chest.

"You're oozing with anxiety. There's something you aren't telling us. We came to help, so out with it."

Tuatha was right. They had come to help. It was the first time she felt like she had actual friends. And if she told them that she was a Terran, it would change everything. Maybe they would hunt her, too. The air took on a sour note, pausing under her nose to make sure she caught it.

"Of course I'm oozing with anxiety. Tamiel tried to kill me because I can flinch! I can't control what abilities I have. I didn't ask for this. What if the other Councillors find out? What will they do to me?"

"Having a Yanisma ability is not a crime, it is just incredibly rare."

"It's more than rare, Keilte. Have you ever heard of anyone other than Carpenter who can flinch?"

"I have not."

"So I'm going to ask the question the rest of you are too scared to drop. What if she can do other Yanisma stuff, too?"

There was a dead moment, like the world had stopped. All eyes fixed on her, a grotesque being wearing a meat suit and an academy tunic. Their expressions flashed with genuine fear that each one tried to hide in their own ways.

Great. They were already turning on her. This couldn't be happening.

"Come on, guys, don't look at me like that."

"Carpenter, with the way you handled Queen Tara, I'm already scared of you."

"But I need your help! Tamiel wants me dead. Does anyone have any idea why?"

"If he did a bad—like a huge bad—and he finds out you're a seer, you're a liability."

"What happens if he did something really bad?"

"He'd be kicked off the Council," Keilte said.

"Kyrrha? What happens to an Atlantian who gets kicked off of the Council?"

"Our society would banish him. He'd be exiled." Her expression, like her assessment, was grave.

Keilte turned his hulking mass toward her, just as solemn. "Atlantians have a strong sense of honour. So we need to know, are you with us, or are you with Tamiel?" Much like the question, his stare brought a challenge.

"Master Eldrin didn't really send me to check on Olivia. He was too busy muttering incoherent nonsense at the walls. I was sure she was involved because nothing's been normal since she showed up, so I followed you. But this…" She pointed at the screen where Olivia had displayed her memories. "Atlantians do not kill, and we do not coerce fellow Atlantians against their will. Lord Tamiel's behaviour is unacceptable. I'm on Team Olivia."

"Tuatha?"

"She speaks truth."

"Great. So how do we keep me safe from a Councillor? Couldn't he just have me arrested and then kill me in jail?"

"What is jail?" It was Keilte who asked, but their expressions all held the same question.

"On my planet, if you commit a crime, they lock you up so you can't commit any more crimes."

"That's barbaric!"

"As barbaric as sending people away to distant colonies, never to be seen again?"

"Ohhhhhhh, you told her about the fringe colonies." Tuatha's acknowledgement made it sound even more ominous. Olivia imagined herself banished to some wasteland, spending the rest of her life in a warehouse, shackled to a sewing machine, making clothes for the elite.

"Could Tamiel ship me off to the fringe colonies?"

"Not without support from the other Councillors. Our system is a fair one." Keilte said it with certainty, but Olivia wasn't convinced.

"What if he mesmerizes the others? What if he takes control of

Queen Tara? He'd have the whole Jin army ready to carry me away."

"Then we need to warn the Jin."

Keilte wanted to play by the rules, but Olivia couldn't trust them. She'd come here for their help, but all they'd done was assault her. AmmaNa hadn't even checked in to make sure Olivia was okay. Unless she hadn't woken up yet. What if bringing Olivia to Sita had been AmmaNa's last act of bravery?

Olivia swallowed a sob. "Not the Jin."

"We could ask Master Eldrin," Kyrrha offered.

"He attacked Liv!" Keilte protested. "What makes you think she wants his help?"

"He didn't *want* to choke her," Kyrrha countered. "Atlantians have honour. He'll do whatever he needs to do to make this right."

"Kyrrha, you weren't there. I begged him to stop, but he didn't hear me. What if he's mesmerized again? Are you going to stop him?"

"Stop playing the victim."

"Excuse me?"

"You couldn't roll a marble one inch, but you had no problem drilling a stone nexus across a room."

"I couldn't focus on the marble with the whole class whispering about what a loser I am. Thanks for that. I do have feelings, you know."

Kyrrha's cheeks went blue with shame.

"I can vouch. Carpenter has more feels than anyone I know. On that note, could you please tone it down?"

"Sorry, Tuatha." Olivia took a deep breath and grew her imaginary roots down into the crystal, pushing the hurt way down deep and out of her, the way Migitju had taught her. It helped. Even though she was four hundred light-years away, Migitju was always helping.

"Wow, Carpenter. That was…interesting."

"Keilte, you know how the system works. What should I do?"

"Reporting this attack will engage a tribunal. That means facing Lord Tamiel, but with a room full of witnesses. Once the Councillors see your memory, they will understand that you need protection."

"From Master Eldrin. I have no proof it was Tamiel. How likely is the Council to find fault in one of their own without direct evidence?"

His silence told her that the odds were not good.

"There has to be another way."

"There is one way around the Council," Kyrrha offered. "If Olivia requests an audience with the Yanisma, she can ask for an oracle to protect her. An oracle overrules all Council decisions."

"Really? Your solution is to ask the Yanisma? Are you insane?"

"Not as insane as facing Lord Tamiel in a tribunal. Olivia is the first Guardian-in-training with Yanisma abilities. I think they'll want to protect that."

"Unless she got their abilities by accident," Keilte mused.

"How would anyone ever get anything from the Yanisma by accident? Think before you say stupid things."

Olivia sighed. Even a threat on her life wasn't enough to stop these two from arguing.

"Just stop! We need to figure out how we get Carpenter an audience with the Yanisma. Oracle requests are only granted by the Council."

"We all have to face the Yanisma as part of our training. Master Eldrin can get her in."

"We don't need Master Eldrin. Any instructor can get her in."

"But Master Eldrin is the only one with a reason to bend the rules."

"Why does it have to be Master Eldrin? So you can feel relevant?"

"At least I'm offering a suggestion that might work. You want to serve Olivia to Lord Tamiel on a platter."

As Olivia tried to drown out their petty arguments and truly consider her options, a small door opened under the screen. It had no decoration, no special carvings to draw attention to its existence; it looked like a storage closet. But this was no storage closet. The smell gusting from its depths gave away its occupant without any need for a label. Her nostrils were assaulted by the smell of a hundred flinches.

"I don't think we need an instructor. The Yanisma already know I'm here."

16 THE ORACLE

ONLY A SMALL wooden door separated Olivia from the answers she desperately wanted. Why did Tamiel want her dead? Why did she have powers that none of the other students had? And most importantly, what was Project Human all about? She stepped forward, excited.

"Are you sure you want to do this, Liv?" Keilte asked.

"What?" Tuatha spun around. "Of course she has to do this. She needs to get an oracle before Tamiel tries to kill her again!"

"There is always room to reconsider, to do the right thing, to get permission first."

"Your obsession with the rules is a total buzzkill, you know that?"

"Are the Deyonns always this rebellious?" Kyrrha was amused by this side of Tuatha.

"When the rules don't make sense, we make our own rules."

"I'm quite sure I'm not breaking any rules. The Yanisma opened the door for me. I don't imagine they need the Council's permission to invite someone in for a visit, do you?"

Keilte's face flushed with deep crimson tones, but he couldn't argue with the logic. "I guess not, but still. Do you really want to go in there?"

"You all keep saying 'face the Yanisma' like it's some kind of terrifying ordeal. What's so terrifying?"

"One boy met a hideous monster who slashed his face open with razor-sharp claws." Tuatha was as serious as Olivia had ever seen. Keilte nodded solemnly.

"If your heart is pure and your soul is worthy, you have nothing to fear."

Olivia remembered her blowup with Miley. Would the Yanisma

pull out a pair of scissors and shred Olivia's face in retribution?

"They can see who you are on the inside," Tuatha explained. "They read you and mimic your vibration."

"They defeated the Draconians by absorbing their murderous hatred and amplifying it back at them a hundred times," Kyrrha added. "Nobody else has ever survived the Draconians."

"You should know," Keilte warned, "that once requested, an oracle must be obeyed. No matter what it says. Even for Tuatha, who likes to rewrite the rules." Tuatha pouted, arms crossed.

"What happens if someone gets a bad oracle?"

"An oracle is never bad. Its advice is always the best path for our collective. That is why it overrules the Council."

"Has an oracle ever banished someone to the fringe colonies?"

"The boy who was slashed ended up being banished, but he had been killing small animals for years. The Yanisma can see. That is why every student must face them before becoming a Guardian."

"Shouldn't they figure out who's dangerous before the training starts instead of after?"

"See? Carpenter questions the things we take for granted, and she's not wrong." Tuatha nodded at the door. "You better go before someone finds us." Tuatha was right. Tamiel was on the prowl.

Beyond the door was blackness. Olivia crossed the threshold and hit the smell of old things, like a musty cellar that hadn't seen sunshine in decades. As the door behind her clicked shut, a pool of light illuminated a lone chair. Olivia took the hint and sat. Another chair appeared only a few feet away, facing away from her. It was already occupied. The chair began to turn.

A chill draft crawled up her spine and settled into her bones. How would the Yanisma appear to a super-weapon from Terra? The illegal entity from a planet that wasn't allowed to exist? Part of her wanted to run all the way back to the quantagate, try to somehow get back to Earth, and pretend that none of this was real. But she was way beyond that. She had come for answers, and despite her fear, she was buzzing with curiosity.

The chair's occupant was shrouded by a long black cloak. Hands reached up to pull down the hood. Olivia braced for the reveal. The hood dropped, and Olivia gasped.

"Percy?"

He was a few years older, but it was definitely Percy Van Houten.

"If you recognize this form, you have already met my clan."

"I met you on my home planet."

"Reach out and take my hand."

Olivia obeyed, and Percy closed his eyes for a few moments, like he was thinking. They burst wide open and gawked at her. "You are from Terra. You were in danger at home. You are also in danger here. You do not come to me as a student. You come for an oracle."

"As long as it's something that protects me and not something that tells me what to do. Because I'm really tired of everyone telling me what I have to do for them instead of asking me what I need."

"What do you need, Olivia Carpenter?"

She didn't hesitate. "I need protection."

"An oracle will tell you your destiny. We do not tell you what to do. We tell you only that which is inevitable. You are special, Olivia Carpenter. Your destiny will protect you. Harm will only befall you when you resist the will of the source."

Percy paused to swing his feet under the chair as he had done outside of the principal's office. This time, his legs were long enough that his shoes scuffed against the floor with each pass. "You have questions. Our kind prefers questions that are asked over answers that are assumed. Proceed."

"How did you grow six inches?"

"I present a reflection of who you are. If I seem older, it means you have matured. This was not the question I was expecting. You may go deeper."

"My grandmother taught me how to see the past of an object. But the other students said this is a Yanisma ability that you don't teach to anyone. How come I can do this?"

"The Yanisma helped create the Terrans. We hid our abilities in your genetic code, the key to the lock, the first of The Twelve. It is an honour to meet you."

"Is that something to do with Project Human? I flinched with the Jin, and there were twelve of you talking about Project Human. Please tell me what that is."

"The Council of Twelve went to Terra and created beings, humanoids in our own image, with genetic code from all twelve tribes. The experiment failed. Tinkering with genes is easy. Combining species is not. We created three-headed dogs, lion-headed eagles, and a myriad of porcine creatures. Something always overwrote the humanoid codes. After many botched attempts, we had to rethink. Instead of one, we made four types of Terrans: red, yellow, black, and white. We taught them the mysteries of the cosmos and then gave them the space they needed to intermix and evolve into something greater than what we could create."

"If you expected us to intermix, as you call it, you're going to be disappointed. A lot of Terrans think intermixing makes their blood impure."

"That is unfortunate."

"Why did you abandon us?"

"The tribe created by Project Human must be neutral. Some of The Twelve wanted to guide your development, but that would have made them too familiar. To protect your impartiality, Terra was hidden."

"What about the Yanisma? I met your kind on my planet."

"We were never forbidden from Terra. We were chosen to stay and watch without interfering."

"What about when a murderous creep eats Terran children? Would that be a good time to interfere?"

"You recognize me. That tells me that we did interfere. And you escaped. Your arrival here is a joyous day for the galaxy and a danger to its enemies."

Percy produced a clear glass object the size of a plum. He took her hand once again and pressed the plum to his forehead, forming a triangle with his eyes.

"I call forth the destiny of Terra-born Olivia Carpenter." He sat in quiet concentration for a long moment, the glass plum filling with a swirling purple mist. The air grew thick with jasmine and cloves, stronger than Olivia had ever smelled. When he was finished, he examined the globe like he was reading a book.

"Unlike other oracles I have created, this one contains many layers. As long as the oracle presents an unfulfilled request, the Council may not interfere in your activities. Each layer of this oracle can only be revealed in its proper time and place. Your path is not an easy one, Olivia Carpenter. As you have so far, you must follow your instincts." He handed her the globe. It contained an object, hidden in the mist, but no matter which way she twisted the globe, the object was always just out of view.

"What do I do about getting home? About the danger on Terra?"

"To get the help you need, you must tell them where home is."

"But the Jin told me not to."

"Only once you reveal your truth, will the truth be revealed to you. You must overcome your fear and claim your seat at the table. If you do not, this oracle cannot protect you. And now I must ask something of you. It will not be an easy task, and it is your choice. It is a favour to me and a kindness to all of the galaxy."

"What do you need me to do?"

"You must unmask the threat."

"How do I do that?"

"A shadow hangs over the Council. Peel back the illusion. Show them the truth. You already have the tools you need. And now you must go. Your time with me is finished. The Council has arrived. They are waiting for both of us. Take your oracle, Olivia Carpenter. Use it well."

Tamiel's icy glare met Olivia as she exited Percy's dark lair, and escorted her across the bright marble floor. He had assembled the other judges, which couldn't be good, but he hadn't expected to find her hanging out with the Yanisma. He was furious. As was Lord Harvarder. With arms folded across his muscular chest, he looked ready to do battle. Queen Tara's smugness said that she'd already won. Only Duchess Damia was calm and unaligned. Olivia clutched her globe tightly. Losing it was not an option.

"The Council did not approve a meeting with the Yanisma! This one has caused trouble since she arrived. She must be expelled immediately."

Clearly, Tamiel didn't want a fair tribunal. He wanted to cover his tracks by disposing of the only witness. If ever there was a time for Olivia to run her mouth, this was it.

"The Yanisma invited me in, to tell me why I have Yanisma abilities."

"Yanisma abilities? You?" He waved his hand dismissively. "Preposterous!"

But Olivia's claim had piqued the interest of the stately Duchess, who rose to her feet, signalling that it was her turn to speak. She was at least fifteen feet tall, dwarfing all of them, commanding silence.

"A Guardian with Yanisma abilities would be a first. If this is true, it is of great interest indeed." Her booming voice came from deep in her belly, like a bass violin. "Why did you not inform us of this? Do you not believe that we would assist you in your development?" The concern in her voice was in stark contrast to Tamiel's abusive tone.

"My apologies, Duchess, but Queen Tara invaded my mind, and then Lord Tamiel saw me being attacked and goaded my attacker instead of helping me. I didn't come to the Council because I didn't feel safe."

"Tamiel? Did you fail to report an attack?" Lord Harvarder was stunned at the suggestion that a Councillor would break the rules.

"That's precisely why I gathered you here. To inform you that Eldrin attacked a student."

"He's lying!" Tuatha cried out from the gallery. Tamiel glowered at the outspoken Deyonn, who cowered into Keilte's shoulder.

"That's the second time he's lied to you today," Olivia added. "He already knows I have a Yanisma ability. The real reason he assembled you is to banish me before I find out why."

"I will not be spoken about with such brazen disrespect!"

Ignoring Lord Tamiel's outburst the way a horse ignores a fly, Duchess Damia continued. "Did the Yanisma shed any light on why you have their ability?"

Unfortunately, Olivia's claim had delivered her to this uncomfortable question. She chewed on the inside of her cheek instead of her lip, conscious of how obvious her nervous habit could be. "He told me that only once I reveal my truth will the truth be revealed to me."

Queen Tara's copper face glowered at her from her perch.

"And what is your truth, child?"

Olivia knew she had to tell them, but with everyone watching her, she lost her nerve. Stalling for time, she produced her oracle. She had been gripping the little glass plum so tightly that relaxing her hand caused daggers of pain to shoot up her arm. Upon seeing it, Tamiel snarled.

"I'm not sure what to do with this."

"You activate an oracle by placing it on a torus."

Keilte strode forward and presented her with the crystal torus he had used to shrink her tunic. Olivia put the torus in her palm, and when she balanced the oracle on top, it activated itself, a projection bursting from its rounded top. A beautiful tree with a tangle of branches formed a large canopy, its roots below mirroring the canopy perfectly, with one key difference. While small pieces of crystal fruit dotted the branches, the roots knotted around a single chunk of crystal the size of a watermelon. The voice of the oracle echoed through the room:

"This child is precious. This child is protected. This child must eat the sacred fruit to learn from the source." The projection vanished.

"THIS IS AN OUTRAGE!" Tamiel was pissed.

"We will have decorum in this chamber!" Duchess Damia towered over him. "You do not speak for the Yanisma. He has made no complaint about the child's visit. That matter is closed. On the other hand, it is well worth investigating the complaint that you witnessed an attack on a student and did not intervene."

Tamiel exploded from his chair, toppling it over, and stormed out through a hidden door behind the other Councillors.

"Allow me to apologize for the disrespect you have endured. What can you tell us of this attack?"

The Yanisma had encouraged her to tell them where she was from, but she was so used to keeping secrets; it was in her very bones. Her mother's people had been keeping secrets for centuries just to survive. But she wasn't being threatened by European colonists. This wasn't Earth. This was a place that seemed to welcome diversity. It was now or never.

"I think it has to do with the reason I can flinch, like the Yanisma. They helped create my people. All of you did. Apparently, my home planet is kind of important."

"And what is your home planet?"

"We call it Earth. But the Yanisma called it…Terra."

There. It was out in the open. They all knew she was from Terra. The weight of the secret was gone, but Tuatha sensed the cloud of relief wrapping Olivia in a hug. Feeling relief meant Olivia knew she'd been keeping this secret.

Realizing this wasn't meant as a joke, Duchess Damia exploded with laughter. Her booming hoots echoed around the tribunal room, filling every hollow space with the sound of her disbelief. "You? A Terran? But you're tiny! You cannot be the issue of Project Human!"

Lord Harvarder, on the other hand, was not amused in the slightest. "Terra is off-limits. Interfering with it is forbidden. I now understand Queen Tara's behaviour. She went looking for the truth because all she heard from your mouth were lies."

"But the Yanisma said that's where I'm from."

"Enough! You have made a mockery of this tribunal, but you will mock us no more. You are dismissed."

His mind was made up, and that was it. There was nothing she could say that he would believe. Even if she used the screen to show him their Yanisma recluse welcoming her as a Terran, he wouldn't watch it. Tuatha whispered something in Keilte's ear, and they shuffled to the exit, pulling Kyrrha along with them. They'd never cared about Kyrrha before, but now they all had something in common; they'd all trusted her. A Terran. A monster.

Olivia left the tribunal hall feeling utterly alone, until she reached the lift. As she stepped onto the platform, the Jin appeared in every hexagonal window and doorway and pointed directly at her. A thousand pairs of slick black eyes watched her every move. She was an exhibit, an animal in a zoo roaming around in a cage, dissected by a mob of accusatory glares.

Take me to the infirmary.

The lift stopped, and Olivia followed the open hallway around the waterfall until she reached a familiar piece of wall.

Open.

A warehouse of glittering coffins stretched out before her, too many to count, too many to comprehend. Olivia prayed that AmmaNa was still alive. She quickly found the bed where she'd been held prisoner, but the one next to it was empty. Was AmmaNa awake? Where was she? What had Queen Tara done with her?

Olivia's stomach growled. The pile of honeycomb on the far table smelled amazing, even from far away, so she helped herself. She didn't care that this was the Queen's food. She was over Queen Tara's power trip. As the honey melted down her throat, coating it in warmth, the fuzziness in her head evaporated. Her skin tingled, and her muscles flexed. She leaned against the wall, wondering *where did AmmaNa go?* and to her shock, the crystal beneath her hands glowed, and the answer came through the walls.

Our AmmaNa is not your kin.

We do not give you leave to speak.

Olivia let go of the wall and ate another chunk of honeycomb, determined to use the mental clarity it created to her advantage. Terra was off-limits, and the closest star to the solar system was four light-years away. AmmaNa had answered her beacon in less than four years, so she had most likely been spying on Earth from somewhere nearby. She would only do that on the orders of her queen. And if that inconvenient truth came out, Queen Tara would face the consequences. That made AmmaNa a liability.

As she paced around, the oracle in her pocket bounced against her leg. It had given her a mission: to eat the sacred fruit and learn from the source. That had to mean the Tree of Life. The experience was supposed to be like knowing everything the Jin knew for a short time. Maybe this was the only way to get answers and clear her name.

She emerged on the surface, bathed by the blue-white glow of Merope on her left, with Alcyone and all of its little cousins as well as Atlas and his twin sisters on her right. She would have found the sky to be quite breathtaking if she hadn't been so preoccupied. The garden was quiet. She sat down next to the lake, feeling like more of an outsider than she ever had back home.

"Are you okay?" Rama's voice made her jump. "You haven't been in lessons since Master Eldrin gave you detention. I've been worried."

"You don't need to worry about me, Rama. Nobody else does."

"What does that mean? Did you get in a fight with the others? They've been missing, too, so I just assumed you were all together, having fun without me."

"We were together, but they ditched me as soon as they found out where I'm from."

"That doesn't sound right. Where are you from then?"

"I call it Earth, but I guess everyone here calls it Terra."

A small gasp escaped his thin blue lips. "You're from Terra?"

"That's right. Go ahead and hate me."

"Hate you? Why would I hate you? I just never expected to meet a Terran! We've all been told that someday... But I never thought in my lifetime..." There was a long pause while he considered this bombshell.

"It would have been better for everyone if the Jin would have just handed me over to the little grey monsters."

"Little grey monsters?" Rama dropped serious.

"A swarm of them attacked the Jin to get at me. So we came here."

"The Greys are on Terra? Do the Councillors know? Olivia, you have to tell them!"

But before she could explain that the Councillors didn't believe her, Kyrrha's shadow suddenly blocked the light of Merope. Keilte and Tuatha waited on the path, and behind them, waves of students began flowing between the pyramids.

"Watch out, Rama. She likes keeping secrets. Big secrets. Even from the people she calls friends."

"Yeah, she's from Terra. She told me."

"Well, it's good to know she trusts you, even though we're the ones who risked everything to help her." She crossed her arms. "Are you coming to Master Scala's lesson, or are you staying with the traitor?"

"I should go," he said apologetically, rising to his feet. "Are you coming?"

"She isn't one of us. She doesn't belong in our lessons. It's just another one of her lies."

"It's fine, Rama. Go. I'm better off alone anyway."

"I'll be back to check on you after Master Scala's lesson, okay?"

Soon, the students were all neatly tucked away in their pyramids, learning skills that she wasn't meant to learn, forming friendships that she wasn't meant to form. She sauntered around the lake, wondering when Maia would rise. Maybe this time she'd stay on the surface to say hello. Maybe that wouldn't be so bad...

She plopped down on the edge of the lake next to Master Scala's pyramid and dug the tuning forks out of her backpack. Striking them against the ground, she held one up to each ear. Maybe if she could get herself in tune, she could stop screwing everything up.

As she listened to the hum, she noticed a canoe tied up a few feet away. Since nobody would need it at least until the next break, she climbed in and pushed off toward the island, tapping her forks once again. She let the canoe drift, focusing instead on the hum from the forks, until she nudged into the island.

The tree was stunning. It towered over her, easily thirty feet tall. It was covered in green leaves shaped like teardrops, but that's where its resemblance to Earth trees ended. Its trunk looked like blobs of molten glass had been poured from the sky and solidified just before reaching the ground, nothing like the cracked skin of a maple or an oak. The bark was almost white with a faint purple hue, but its fruit was what made this tree truly magnificent. Hanging from every branch was a small pink apple that sparkled, causing the whole tree to twinkle like a chandelier. Four students in coral tunics tended to the tree; one Atlantian, two Vegans, and a Doggo. They polished the smooth bark with sponges and buckets of water they filled from the lake.

"Are you polishing the tree for a special occasion?"

"We aren't polishing the tree, we're watering it," replied one of the Vegans.

"Oh. I'm used to trees that drink through their roots."

"How can you wear the tunic if you don't know how to care for the tree?"

"They let all sorts of riff-raff in these days," said the Atlantian, turning up his nose. Ignoring his elitism, she reached up for a piece of fruit, but he jumped to his feet and swatted her hand away. "Eating the fruit is forbidden without the guidance of a Master."

Olivia was done with being bossed around. This Atlantian snob could say whatever he wanted, but sharing his opinion invited a rebuttal, and Olivia wasted no time putting these jerks in their place. She whipped out her oracle, placed it on the torus Keilte had abandoned, and let it speak for itself. When the projection finished, she put the oracle safely in her pocket and smirked. "Maybe you need a chaperone to eat the fruit, but clearly I don't. Now get out of my way."

As if the tree was listening, it lowered a branch willingly, offering Olivia a sparkly apple. Stunned, the watering crew dropped their buckets and stepped back, giving her room. She put the fruit to her lips expecting to shatter her teeth, but its skin gave easily under the pressure of her hesitant bite, the juice bursting into her mouth, overwhelming her taste buds with the bite of ginger and the sweetness of honey all rolled into one. It made her mouth and throat tingle and go numb.

The world went black. She was alone, falling face-first through a void. Out of the nothing, shapes began to appear. A red hexagon formed to her left, a yellow one to her right. They multiplied until she was surrounded by hexagons in a tunnel of primary colours. She whizzed forward, the colours whipping by so quickly that they blended into greens and purples and oranges. The tunnel ended in a massive chamber, its floor and ceiling made of geometric shapes that melted into a distant horizon. A pulsing ball of white energy appeared on the horizon and grew with each beat. It had a steady rhythm, a small pulse followed by a larger one.

Da-DUM, Da-DUM, Da-DUM.

It grew and grew until it was as bright as a star, and then it exploded, sending a shower of light in all directions. Clumps of atoms crashed into each other, forming larger clumps. Again, she fell. She landed in another chamber, but this time the pattern was more complex, with circles and triangles adding extra layers. Two triangles overlapped to form a star, which was enclosed in a hexagon and surrounded by a circle. Circles overlapped from one hexagon to the next, meeting each other at the points of the stars. The pattern repeated all around her, as far as she could see. It was magnificent.

A floating nexus appeared, similar to the ones in Master Eldrin's collection, but this one was made of amethyst. The nexus sprouted a leaf. The leaf grew into a sapling. Its branches twisted upward into corkscrews, sprouting new corkscrews as they went. The base of the tree grew down in the same way, trapping the amethyst nexus in a claw of tangled roots. Olivia could feel a rhythm, like the inhale and exhale of breath.

Da-DUM, Da-DUM, Da-DUM.

The tree grew. Its leaves and fruit turned blue and swelled with each beat, filling in the gaps. Soon, the tree grew into a solid sphere. A planet. The bottom half of the planet fell away, leaving the tree's roots exposed. A frostbitten hand reached in, took hold of a root, and snapped it off. Ten thousand voices howled in pain. Another hand, a golden one, grabbed a second root and snapped it off, leaving an ugly wound at the base of the tree. The voices howled again, much louder and full of terror.

Da-DUM, Da-DUM, Da-DUM, Da-DUM, Da-DUM.

A red hand reached in, and so did a blue one.

"Please stop! You're hurting it!" Olivia's pleas had no effect. The carnage continued, root after root amputated until the tree barely had any roots left. She felt every break as if her own bones were snapping. The pain filled every cell of her being, intensifying with every beat.

Da-DUM, Da-DUM, Da-DUM, Da-DUM, Da-DUM!

Da-DUM, Da-DUM, Da-DUM, Da-DUM, Da-DUM!

It overwrote everything. There was only pain. Drowning, she called on every ounce of strength she had and pushed back against the carnage.

"NOOOOOOOOOOO! STOOOOOPPPPPP!"

A bright light shot down from the sky. A million tiny bolts of lightning spinning inside a tornado twisted directly towards the island. The lightning tornado touched down at the base of the tree, the shock of its impact sending Olivia and the watering team tumbling to the ground. The entire moon trembled.

A crack appeared at the base of the tree. It grew and grew, splitting the island in two, picking up speed as it went. It raced across the lakebed, water rushing into the open wound as it headed for the edge. When it reached the canyon, the ground pulled apart, opening like the petals of a flower to expose the pollen beneath. Hundreds of hexagonal windows, once protected inside the cliff, now lay exposed to the burning rays of Maia.

17 AFTERSHOCKS

AS OLIVIA TRIED to shake off the mental fog clinging to her brain cells like gum in hair, one of the Vegans pounced, snatching her arms and twisting them behind her back.

"Hey! Let me go!"

But with four arms, his grip was much too strong for Olivia to wiggle free.

"You tried to kill the tree!"

"You destroyed our home! We're taking you in!"

Their hostility was understandable. The lakebed was dry, the water now disappearing at the base of the tree. The hive was cracked wide open and Maia would be rising soon.

"We told you not to eat the fruit without a Master," said the Vegan, his fingers puncturing her flesh.

"I didn't do this! Didn't you see the lightning tornado?"

"It all started when you screamed," said the Atlantian.

"If you don't let me go, I'll scream again!"

She inhaled deeply and the Vegan let her go, afraid that she was about to deliver on her threat. Terrified, he scrambled away across the lakebed. The rest of the watering crew gave chase, leaving Olivia alone on the island. Swarms of students poured out of the pyramids, a wave of panic crashing across the plaza as each one absorbed the magnitude of the devastation. Some darted for the lifts while others hesitated, unsure if it was safe to go underground. Olivia picked her way down the bank and across the lakebed. As she climbed up the other side, she came face to face with Keilte, Tuatha, and Kyrrha.

"Why would you do this?" Keilte asked, his face painted with hurt.

“Oh, so it’s gotta be my fault. Thanks.”

“Of course it’s your fault. Who else could do this? You’re the TERRAN.” Kyrrha spat out the word like rotten food. Nearby students approached, wondering if they’d heard correctly.

“She’s a Terran? Like, the forbidden planet? For real?”

“So she says. And she’s been lying to everyone about it. So much for the promise that Terrans would bring peace to the galaxy. All this one brings is lies and destruction.”

“I don’t call my home Terra. Queen Tara said I was Terran and ordered me not to tell anyone because the Jin weren’t supposed to interfere. What would you do, Kyrrha? Would you ignore a Councillor’s order?”

Kyrrha’s cheeks went blue and her eyebrows tented in astonishment. She hadn’t imagined that Olivia might have a valid reason for being secretive. But it was too late. Enough students had heard the accusation that a small crowd was now forming to peek at the freak.

“Keilte? Aren’t you all about the rules? I was following an order.”

“Only until you decided not to.”

“Only until the Yanisma gave me permission. I hated keeping secrets from you. Tuatha? You know that’s the truth!”

Tuatha nodded reluctantly, but Keilte didn’t care. He turned away. It didn’t matter that she had followed the rules. It didn’t matter that she had come clean as soon as she was allowed. All that mattered was that she was a Terran. A freak. Some weird science project who didn’t fit in.

Tamiel would blame her for the moonquake and use it to send her away to the fringe colonies. She needed a quiet corner where she could assess her options. She pushed through the crowd and ran for the nearest lift. Thankfully, it was undamaged.

Olivia expected the interior of the city to be immersed in chaos. Instead, the Jin buzzed from balcony to balcony in an orderly fashion, filling in windows, turning them into walls. The crystal glowed under their touch, spiderwebs of light emanating from the point of contact. It was a relief to see the repairs underway so quickly, but as Olivia travelled down into the belly, the immensity of the damage revealed itself. The city's innards lay open to the elements. Rows upon rows of hexagonal windows were, for the first time, illuminated by starlight from Alcyone and Atlas. It penetrated the hive one hundred floors deep, a slice of daylight cutting through a dark closet. The exposed crystal glowed in the starlight. Without the waterfall to cool the air, things were getting a bit clammy. Olivia shed the extra burgundy tunic; wearing two was too much. A wisp of cool tickled across her wrists.

Stop.

She followed it across the concourse, a chill wind that came from deep in the cracked crystal luring her into the wound. She stepped carefully, leaning into the wall along a cliff's edge that brought her to a grotto where the wound ended. Part of the waterfall now lived here, splashing down over the newly exposed crystal. The new cascade was beautiful, bouncing from rock to rock instead of falling in one great chute. But as she approached it to get a better look, her foot slipped, and she skidded across the floor, landing hard on her left hip. That would leave a nasty bruise. As she pushed herself up, she palmed the most interesting crystal, a long mauve shard that hooked on the end like a claw. She tucked it away inside the spare tunic in her backpack, grateful that she'd brought one.

As she fumbled around in her backpack, her hand brushed against something smooth and unfamiliar. It was a leather case, but nothing she recognized. She popped open the button and found the glasses Percy Van Houten had insisted she take. He'd given them to her right before the flinch with Creepy McSlenderman, and then Miley had happened, and then she'd run away… There had been so much chaos she'd forgotten all about these. But now, knowing that Percy was Yanisma, they became a definite curiosity. They were way too big for her but she put them on anyway, hoping she'd be able to see through the crystal or something cool like that. Nothing happened. Maybe they were a slow burn. Maybe she'd have to wear them for a while to figure out their purpose.

The grotto was a natural cavern in the rock, like the inside of a geode cracked open during the moonquake. The pebbles she'd tripped on were scattered all over the grotto, evidence of the damage done. She didn't think this damage was her fault, but it really didn't matter who was to blame. The land was hurting and it was her responsibility to try and help it heal. Migitju believed that the land and the trees knew what they needed to thrive. Maybe this moon could tell her what it needed. Olivia put her hands on the crystal to listen, the way Migitju listened to her trees. The crystal glowed and Olivia asked it:

What do you need to heal?

There was a long moment of nothing, followed by the unmistakable voice of Queen Tara:

Go out and find the child that caused our precious moon to quake.
Bring her to the tribunal room to pay for this mistake.

Great. The crystal doubled as Queen Tara's social media channel. So much for helping the moon. The Jin were on the hunt, and Olivia was their prey. Deflated, she pulled the oracle from her pocket. A swirly mist still hid the object inside, but the mist was now pine green instead of purple. Curious, she rummaged in her backpack for the torus and rested the orb on top.

The projection burst upward, showing Dr. Retchen sitting in a black SUV, watching Eagle Crest Farm through a pair of binoculars. He reached into a cooler perched on the passenger seat and pulled out a long strip of bloody meat. He lowered it into his mouth bit by bit, ripping at it with razor-sharp teeth.

"You must return to Terra and defeat the one who threatens your family," the oracle boomed.

WHAT? She had just barely escaped this creep and now she had to go back to defeat him? This was insane! And then she realized…the Council couldn't override an oracle. Queen Tara would have to let her use the quantagate. Suddenly, it didn't matter that all of her so-called friends had abandoned her. She was going home. The only thing to do was to present her new mission to the Council.

Moments later, as Olivia shimmied back along the cliff's edge, a scuffling noise on the concourse alerted her to their arrival. The crystal must have led them here. It was alive, after all, and it probably blamed her, too. None of it mattered anymore.

Your actions caused our moon to break,

our water source lost to the quake.

You will come answer for your crime,

or we will scream again.

Olivia's head ached just at the suggestion that they might scream. She wondered if her tower could protect her, but any protection would only be temporary anyway. She couldn't rely on it. She didn't want to end up sleeping forever.

There's no need to scream. I'm already coming.

Much to her relief, the tribunal room was untouched. It was far enough from the crack that nothing was out of place. The marble floor was perfect. But unlike the other times she'd been in this room, today, thousands of bodies crammed into the bleachers, a patchwork quilt of at least fifty colours carpeting the risers from wall to wall. An auditorium full of nerves and fidgeting. The moonquake had left everyone unsettled, and although the tribunal room made an excellent shelter, it was more likely that they had gathered to get a peek at the freak. Her former friends populated the front row, anxious to see her pay for her crimes.

The Yanisma door opened and Percy emerged, fully hidden under his cloak. It made sense. If he appeared differently to each person, keeping himself hidden likely avoided a lot of confusion. He climbed the twelve stairs and took one of the ornate chairs at the top. It gave Olivia small comfort to know she had at least one ally among the Councillors. She clutched her oracle, praying that it really had the power to send her home.

Unlike her last visit, this time, all twelve chairs were occupied. Percy, Duchess Damia, Lord Harvarder, and Queen Tara had been joined by a Vegan, a Deyonn, a Doggo, and five other beings Olivia did not recognize. Tamiel was not among them. His chair was occupied by a giant with a muscular chest partially covered by a long beard of ebony ringlets. His skin was dry tobacco that reflected the light, much like the golden helmet on his head and his long golden robes. If it weren't for his size and the wings protruding from his back, he could've easily been mistaken for human. He looked like the biblical depictions of angels Olivia had seen on a field trip to an art gallery in

Regina. Seeing him in Tamiel's chair was a relief. Maybe they'd already kicked Tamiel out for his attempt on her life. Wouldn't that be a refreshing twist?

Of the remaining four, one was impossible to describe because it wasn't fully there, like it was trying to download but couldn't quite connect. To its right, a feline woman with warm nutmeg fur and striking pink eyes wore an ebony jewel in the middle of her forehead that stared down into Olivia's soul. To the left of the flickering download was a woman with orchid skin and a long face topped with short blueish-white hair, and to the right of the Deyonn Councillor, a reptoid being sat calmly with her hands crossed in her lap. Her stare was frightening, her yellow eyes punctuated by black pupils that morphed from round to vertical slits every time she blinked.

Lord Harvarder stood, commanding the room. "This Tribunal has been called by Queen Tara. She accuses Olivia Carpenter of causing a moonquake that has put the city of Sita on the edge of ruin."

After the way he had dismissed her earlier, Olivia wasn't interested in playing by his rules. She would speak when she wanted to and for as long as she needed. This time, she'd write her own rules.

"Her tribunal will have to wait. My oracle says I have a mission to complete, and the Council cannot over rule an oracle." She produced the oracle, put it on Keilte's torus, and let them see for themselves.

"You must return to Terra and defeat the one who threatens your family,"the oracle boomed.

"My oracle says I have to return to Terra. Return. Because that's where I came from."

Lord Harvarder could not argue with the oracle's revelation. "The oracle has confirmed it, so it must be…" He trailed off, bewildered.

"If Terrans are important to you, laughing at me was a really crap way of showing it."

"Terra is four hundred light-years away," protested the Duchess. "How have you travelled such a distance? How will you return?"

Olivia shot Queen Tara a challenging look. "I'm going back the way I came, through the Jin quantagate."

"What?!" They all turned to the Queen, who glared down at

Olivia. “Taking a Terran off-planet without the Council’s permission is a betrayal of the highest order!”

We only learned about this child
when she arrived and breached our wall.
We tried to keep her in a shell,
but she was able to escape.

“AmmaNa rescued me. She said her queen would protect me, but instead I’ve been treated like a dirty little secret Queen Tara doesn’t want you to know about. I don’t know why she’s ashamed. AmmaNa is a hero. She saved me from the grey monsters terrorizing my planet.”

“Grey monsters? What grey monsters?” The mention of the Greys affected Lord Harvarder the same way it had affected Keilte.

“They’re all through our culture, abducting adults and children, doing weird experiments on our people. They’re so common back on Earth that we have posters and movies and television shows all about them. I thought they were fiction until they attacked AmmaNa’s ship to try and stop me from leaving. Queen Tara can show you the memory.”

We do not have that memory.
It never was transferred.

“I don’t understand. Don’t the Jin have one singular mind? Don’t you all share your thoughts?”

We did not tap those memories
so we could judge with virgin eyes.

“Well, I’m too tired to run the screen again, and I don’t owe you any more answers. Call AmmaNa in. She can show the Council everything. I’m not doing it.”

“This is preposterous! Are we to ignore the destruction this Terran has caused to our city, our academy? Terran or not, her betrayal must be punished.”

Something about his voice was familiar, but Olivia couldn’t place it. She’d met so many people in the past few days it was hard to remember every voice. And she’d met twelve new alien tribes, but not his. He was memorable. It had to be a coincidence. Like a doppelgänger. A vocalgänger? Could that be a thing?

“Please, Lord Tamiel, control your outbursts. We must have

decorum."

Lord Tamiel? But… He wasn't Tamiel. She reached up to rub her eyes, her hand bumping into Percy's glasses. They fit so comfortably that she'd forgotten she was even wearing them. When she took them off and looked at him again, it was Tamiel.

The realization was a punch in the gut. He was the threat the Yanisma wanted her to unmask. She already had the tools; her glasses and the ability to run Jin tech. She'd come here determined to show them her new oracle and go home, but she couldn't leave them like this. An impostor with the power to mesmerize was sitting in a Councillor's chair, and that put the entire moon in danger. She had no choice. She had to expose him.

She walked over to the wall and made contact with the crystal. If contact amplified the Jin signal, chances were it would work the same for her. Spiderwebs of light appeared around her hand.

Show what I see onscreen.

The screen flickered to life, showing the hall from Olivia's point of view. From high above, the cloaked figure next to Lord Tamiel nodded his head.

"This is my point of view. I'm running the screen. Look." Olivia put her glasses back on, and Tamiel disappeared. In his place, the golden-angel-impostor was revealed to all in his true form.

Panic erupted in the gallery.

Screams echoed off the crystal walls, creating a cacophony of terror. Students and Masters alike dashed for the exit. The impostor wasted no time trying to regain control of the room. He leaned toward Lord Harvarder and whispered something in the Teuton's ear, but instead of blindly repeating it, Lord Harvarder turned and confronted him, full of shock.

"What did you just tell me to do?"

In his haste, the impostor had forgotten that Teutons protected themselves with Mindshield. He turned to his right, coming face to face with the shadows under Percy's hood, but decided it was pointless. He'd already lost control. Trying to mesmerize a Yanisma wouldn't help. Instead, he lunged from his chair and opened his mighty wings, swooping down like an eagle, his sharp talons aimed directly at Olivia.

She would not be easy prey. Not today. She took a deep breath and silently called on Migitju and on all of Migitju's warrior ancestors to come lend her their strength and their bravery. Venom bubbled inside her, racing through her veins, demanding to be unleashed.

He landed and snatched for her throat all in one graceful and terrifying movement, but she was ready. She ducked and rolled sideways, avoiding the snatch of his claws. She could have used his brief moment of confusion to run and hide, but she had called on her warrior ancestors for a reason. She lunged at his feet, grabbing his ankle. He wanted her dead, and she was going to find out why.

Amid the chaos of her emotions, there was power, and this time Olivia didn't shy away from it. This time, she called on that power to be useful.

Why do you hate Terrans?

The tribunal room exploded, swirling around her like confetti, reforming as a tan landscape with low shrubs and distant hills. The impostor and another like him crawled out of a large hole and wiped at the dirt caking their skin.

"I'm sick of digging in the bowels of this vile planet!"

"Agreed. Let us go find some lesser creatures to do this dirty work for us."

The two spread their mighty wings and flew for a distance until a plume of smoke led them to a small village.

"Enki, these creatures are too big. Surely they will reject our slavery and destroy us."

"Fear not, brother. We will take their females to Ninhursag and have her breed an army of smaller creatures with shorter lives. They will not be able to overthrow us, and when they wear out, she will make more."

The brothers waited until the village slept. When the fires had burned down to embers, they crept into the huts, and each of them kidnapped one of the females. When they presented their captives to Ninhursag and explained their plan, she was skeptical. "If I breed an army, what will stop them from using their numbers to overthrow us?"

"Tweak their genes, sister. Fill them full of greed, violence, and jealousy. We will choose a king from among them, a target for their hatred. We will vanish into the shadows while they mine every last atom of gold on this planet. And then, we will claim our reward and return home to enjoy the hero's welcome we deserve."

Ninhursag nodded in agreement and set to work creating an army of human slaves. Day after day, the slaves crawled into the earth and resurfaced, their backs bent under heavy bags of rocks that they turned over to their masters. Enki put a golden crown on one of the men and taught the new king to make his subjects work harder by the whip.

The vision ended. Olivia was stunned.

Enki inhaled deeply, savouring her flinch. "I knew you were different as soon as I smelled you in Eldrin's office." He snatched at the hand gripping his ankle with six scaly fingers ending in sharp talons. They pressed into her skin, drawing blood, ensuring she could not evade him a second time. With her pinned, his other claw snatched at her throat. He leered, closing his leathery fingers, shutting off her breath. "Unlike your weak-minded instructor, I will not fail."

She gasped, clawing at his arm, but her efforts had no effect. Beyond the scales on his fingers, his skin was covered in a layer of downy feathers—it was like scratching a chicken.

Keilte burst from the gallery and lunged at Enki, landing a hard punch on his shoulder. Enki's claws retracted from the flesh of her arm, but he still had Olivia by the throat, suffocating the last few moments of life out of her. Enki raised his free hand to do battle with Keilte, but Tuatha flew in overhead and began shaking, causing a downpour of shimmer to engulf him. He sneezed violently, and again, and again, unable to stop. He took to the air with his mighty wings and punched Tuatha to the ground, ending the shimmer storm.

Behind Enki, a head with yellow eyes and a large hooked beak emerged from the shadows of the Yanisma's hood. It screeched, and those still in the gallery screamed even louder than before. Startled, Enki looked over his shoulder, loosening his grip just enough for Olivia to fill her lungs. Determined to use every extra second this new breath gave her, she scanned the room for something she could use to knock him out. Her eyes locked onto the impostor's chair, toppled over by the momentum of his lunge. She pointed her fingers at it, searching for the invisible strings, but she couldn't find them.

Enki didn't notice. His attention belonged to the raptor. "How dare you mock me! You'll pay for this insult with your life!"

The raptor stretched his neck high above, then whipped his head down, blasting a piercing screech right in Enki's face. And just as the screech ended…

SNAP!

The raptor's open beak clamped down over Enki's head. The grip on Olivia's neck went slack and Olivia scrambled away. The raptor tossed Enki to the left, then the right, then to the left again, until the bronze flesh of his neck gave way. Blue blood sprayed everywhere, his flesh shredding more with each toss until…

THUD.

Enki's headless body dropped to the marble floor, a river of blue gushing from the stump. The smell of decay followed, the rot from his blood overpowering her flinch. The raptor spat Enki's head across the room and his neck began shrinking. In moments, the head disappeared under the hood, leaving the cloaked Yanisma sitting calmly in his chair as if nothing had happened. But the carnage he had left behind was undeniable.

Olivia now understood why everyone was terrified to face the Yanisma. The tribunal room was steeped in chaos. Some spectators huddled on the top bleachers sobbing, while others crept down for a glimpse of the body. A few dozen Jin scurried around the pit, cleaning up the headless mess and the blue still oozing from the corpse.

Keilte pulled himself off the floor and rushed to Olivia, helping her up. "Are you okay?" Blood was dripping from the lacerations in her arm.

"I'm fine."

But she wasn't. She'd been strangled for the second time today. She'd witnessed her attacker's decapitation by the Yanisma, who was now calmly watching the cleanup as if it was no big deal. None of this was okay. She was only barely holding everything together on the outside, but on the inside, she was turning to goo, like chocolates left on the dash, like a Jin melted by Maia. She smoothed out her tunic, and tried to steady her breathing, the way Migitju had taught her. One long breath in. Hold for three. Exhale. Another long breath. Hold for three. Exhale.

"Listen, Olivia, I'm really sorry, I—"

"Whatever. I'm used to being ditched."

But she wasn't used to it at all. This was the first time she'd ever had friends, and their rejection hurt worse than anything Miley had ever done. Having friends was pointless if they could turn against her so easily. She was better off alone. She squared her shoulders. They would never hurt her like this again. She would adapt like the river but stand firm like the rock. She was Olivia Carpenter, the girl with two names. The girl from Terra.

Lord Harvarder, clearly affected by the decapitation, cleared his throat and tried to recover the meeting with a commanding tone. "The Council thanks you for revealing the impostor."

Olivia, still bleeding, saw her moment and took it. "As a reward, I request an audience with the Jin named AmmaNa."

Queen Tara had been interfering with this reunion from day one, and Olivia enjoyed watching her plump body shift uncomfortably under the gaze of the ten remaining Councillors. Finally, she placed her hands on the crystal wall and made it glow. Within moments, the door opened and AmmaNa entered, alive and healthy. Olivia squinted away her tears—she was not about to cry in front of a whole gallery of students—but she ran to her golden friend and wrapped her in a giant hug. Her leathery skin had recovered its sparkle and she radiated a warmth that was almost uncomfortable, given the current temperature control issues in the hive. AmmaNa returned the hug, and when they parted, the Jin's tiny mouth was all smiles.

I owe you thanks for saving me.

I stand and breathe because of you.

The Council gasped, a sound that bounced off the walls, hushing the murmur of those filing back into the gallery now that the threat had been eliminated. Queen Tara's embarrassment deepened. Everyone had heard this heartfelt thank you that AmmaNa delivered in her own voice —in the first person instead of as part of the collective. Olivia didn't understand enough about Jin culture to fully grasp the gravity of this act, but the reactions around her told her it was a big deal. Was this why AmmaNa had been hidden away?

"AmmaNa, can you please show what happened when you found me?"

The screen flickered, bringing them into the ship's lab. The ship was parked on a lump of ice in dark space. At a great distance were twin yellow stars, one with a red dwarf nearby.

"The Centauri system." Duchess Damia recognized it instantly.

Suddenly, a beam of light exploded through the darkness, barely missing the ship. The Jin crew flew into action, followed the beacon, but it soon disappeared.

We knew not what it was, or how to find its source.

We waited quite a pause, and then the beam returned.

It led us to a star—surrounded by a void.

A planet full of life, but missing from our maps.

The ship passed a lump of ice and a large planet with rings, towards a giant red planet with many moons. Once again, the beacon stopped, but this time, the Jin continued. They passed over an asteroid belt, then a small red planet, and slowed at a blue planet orbiting a warm yellow sun. Its outer atmosphere was a tangle of metal objects with blinking lights. When the beacon sliced through the darkness a third time, the Jin made their move, dodging between the mess of satellites that watched every moment of life on the surface. They found the source of the beacon to be a red-headed girl dancing in a cornfield.

Olivia's jaw dropped open. "I did that? For real? That's intense."

"She commands the light like a Teuton!" But Lord Harvarder's jubilation quickly evaporated as the Greys appeared onscreen, demanding Olivia's return. The saucers fired. Olivia's thoughts commanded the ship for all to hear, and within moments, the yellow sun and its eight planets were a distant memory.

Duchess Damia rose to address the Council, racked with apprehension. "According to the testimony of this Jin Science Officer, the Greys have infiltrated Terra. This planet was meant to be invisible."

"Who wouldn't find a planet with that much junk in orbit?" asked the Vegan Councillor, silent until now.

"The Greys aren't the only ones. The creep in my oracle who's threatening my family—I'm quite sure he's not human at all. I flinched with him, and he eats Terran children."

"Something must be done!" Duchess Damia was outraged, even if Terrans were much smaller than she had expected.

"Like my oracle says, I have to go home and deal with him. And before I go, I need to know all about Project Human."

"Where did you hear that name, child?"

"When I grabbed Queen Tara's ankle, I flinched. I saw the twelve tribes planning something called Project Human. What I saw was real, and I want to know what it is."

"That information is classified." Lord Harvarder would not bend his precious rules.

"Nobody is supposed to know about it, but for some reason, everyone does. Everyone except me. I'm not just a part of this; I'm here because of it, and I deserve the truth."

The Yanisma stood and reached for his hood. Everyone sucked in, bracing for whatever might appear. There was a communal exhale as he revealed Percy Van Houten, who once again looked a little older than before.

"Olivia Carpenter has asked for the truth. Her request is a fair one." He sat back down, hiding once again in his own self-made shadows.

Lord Harvarder looked around. "Are there any objections?" They all shook their heads, except for Queen Tara, who pouted from the corner. He addressed Olivia. "There is another tribe that lives exclusively on Terra, a very powerful tribe that we believe has the ability to defeat the Draconians, the Greys, and other enemies of peace. When we first discovered their existence, our goal was to commune with this thirteenth tribe. But as they are microscopic and live symbiotically inside the simians on Terra, we had no means of communication. We therefore set out to create a fusion between Terran simians and ourselves, with kinship to all and affinity to none. A new tribe that can be the voice of the thirteenth tribe. It is an honour to meet a real Terran."

Wait a minute. She had some kind of teeny-weeny tadpoles swimming around inside her blood? This wasn't just extra, this was beyond extra. This was life-altering, earth-shattering information. Migitju believed that star people brought their people to Earth and would come back for them someday. And now here she was, halfway across the galaxy, hearing the other side of the same story. The star people were real, and they had been tinkering with the human gene pool to commune with tiny tadpoles. Humanity had an actual purpose. There was a reason for her, for her mom and dad, for Migitju, for everyone she knew. This was way better than being a super-weapon.

"Okay, so if you all had a hand in creating my people, could I get some introductions?"

"Yes, yes. That is an oversight on my part." Lord Harvarder seemed suddenly redder in the jowls. "Allow me. Starting on your left, we have the Jin, the Doggos, the Polarians, the Telosians, and the Yanisma. The Atlantians are not currently represented. I speak for the Teutons. Beyond me, we have the Deyonns, the Saurians, the Procyons, the Felicians, and the Vegans."

"So, we Terrans got genes from all of you?"

"That is correct."

"You chose what genes to give us, but you didn't give us Deyonn wings? Epic fail."

The Deyonn folded her wings around her face to hide a smile blossoming from cheek to rosy cheek. But Olivia's joking faded into the shadows of her mind as her flinch with Enki came flooding back. Ninhursag had tinkered with the same gene pool. She'd made humans smaller than the originals. She'd made kings who took wives and had families—vast families with many children. Duchess Damia was surprised at how small Olivia was—what if that meant she had Annunaki genes too? What if all Terrans did? Would they close down the experiment? Would they dispose of the tainted Terrans? They couldn't possibly know—they hadn't seen her flinch with Enki, and she wasn't going to hang around waiting for Queen Tara to steal it from her mind.

"I'm not sure how I feel about being your number one lab rat, but I've got this oracle," she waved it around for emphasis, "and it says I'm going home, so I need to go plan my trip."

Before she could make it to the door, the Deyonn Queen put up her hand and rose, floating above her chair, her wings softly rippling like wind across a hay field.

"Olivia Carpenter. I am Fae Morgana, chief of the Deyonns. It is lovely to meet you. The story of your ordeal has been quite a lot to consider. Now that I possess a new level of clarity surrounding your arrival and the attempt that was made by the Greys to capture you, may I ask you to present your oracle once again?"

The Fae's voice was hypnotic. It was impossible to refuse such a simple request, so Olivia activated the orb once more. Dr. Retchen sat in the driver's seat of a black SUV, watching Eagle Crest Farm through a pair of binoculars. He reached into a cooler perched on the passenger seat and pulled out a long strip of bloody meat. He lowered it into his mouth bit by bit, ripping at it with razor-sharp teeth.

"You must return to Terra and defeat the one who threatens your family," the oracle boomed.

Fae Morgana raised a hand once again and floated for a few moments, eyes closed, the other Councillors waiting respectfully.

"The Twelve expected much from Project Human. Although you have only begun to learn about the importance and the potential of your people, you are as brave as the Deyonns had hoped you would be. Go prepare for your mission, Olivia Carpenter. Let me know if my people can assist your cause in any way."

18 THE EXCEPTION

DR. RETCHEN CREPT along the side of a barn, its wooden slats weathered and grey from decades of Canadian winters. Nobody saw him slip into the barn carrying a large duffle bag. It wasn't like in the cities, where something was always watching. Not yet.

He climbed to the loft and did a quick inventory of her possessions. He didn't need a light to see; his eyes were well suited to this environment. He opened the duffle and grabbed a few items, then hoisted himself easily into the rafters. Nobody saw him attach three electronic eyes overhead, and he was confident that no one would ever find them.

Back on ground level, he installed a motion sensor on the second stair and another on the barn door, sandwiched between the door and its frame, out of sight.

Deep in the cornfield, he found the circle where Olivia's abandoned bike waited for her return. He pulled out his monkey wrench and pounded long stakes into the ground, on top of which he installed more motion sensors. He added a final one, under her bicycle, just in case.

Retiring to the discomfort of his motel room, he opened a laptop and made a video call. A Grey appeared on the screen.

"What have you learned about her DNA?"

"This specimen contains a combination of African, European, Asian, and American DNA." Its voice was nasal and gravelly, similar to the voice that had threatened Olivia. Forming audible words was a chore. "None of the DNA is extra-human, but two sequences that are normally dormant have been activated in this sample."

"Activated?"

"Able to express proteins when stress is applied. Able to replicate."

"Is this active DNA a sequence donated by the Yanisma?"

"One of the two is, yes."

This was exactly what he needed to hear. Harnessing a subject with an active Yanisma sequence could elevate his status and get him out of this bunker. No longer would he be their errand boy.

"You know what to do next."

OLIVIA SAT ON a bed in the academy's infirmary. Thankfully, this place was nothing like the Jin infirmary, primarily in that it had no crystal coffins. It was built like the commons, large rooms connected to each other via thick doorways that stretched around the waterfall on the level below the dorms. Olivia hadn't thought her injuries were a big deal, but now that her adrenaline was going back to normal levels, she was ready to pass out.

"You're still dripping, which means we need to patch you up before you run dry." The healer, a female Felician, spoke to the puncture marks in Olivia's arm and neck rather than to the owner of these wounds. When she looked up, her pink eyes were at once very intense, but also very caring. "You are the one who fought the Annu, no? You are very brave. Possibly stupid, too."

She put a fur-covered paw on Olivia's arm, and Olivia felt her finger pads, warm and leathery, stretch over the wounds. The paw began to rumble, accompanied by the sound of a low purr coming from the base of the healer's throat. Four claws extended from her fingers, coated in beautiful red tips. When she withdrew her paw, the bleeding had stopped and the wounds were fused into scabs. She reached for Olivia's neck, and Olivia sat still for the treatment, entranced by the healer's ability to transfer the vibration from her throat to her paw.

"Did you just stitch me up without stitches?"

"Why would I use stitches? You're not a piece of fabric."

Olivia just stared at the woman, her head too woozy to decipher the cryptic answer, until finally, a real answer was given.

"You must rest for a few days. The healing points are fresh, and you've lost a lot of blood. I can't say that I ever expected to work on a Terran, but we all operate on similar frequencies."

"Your healing has to do with frequencies?"

"Yes. As we are all water-based life-forms, we are all positively affected by the frequencies that cause water to organize into healthy shapes. I am able to generate these frequencies with my purr and transfer them to your wounds. The water hears the frequency and organizes the system to find harmony. Harmony is health."

On the next bed over, Tuatha was being treated for a face-plant into the marble floor, while Keilte was treated for three broken bones in his fist. They'd jumped in, risking their lives when hers was threatened, and now that she'd had some time to process, gratitude had erased the hurt.

In the aftermath of the impostor's defeat, she'd foolishly believed that she had the power to fulfill the oracle's next quest. But with hindsight, it was pretty clear that she hadn't defeated the impostor at all. That was all Percy. There was another Percy back on Earth, so why did she have to defeat Dr. Creepy McSlenderman? Why couldn't Percy copy his shark teeth and bite his head off, too? But Percy had been on the other side of the door from him outside the principal's office. He could have bitten Retchen's head off days ago. It was her responsibility, so she could either curl up in a ball and cry about it, or she could show up for humanity and deal with him, whoever he was.

She looked at her oracle, its green smoke swirling in an ever-changing storm. It believed she could do this. Maybe it was time for her to believe it as well.

Her self-pep-talk was interrupted by the Telosian Councillor. She was eight feet tall, and although she stood very straight, she still managed to look completely relaxed. Her head was egg-shaped and as large as her chest, while her torso was as big as both combined. Her orchid skin had jewel undertones, which made her blue eyes striking. Short powder-puff hair shocked out in all directions, but she spoke with a soft and calming tone. Everything about her seemed to be a balance of opposites.

"I am Shakkar. I have come to ask how the Telosians can help."

Overwhelmed with gratitude, Olivia took a moment to consider what her biggest problem was, what she needed most. She knew what it was. It seemed like a crazy thing to ask, but so far, this galactic adventure had overturned so many things she had taken as fact that she chose instead to lean into pure possibility.

"The quantagate will take me back to the ship, but the Greys will be waiting for me. Do you have any way to hide a whole ship?"

"Yes. Stealth within your mission will bring better outcomes for all involved. The Procyons have a quantum cloak that can disguise it, making it look like empty space. My people have good relations with them; I will ask for their help."

"Thank you, Councillor Shakkar, that's a huge help."

"Please call me Shakkar. My people don't carry titles—we are all equal. Being a Councillor is only relevant when the rest of the Council is present."

Olivia nodded and smiled. "Thank you, Shakkar."

Keilte waited a moment to be sure their conversation was over, but soon his need to speak took over.

"I know you are mad, but I do not care. I am here to help. I want to help."

"I have to admit, I was really upset with both of you, but I've also realized that all of this is a lot. It's a lot for me to understand and accept, but it's been a lot for you and Tuatha as well. I'm not going to represent my people very well if I can't get over shit. So I'm over it. And thank you. Your interference probably saved my life."

"I saved the life of the first Terran?" Keilte beamed with pride.

"So we can come with? We can help on the mission? Wheeee!" Tuatha sang, fluttering up from the bed, only to get dizzy and drop out of the air with a soft thud. "Team Olivia is back on!"

"The healer says you need to rest."

"Whatever. Before Maia rises, I'll be as right as starlight. And everyone knows you can't have a great team without a Deyonn, so you'd better count me in for the upcoming shenanigans!"

"Shenanigans?"

"It's a Deyonn word for trickery and spirited undertakings."

"I know what it means—we say it on Terra."

"A Deyonn word is used by Terrans? Interstellar!"

"I want to be part of the mission!" Rama poked his face into the infirmary. His skin was a bright shade of leaf green. Before Olivia could answer, he scrambled in, crossed his legs and his four arms, and immediately launched into his normal line of questions. "What's the plan? What can I do?"

"I'm still trying to figure out how to find Mr. Creepy McSlenderman."

"Is that really his name?"

"That's what I call him. He calls himself Dr. Retchen."

"Have you actually met him?"

"Yup. I flinched with him, and I'm pretty sure he eats Terran children."

This revelation halted Rama's next question in his throat. He swallowed it back down, his expression finally showing awareness at the gravity of the situation.

"Shakkar has graciously helped to solve our biggest problem. But I have to find this creepo before I can defeat him. Maybe I can find his hideout by flinching with his brochure. Or maybe he'll be up the road, stalking my house like the oracle showed me. It's all a guessing game, and I much prefer a concrete plan."

"What are you going to do when you find his hideout? Knock on the front door? Won't that just get you snatched?"

"Great question, Rama."

"What if I go with you as a decoy?" Rama blinked, and suddenly Olivia was staring at herself.

"That's amazing, but I can't ask you to put yourself in danger."

"You didn't ask me to, I offered. I can distract everyone long enough for you to slip in, but you have to promise to come back for me."

"If Rama gets to visit Terra, I'm going too."

"Fair warning, I have no idea what kind of abilities Creepy McSlenderman has. And all I know about the Greys is the telepathy thing. What if they have other abilities?"

The Greys were once a sister hive.

Everyone gasped as AmmaNa entered, all except Keilte, who stood with fists clenched.

"I should have known Queen Tara would send a spy."

Olivia patted his seat, imploring him to sit back down. "AmmaNa came to my rescue on Terra and at the tribunal. She's a friend."

"Oh really?" He wasn't convinced. "How do you know this is AmmaNa? They all look alike."

I think the Queen is incorrect;

I can't support her disrespect.

The Jin cannot afford to forge bad blood with yet another tribe.

Olivia has taught me how to see this from her point of view.

I come to ask to join your team and pay the debt I owe to you.

Shakkar's cheeks and antennae brightened from orchid to magenta. "Never in a million generations did I think I would witness a Jin exception." Her concern sent a tingle through the air.

"A Jin exception?" asked Olivia.

"Each Jin is born with unique personality traits. They are almost always overshadowed by the need for survival within a hive, but it seems like AmmaNa is loyal and has a strong sense of justice. You saved her life, shifting her loyalty to you, and she sees injustice in the way you've been treated. She's risking her life to create an exception within the hive."

Queen Tara wants no more of me.

I am not welcome in her world.

Olivia had much to learn about Jin culture and much to be grateful for. AmmaNa was risking her life to defend Olivia.

"So you're able to survive even though the Queen doesn't accept you?"

As long as I am in the hive,

I can recharge and stay alive.

"And once we get you back to your ship," Olivia added, "you'll reconnect with your siblings." She imagined all of them travelling the galaxy together, having amazing adventures.

AmmaNa put her hands on the wall. It glowed, and AmmaNa's tiny smile quickly faded.

The Queen has charged her three best guards to follow every move you make.

Your every breath will now be watched, your every action known.

"That complicates things, but she doesn't know that we know she's watching. I'll come up with something. I'm pretty good at sneaking away."

"What about this child-eater? What are we going to do to him?" Keilte was gunning for a fight. Thinking about it made Olivia's stomach all twisty. Confronting him terrified her. She didn't want to find out how deep his evil went.

"I don't know. My oracle says I have to defeat him, but…" And that's when it clicked. She saw all the possible choices floating in front of her. She saw the outcome of each choice and what lay beyond. It was a giant tree of decisions with a clear path to victory.

"What's going on?" Tuatha asked. "Something's changed. Out with it."

"Keilte, can you create a big beam of energy like the one we saw in the playback?"

"Of course. Teutons command the light."

"Great. Rama, you're not going to be my double. You're going to be the hard hand of the law."

"What?" They were all confused.

"Keilte makes a big light in my dad's backyard, luring Creepy McSlenderman into our trap. When he comes chasing us, Rama makes himself look like a police officer. He'll be surprised and have to explain why he's trespassing. That will distract him long enough for Tuatha to mesmerize him. Once he's under Tuatha's spell, defeating him shouldn't be that hard. It'll be gross," she shuddered, thinking of Enki's headless fate, "but no worse than what he's been doing."

"AmmaNa, will you fly the ship?"

AmmaNa nodded in agreement.

"Okay, once Shakkar gets us a cloaking device from the Procyons, we'll be ready to go."

19 SPEEDBUMPS

DR. RETCHEN SAT in the driver seat of his black SUV, snacking on strips of bloody steak, binoculars pointed at the next hill over. As dusk fell and the lights went on inside Eagle Crest, the Carpenters' shadows moved around, unaware that they were being watched.

Three hours later, a second SUV arrived with his team. Both vehicles climbed the Carpenters' driveway together. Parked to block any escape, Retchen fronted his men, all fully armed but careful that their weapons were not visible from the road. They marched up to the door as a unit, but only Dr. Retchen lifted a hand to knock.

OLIVIA STOOD BY the twelve pools as the Jin reached into the water and made it bubble. But before they could extract the human babies, their skin turned grey, their eyes spiteful. The pools turned into bathtubs. Instead of babies being born, they were being basted for the spit.

Olivia woke up, clammy and trembling. She didn't recognize her surroundings. Her heart thumped out the rhythm of her anxiety. Her eyes searched the room, and when they found the backpack Migitju had made, the entire week came rushing back. It was a lot to process again. Would she ever fully come to terms with a galaxy full of intelligent life that had given her powers she didn't understand? She was grateful for the knock on her door.

Open.

"Master Eldrin requests an audience."

"I don't want to see him."

Kyrrha looked up, revealing two dark streaks staining her cheeks.

She'd been crying. "Please, Olivia? He's really sorry. You can't leave without at least letting him apologize."

He had been a pawn in the ordeal, sure, but a pawn who had almost ended her. The thought of meeting with him sent a surge of adrenaline racing through her veins, and that was exactly why facing him was a good idea. She needed nerves of granite to face Creepy McSlenderman, and this was a good way to work on breathing through the panic. As she travelled to the surface, trying to pretend she didn't notice thousands of Jin watching her, her stomach writhed in protest.

A long breath in. Hold for three. A long breath out. Relax.

A long breath in. Hold for three. A long breath out. Relax.

A long breath in. Hold for three. A long breath out. Relax.

When she crossed the threshold into the pyramid, she felt calm. Kyrrha hadn't told Olivia why he wanted to see her, but at least it wasn't to finish her off. That had been Tamiel's plan, and Tamiel was gone. He sat alone, his face sharp with emotion, but as soon as he saw her, his expression relaxed into relief.

"After our troubled beginnings, I worried that you wouldn't come. Please, sit."

"Why am I here?"

"It seems that your abilities have progressed drastically since our last lesson. I would like to help you practice your skill before you return to Terra, in case you need to use it." He placed the marble on the pedestal in front of her. "Please, allow me to be the teacher you asked me to be."

Olivia reached toward the marble and tried to conjure the invisible string from her fingers, but even without the other students jeering at her, nothing happened. It didn't make any sense. She was able to whip a stone nexus across a room like a baseball. Why couldn't she move a marble? After what seemed like an eternity of frustrating attempts, he stopped her.

"Let's figure this out together, shall we? The first object you moved was my nexus?"

Olivia nodded.

"What occurred immediately before you found the invisible

string?"

"You were choking me, and the world was turning black."

He dropped his gaze to his hands. "I am so sorry. You must have been terrified." He cleared his throat. "What about when you sent out your beacon?"

"I was dancing. I didn't even know I did that until I saw it onscreen."

"And what were you doing before you ate from the Tree of Life?"

"I was sitting beside the lake, listening to my tuning forks. Master Yamma says I can't do any of her lessons because I'm out of tune."

"Interesting. Please show me."

Olivia produced the tuning forks and, striking each one, held them to her ears. Master Eldrin waited for her to finish, then returned the marble to its perch.

"Try it now. Find the string of energy. Listen for the vibration."

Olivia listened, and this time, she heard a faint tone. A low hum in the background. A long note on a cello. She reached toward the marble and the vibration intensified. She swiped her hand to the right. The marble whizzed across the room. CRACK! It embedded itself in the crystal wall of the pyramid, hitting with such force that it left a shatter print like a rock hitting a windshield.

"Fascinating! Master Yamma was correct. When you adjust your frequency, look at what you can accomplish!"

"What does frequency have to do with anything?"

"Every object vibrates at a specific frequency. The frequencies that create water-based life are all in harmony with each other. Our frequencies allow us to communicate with plants and animals, to know when they are in distress."

"Does this moon's crystal have a frequency?"

"The crystal, the bees, the gardens, they all react to frequency. But the crystal here is special. Living microorganisms secrete this crystal as a shell. The Jin have a symbiotic relationship with the microorganisms. When they ask the crystal to move, they're actually asking the microorganisms to break apart their shells and reform them in other ways. That's how the city and the academy were built."

"So why don't the Jin repair the crack?"

"But surely you have seen them hard at work. For them, this is a slow process."

He put a new marble on the pedestal and had her practise again and again, spending most of the time focused on making and maintaining the connection. After about fifteen minutes, her control began to fade, but once she re-calibrated with the tuning forks, she was good for another fifteen minutes. He kept drilling her until her head began to throb and she tapped out. Picking up the marble, he rolled it around. It hovered over his fingers, moving smoothly from one to the next without ever touching his pale skin.

"There is something else I would like to discuss before your journey." He sat still, deep in thought. Olivia waited, still amazed by how easily the marble floated from finger to finger.

"Your arrival has brought hope to many, but to me in particular. You have many reasons to refuse, but I hope you will consider my request." He let the marble drop into his other palm, and with a beckoning of his finger, the flap of his bag opened, and the amethyst nexus floated up to hover between them. "This was given to me by my brother just before he vanished. He boarded a ship headed for a star system we call the Centauri Triad, but the ship disappeared. Many search parties have been sent without success. When the Jin saw your beacon, they were near the Triad." He produced a crystal apple from the bag at his feet. "Once you have completed your mission, would you consider passing through the Triad to check for my people, for my brother?"

"You think that fruit will help me find your brother?"

"This fruit will allow you to hear every nearby thought all at once. As I said, this is a lot for me to ask of you."

"That fruit doesn't work on me the way you want it to. There are thousands of Jin on Sita, but I didn't hear any of them."

"So you didn't hear da-DUM-da-DUM-da-DUM?"

"Oh, sure. I heard that loud and clear."

"Exactly. That was every single Jin on Sita thinking in unison. That rhythm is the cadence of their tribe. Did you not notice that it governs everything they say?"

She had to admit that their thoughts always seemed to have a rhythm, but she hadn't connected it to the voice of the tree. With a swish of his finger, the fruit floated over to her, landing in her palm.

"The Atlantian people are already in your debt for saving our reputation with the Council. We already owe you more gratitude than we can repay, but please consider my request. I miss my brother."

Olivia left the pyramid, surprised at how Master Eldrin's plea had affected her. As an only child, she didn't know what it was like to lose a sibling, but she couldn't stand the thought of ever losing Migitju. Master Eldrin had said the City of Atlantis was headed for the Centauri system, but her flinch with Kyrrha had revealed that it was actually headed for a single star in a desert of stars. It had to be her solar system, because why else would Olivia know about a lost City of Atlantis? She needed to hide this memory before anyone had a chance to extract this information. Keilte had helped her practise turning memories into objects so that she could hide them in her tower, safe from telepathic intrusion.

She sat down on the edge of the dry lakebed, took a deep breath, and for the first time, began a Mindshield visit on her own. Finding the clearing in the forest was easy this time because Keilte had trained her to use smells instead of visuals. She created an amethyst nexus to house Master Eldrin's memory and attached Kyrrha's bedtime story to a book.

Once both items were safely tucked away in her tower, she spent some time roaming in the clearing. She missed Earth. She missed the simple things, like picking a blade of grass to make a thumb whistle or hearing the crows caw and calling back to them. All of these things made her think of Migitju. She couldn't wait to see her grandmother again, to tell her the news that she'd met the people from the stars. Maybe Migitju would want to come with her to Sita to meet all of her new friends. And because Migitju was so important, Olivia had to protect her, too.

She conjured up a blanket, large and round and made of patches. It looked just like the blanket Migitju had inherited from her own grandmother, complete with stitches that had been replaced after years of loving use. Olivia folded the blanket and hugged it. It even smelled of sage and cinnamon, just like Migitju's kitchen. Olivia brought the blanket to the top of her tower and placed it carefully on the second recliner. It made sense to give her grandmother a place of respect, a comfortable chair. It felt right.

Olivia felt much better about her private thoughts as she stepped onto the lift and dropped back into the hive. A trio of Jin who were helping a window turn into a wall shifted their attention to her, and the crystal stopped repairing itself. She couldn't help but wonder if these microscopic beings did what the Jin asked because the exchange of energy gave them no choice. When she stepped off the lift, an escort waited for her, following her all the way to the teal wing. She was so distracted that she didn't notice the cloaked figure waiting in her room until the door was already shut.

"What the?!" Had Percy come to tell her that she had to go back to Earth alone? But a golden hand pulled back the hood, revealing AmmaNa's smiling face.

To meet you here, I hid in this:

the best disguise that I could find.

"Maybe you should stay hidden. They followed me here, and I wouldn't put it past them to invite themselves in."

AmmaNa disappeared back under the cloak just as Shakkar arrived. She nodded just as she had done to the Yanisma in the tribunal room. The hood nodded back.

"The Quantum Lords support your quest." She produced a small device that looked like a fried egg. "Press this side to turn it on and this side to turn it off. I understand you leave the next time Maia sets. May success be yours, Olivia Carpenter."

"Thank you for your help." Olivia took the device, full of genuine gratitude, hoping Shakkar would forgive the deception. They were actually leaving within the hour, right before Maia rose, but Olivia didn't know Shakkar well enough to trust her with the real plan. Olivia couldn't risk Queen Tara learning of it, either by willing disclosure or by telepathy. And with a little luck, they'd be back before anybody even noticed they were gone. Even if they were spotted, Maia would stop anyone from following.

The rest of the gang showed up soon after the Telosian Councillor's departure.

"We're bringing the Yanisma?" Keilte asked, voicing the shock that everyone else was feeling at the sight of the cloaked figure sitting with Olivia. "Is this a backup-secret-weapon thing?"

AmmaNa revealed her face just enough to wink at him.

"Clever disguise," he admitted.

"If anyone's having second thoughts, voice them now."

Nobody did. They were ready to put their lives in danger to help her. Olivia swallowed hard against a sob, pushing it back down. For the first time ever, she had real friends. She wasn't going to screw up the moment with tears.

Tuatha went ahead of them through the halls to the lift, clearing the way with starlight. To add an extra layer of deception, they all held Rama's hands. He blinked, and suddenly, they were a group of Jin guards.

The trip to the bottom of the city was eerie. Now that the water wound its way down through the crystal and found the canyon floor elsewhere, the thunder that had once rumbled up from the base of the waterfall was gone. For the first time ever, Olivia became aware that silence was an actual sound, a hollow emptiness that hurt her ears. Olivia looked up at the barrel of the hive stretching into oblivion. It was breathtaking to behold, but the quiet whispered of a place long dead, and without the falls to cool the air, the deeper they went, the more suffocating the place became. At the base of the lift, a long tunnel through the crystal brought them to a dead end.

"When I open this door, we have to run. AmmaNa will lose strength really fast once we leave the hive. We have to get to her siblings quickly. Keilte, do you think you can piggyback AmmaNa and still run?"

It was a big request, considering the history between the Teutons and the Jin, but his eyes met Olivia's, and he dropped to one knee, prepared to do whatever he could to help. "You are as brave as any

Teuton, little Jin captain. Climb on."

Though it was not the Jin way to make physical contact of any kind with another species, she accepted his help without argument. Her tiny arms couldn't wrap all the way around his hulking shoulders, so she grabbed onto them like bike handles.

Open.

As they raced out across the canyon, Olivia felt the tension in her shoulders drain through her feet and into the ground. She missed her bike, but in many ways, this run was better. She was racing alongside allies, heading out on an adventure, just like the heroes in her books, but this time, the end of the story was hers to write. The run to the cave went off without issue, and when she pulled aside the curtain of vines hiding its entrance, they all bustled in, unprepared for Queen Tara's trap. Three guards surrounded the gate, blocking their path.

Who dares to use our quantagate
without permission of our queen?

Maybe Queen Tara had anticipated their deception, or maybe this was to contain AmmaNa's exception. Either way, Olivia had to do something. AmmaNa was already losing her sparkle. She remembered Shakkar's explanation of Jin loyalty, that it was linked to their instinct to survive. Maybe she could awaken that instinct.

"Did Queen Tara tell you this was a suicide mission?"

We do not ask for reasons why.
We always trust the greater good.

"When Maia rises, this cave turns into an oven. You'll bake. You'll fry. You'll melt into piles of goo."

If our success must cost our lives,
we gladly give them for the hive.

She had to try again. Maia was coming. None of them would last long in this cave, and they didn't have time to run back to the city. Maybe the guards would feel loyalty for their siblings hibernating on the ship. "Your sisters are out in space. They're alone and vulnerable to attack. Don't you want us to bring them home safely?"

We do not ask for reasons why.
We always trust the greater good.

If our success must cost our lives,
we gladly give them for the hive.

It was a program. There was no reasoning with them. Queen Tara knew her hive very well—these Jin had likely been hand-picked for their blind obedience.

Maia's tentacles snaked in under the vines that didn't quite hang all the way to the ground. They were out of time. They had to go now, or they would all be roasted like turkeys.

Olivia called on every ounce of strength she had and rushed at the guard directly in front of the gate, dropping her shoulder to make contact. The guard's small body flew backwards, hit the quantagate, and disappeared. The other two guards lunged at Olivia.

"Keilte, now!"

He launched himself at the gate and had AmmaNa through before the guards could react. They saw their error and backed up, linking elbows, blocking the gate.

"There's only two of you now," Olivia reminded them. "Soon, you'll hibernate whether you want to or not. Nobody's coming with backup. Either you let us pass and we save your lives, or we wait until you sleep and walk past you anyway."

They didn't even twitch; they were ready to die for their queen.

Olivia looked at Tuatha and snapped her eyes shut, hoping her friend would understand. She was not disappointed. In a blink, Tuatha shrank down, blinding the Jin. Olivia shoved both guards to the ground, grabbed Rama, and pushed him into the jelly. Going in headfirst was not ideal, as he soon found out. When he emerged, his momentum sent him tumbling across the lab. For Olivia, the second time through was much easier, like stepping off an escalator. She popped out and went straight to Rama.

"Sorry about shoving you. I didn't have time to warn you."

"I just dove through a quantagate! That was awesome!"

Tuatha arrived last, dizzy and slightly bewildered. Keilte had already detained the Queen's guard, and Olivia was relieved to see that AmmaNa had opened the hibernation pods to wake up her sisters. They climbed out and crouched on the floor together, all three joining hands.

Olivia felt a ripple pass through her body as their minds shared experiences and memories.

"What will you do about this one?" Olivia nodded at Keilte's prisoner.

We must allow the chance for every Jin to choose to live.

Please bring him to our circle for the transfer to begin.

"Why should we save him?" Keilte was not a fan of this idea. "He was ready to let us fry!"

The Jin will do as we are told in order to survive.

He was not shown the truth of what Olivia will be.

He needs to see the moment that you showed us in our flinch.

AmmaNa and her crew all bowed their heads at Olivia. Her cheeks felt hot. She couldn't let a Jin die. This mission was about saving lives, not taking them.

"Come on, Keilte, we can't judge their ways, just like they shouldn't judge ours. Let the Jin be Jin."

Keilte brought his captive to AmmaNa's sisters. Each one took a hand, completing the circle, and again, Olivia felt a ripple like a single wave travelling over a calm pond. The four Jin nodded in unison.

We did not understand your quest.

Your origins had not been shared.

We ask you to forgive our blindly following our queen.

"AmmaNa! He spoke in his own voice!"

We feel there is a benefit

to studying the Terran way.

The things that we can emulate

will help us learn how to relate.

"What about the other guards? If we bring them through the gate, do you think we can save them, too?"

By now they're overwhelmed with sleep

and scorching in our star's white heat.

Is this a risk you wish to take?

"Yes. They haven't committed any crime, they're just doing what the Jin do."

"If you're sure," Keilte said, stepping up to the quantagate, "I'll be right back."

"Be careful," Olivia implored. Within moments, he was back with a guard draped over each shoulder. He lowered them to the floor, adding their limp bodies to the circle.

"Are you good?" Olivia asked. He smelled like burnt hair.

"I'm made for this kind of stuff," he declared, puffing himself up a little as he dusted away a few embers.

Olivia felt the ripple pass through her a third time. The rescued Jin opened their eyes, and the sparkle returned to their golden skin. They looked at AmmaNa as if they had found home. Was Olivia watching the birth of a new hive?

Olivia, the time draws on.

Are you prepared for what comes next?

The thought of facing Dr. Creepy McSlenderman turned her blood to sludge. But the oracle had said this was her destiny. If she was going to be part of this galactic community, she needed to trust that the Yanisma would not send her to the slaughter. The oracle had also said her family was being threatened, and that made her want to destroy him.

Tuatha shivered. "Carpenter's ready. She means business."

"Yes, AmmaNa. I'm ready. Take us back to Terra."

20 A TENSE REUNION

FROM THE OUTSIDE looking in, it was easy to see why Terra was so difficult to find. The entire solar system was protected by the Oort cloud, a shell of ice chunks the size of mountains. Penetrating it was as dangerous as flying though an asteroid field. Nobody would risk it without a good reason.

Olivia turned on the quantum cloak before approaching this first line of defence. Retchen likely had scouts watching for their return, and she wasn't taking any chances.

Her instincts were correct. As soon as they were clear of the dangerous Oort cloud, a saucer whizzed by so close that the two ships almost collided. The saucer must have felt the turbulence of this near-collision, because it turned and began retracing its path.

AmmaNa dropped slowly away while everyone held still on instinct. Starting their mission with a full-out space battle would totally blow their cover. A rush of anxiety flooded Olivia's veins, making her buzz all over. She was used to being triggered like this by Miley, but Miley was a joke compared to the Greys. The saucer zipped back and forth, up and down, searching every inch of space, but with the quantum cloak engaged, they were invisible. Finding nothing, the saucer gave up and went back on patrol.

"Are you some kind of magnet for danger?" Rama asked, shaken.

"You're just figuring that out now?" Tuatha countered. "Give the kid a gold star!"

"At least we know the quantum cloak works."

Unlike their escape from the solar system, AmmaNa brought them in at an angle to the planetary orbits, allowing her to miss both the Kuiper belt and the asteroid field. As they approached Earth, Olivia went over the plan one last time.

"Why is Keilte making the beam? Why don't you dance like you did before?" Rama's question was a good one, and that was a problem.

"Keilte has more control than I do. It's better if he does it."

"But what if his light beam looks different? What if he can't call the light on Terra?"

"Teutons can call the light anywhere we go."

How could she explain that her dancing was private, that she didn't dance in front of other people? They wouldn't understand—none of them had spent their lives being everyone's favourite joke. She needed to shut down this distraction.

"I don't know how I did it, okay? We could be waiting hours for me to figure it out. We don't have that kind of time."

"Don't know how you did it, or don't want to admit it? Looks to me like all you have to do is dance."

Olivia scowled at Tuatha. "Maybe I do know how to do it, but I'm scared as hell I might crack another planet in two. So can we just drop it and let Keilte do his part?"

"Ooh, some seriously angry vibes there, Carpenter. You're ready to explode. I think you should dance it out." Tuatha flitted high overhead, where Olivia couldn't reach, giggling the whole way. "You need to embrace your awesomeness."

"Moving on. Once Creepy McSlenderman arrives, Rama will make himself look like a cop and start grilling him about why he's on the property. This is your expertise, Rama. Just keep asking questions. Use words like permission, trespass, legal action…"

"That won't work. You can understand me because of your translator." He pointed to her ear. "I don't speak Terran. But I can distract him long enough for Tuatha to get in there."

"Okay, so Tuatha will sneak up from behind and mesmerize him. Once he's under your spell, Keilte and I will pop up with plastic wrap and wrap him like a mummy."

"If I'm going to be a cop, I need to know what a cop looks like."

"AmmaNa, does this ship have a viewing screen like the tribunal room?"

AmmaNa nodded, and a screen appeared on a large, flat section of the wall.

Show the RCMP knocking on my door last year.

They all watched the memory of two uniformed officers, a man and a woman, talking to Olivia's dad, blaming Olivia for vandalizing her middle school. It was hard to see her dad agreeing with the officers who had no actual proof, just Miley's accusation.

"Can you make yourself look like one of them?"

Rama studied the image for a moment, then blinked, becoming a perfect replica of the male officer. "Does this work?"

Olivia nodded.

"So what about this Creepy McSlenderman? I need to know which Terran I'm supposed to distract."

"He's not a Terran. He'll probably have Terrans with him for security, but he isn't one of us."

"What's the difference?"

"He's tall. Taller than Keilte."

"So not super tall," Tuatha snickered as Keilte straightened himself, stretching to become as tall as possible.

"This is not my maximum height. Teutons grow until our bronze age."

"Your bronze age?" Olivia had to know.

"Our hair turns bronze as we get older."

That explained why Lord Harvarder's mane was a few shades lighter than Keilte's. She tried to imagine Keilte as an elderly Teuton, but she had no context.

Show Dr. Retchen.

The image made her stomach do a cartwheel. Onscreen he looked much less human than she remembered. Not only did his thickly gelled hair and eyebrows look unnatural, but he was taller and thinner, with a head two sizes too small for a man of his height.

"Rama, this is our target. This is the monster who eats Terran children."

AmmaNa slowed the ship and implored everyone to hold on as she descended through the maze of junk humans had launched into space. Approaching Swift Current from above, the farmlands reminded Olivia of a diorama Randall Shepherd had built in grade seven for a project on local agriculture. The town was sleepy and at peace, unaware their planet was a Petri dish, tucked away and forgotten, collecting dust. Olivia gave AmmaNa a quiet instruction, not wanting to share more anxiety with the group.

"Don't land in the circle where you found me. Land right in the corn, just in case." Though the townsfolk would not see the ship this time, thanks to the quantum cloak, the circular mark it would leave would have them gossiping for months. Her dad would just have to get over it. But how would she explain this to her folks? By telling them that twelve alien races had created humans as their science project, and somehow, she was the first to get beamed up? That sounded like a Hollywood movie. It was too crazy for him to believe it. Unless…

"Will you come with me? To the house?"

Nobody stepped forward, likely sensing her anxiety. Only Tuatha spoke up, determined not to make Olivia face this alone. "Really, guys? We get to be the first ones in the galaxy to see an actual Terran dwelling from the inside, and you're all going to chicken out?"

Tuatha's chiding had the desired effect, and suddenly they were all eager to explore a Terran home. Olivia led them through the corn stalks and the boneyard, pausing at the back door to listen. All was quiet, so they crept inside. As soon as the door clicked shut, her dad lunged from the other room, his shotgun pointed directly at Keilte.

"You better get the hell outta my house before I blow your brains all over the wall."

"Dad, they're friends!"

"Olivia?" In his shock, he dropped the gun, which hit the floor and went off, blowing a hole in the back door, barely missing Tuatha's feet. Rama screamed, and Olivia dove for the gun, worried her father had loaded two shells.

"What in the sparkling stars was that?" Tuatha whimpered.

"Dad, it's me. You don't need the gun."

In an instant he had her head in his hands, pushing back her tangled hair, searching her face. "Olivia. Are you okay?"

"Yes, Dad, I'm fine."

"Then explain yourself. Where on God's green Earth have you been? Why are your friends dressed up for Halloween?"

"Well, for starters, I haven't been on God's green Earth. And it's not Halloween."

She did her best to relay the events since their last fight. When she got to the part about a school on another planet full of people that looked like they were dressed up for Halloween, his eyes scanned the room. Realizing that these were not costumes, he plopped down at the kitchen table, overwhelmed, shaking his head. "He took Mom."

"What?"

"That guy from the school. He came here, knocked me out, and took your mother. Said he didn't need you if he had her. What does that mean?"

Olivia didn't know what it meant, but it couldn't be good. "Dad, I need to see what you saw." She took his hand into hers, shocked by the tremble he'd acquired.

What happened when Dr. Retchen came back?

The kitchen exploded into blackness, then reformed itself into the front entryway. A sharp triple knock on the door sent Brooke Carpenter scrambling for shelter behind John.

"Mr. Carpenter," came the slick, honeyed voice. "I've heard that Olivia is missing. Have you reconsidered the idea of a more structured learning environment for your daughter?"

"I don't trust him, John. Don't tell him anything. Don't open the door."

"We don't need your help parenting our daughter."

"May I speak with her?"

"No. She's grounded. No TV, no phone, no visitors. It's too bad you drove all the way out here instead of calling first. I could have saved you the hassle."

"If she's at home, I'd really like to speak with her. Please." The last word stung, acid burning his tongue.

"I've had enough of this," John growled. "I'm calling 911."

The call connected, but it was Retchen's voice in the receiver.

"911 can't help you." The line went dead. "Open this door NOW!"

Brooke dove into the closet behind her husband. There was a *click* and then a deafening *BANG* as the door frame around the deadbolt exploded, peppering John's farm-weathered hands with thousands of tiny wooden splinters. Five men in black suits surrounded him. They all wore sunglasses despite the late hour, and two of them cocked their shotguns, aiming at his head.

"I tried to be nice. A waste of time." Retchen paused for a moment, enjoying the look on John's face. "Where is she?"

"She's not here."

"Lies. Check everywhere. The basement. The attic. Trap doors under rugs. Fake walls in closets. Old houses are built with hiding spots."

His men scurried off in all directions like rats in a maze.

"She's not here," John growled, leaning against the closet to shield Brooke's hiding spot. "She ran away five days ago. Wouldn't matter anyway. She isn't going with you."

Retchen's closed fist came down hard on John's shoulder. He crumpled to the floor, biting back the pain, cradling his crushed collarbone. Retchen yanked him away from the closet door. "What are you hiding?"

He opened the door, and Brooke spat in his face, hoping to create enough of a distraction to pull her husband away. Disgusted, Retchen retrieved a cotton handkerchief from an inside pocket, wiped away the spit, and along with it, some peach-toned foundation, revealing a patch of grey underneath. Capitalizing on her surprise, he grabbed Brooke by the sides of her head and pushed his fingers into her skull. Brooke howled in agony.

The henchmen returned. "No sign of the girl, sir."

"Tie this one up." He looked down at John, wincing on the floor. "Call the police, and she's dead."

Brooke cursed Retchen's existence through the gag his men stuffed in her mouth. He sneered at her, enjoying her struggle. "If I have the mother, I don't need the girl."

Olivia let go and the flinch ended. She stared at her friends, feeling herself fading out of existence, like the tribe that couldn't quite seem to download in the tribunal room.

"What's going on, Carpenter? What did you see?"

"Our plan won't work. We have to come up with something else."

"Why not?" Rama needed more.

"He doesn't need me if he has my mom. And he has my mom, so our plan to lure him away won't work. We have to find him. We have to get her out of there before he…" She couldn't finish. Even thinking about what he would do to her was too much. She'd thought she'd found her strength. She'd believed she could handle this mission. But now, she wasn't even sure that she could hold herself together long enough to make it back to the ship. Her shell was intact, but her insides were turning to goo faster than the melting rays of Maia ever could.

Thankfully, Tuatha could see that she needed help and stepped in. "The oracle wouldn't have given you this mission if you couldn't handle it. So we change the plan. We figure out how to find this creep, and then we rescue Mama Carpenter. Am I right?"

Olivia nodded weakly.

"Okay, Carpenter, stay with me. We have to find this creep. How do we do that?"

AmmaNa produced a small cloth bag. When she opened it and presented its contents to the group, they all gasped. It was full of crystal fruit harvested from the Tree of Life.

"Did you ask permission to take those?"

Tuatha let out an exasperated sigh. "Seriously, Keilte! We're living on the edge. We've gone rogue. The Jin tried to stop us from leaving, remember? Let go of the rules so we can focus on rescuing Mama Carpenter. Got it?"

"Right, right. Got it." But he continued to eye the satchel with suspicion.

Olivia's attention was also fixed on the fruit. Under its spell, she'd cracked a moon wide open. She chewed on the inside of her cheek.

The sacred fruit will help your mind
locate the ones you wish to find.
Your brain will open up to hear their voices from afar.

"This is a bad idea. There has to be another way."

"Come on, Carpenter. This is part of the plan. You can't go all jelly on us now."

"I'm not going all jelly."

"So just eat it already before Maia sets. You know the Jin are gonna march through that gate and take over our ship as soon as they can, right? Do you want your first big mission to be hijacked because you were scared of a piece of fruit?"

"But what if my brain explodes? What if I rip the Earth in two?"

"Not going to happen. I'd offer to calm you down, because Deyonns can do that, but you need all of your twisty tangled emotions to fight this bad guy. So stop stalling, eat the fruit already, and let's get this show started."

With all of them watching expectantly, she begrudgingly took a piece.

I must prepare you for this task. This will not be an easy road.
One bite will open you to hear eight billion minds on overload.
You need to turn the volume down
and listen for the voice to speak.
Once you have locked onto that voice,
the Jin will find the one you seek.

Silence blanketed the group as Olivia put the fruit to her lips. She took a deep breath to steel her nerves before sinking her teeth into its flesh. Once again, her taste buds exploded with its fragrant sweetness, but the pleasure was short-lived. A cacophony blasted into her mind, people screaming, crying, and cursing. It was like walking into a TV warehouse with every set tuned into a different channel, all screaming over top of each other.

Why does he hit me?... I love her so much... They're right, I am fat... Why won't they focus on me?... What did I do to deserve this?... Please don't take my baby... Nobody loves me... I'll show her, I'll show every stupid woman... All I want is a million followers, is that so much to ask?... I'm never gonna be good enough... I'll cancel that bitch if it kills me!... Please don't let them find me... Why won't they do what I want?

Olivia dropped to her knees and clawed at her temples as eight billion voices full of loathing assaulted her brain all at once. "Make it stop! Please, AmmaNa, make it stop!"

AmmaNa's voice pushed through over the noise.

Decide to turn the volume down.

"How?" Olivia whimpered, tears welling up, every neuron on fire. A drop of blood trickled from her nose to the floor.

You gave an order to our ship,
so give the order to your mind.

Olivia imagined a volume button and turned it down. Surprisingly, it worked. The cacophony subsided. "Is that really what we sound like?" She was horrified by the amount of negativity her people were releasing into the universe.

Let's hope that Dr. Retchen thinks
as loudly as the rest of you.

Right. Focus on Retchen's voice. Her head was already throbbing, but she focused on the soothing veneer he had used when interviewing her at the school. But every time she turned up the volume, all she heard was a planet seething with negativity. She took a deep breath, imagined a remote control, and pressed the button to change the channel to Retchen. It was no use. She strained, searching until she was exhausted. A small puddle of blood had congealed by her feet.

"This isn't working. I can't find him. What do we do?"

If you can focus on his voice, then we can filter out the rest.
Please let us work on this as one. Cooperation breeds success.

Olivia's head throbbed from the exhausting search, but a headache was not going to stop her from finding her mother. AmmaNa put her hands on Olivia's temples and she felt a tingle pass through her, like a single wave rippling across a calm lake. She focused on the flinch with him, on his voice when he wasn't trying to coax her into his clutches.

"Prepare my roasting spit." The Greys scurried out of the room. He poked at the boy in the bathtub with an electric cattle prod. "Let's tenderize you a little."

She kept her focus on the flinch, repeating it over and over in her mind, but when AmmaNa let go of her temples, she had only found disappointment.

We cannot find the voice you seek.

He may have left the planet, or

he may know how to shield his thoughts.

"Do you think he can Mindshield like Keilte?"

"Hey! The Teutons would never eat a Terran! We do not eat flesh."

"I've met him, Keilte. Being able to shield his thoughts doesn't make him anything like you."

"Does it make him more dangerous than you thought he was?" Rama seemed worried.

"Most definitely. But I'm quite sure he isn't telepathic, because he didn't see my flinch."

"Are you sure?"

"If he knew that I knew his secret, I wouldn't have walked away."

"What's all this flinching nonsense?" John Carpenter had been trying to follow the strange conversation in his kitchen between these strange beings that still didn't seem real, and he didn't like feeling confused. He liked being in control. He liked knowing what was what.

"Flinching is my superpower, Dad. It lets me see things that have already happened. It's something Migitju showed me how to do, so I know you're going to think it's crazy bullshit, but aliens are standing in your kitchen. For once, you're just going to have to admit that you don't know everything."

"I don't even know my own daughter."

"It's true. And I don't have time to help you fix that, because Mom's in trouble. When Retchen came here, even the first time, did he give you any paperwork about his school?"

"All he left us was this." John handed her a brochure he'd discarded on the counter.

"This is great, Dad. Thanks." Olivia headed for the back door, brochure firmly clutched in her hand.

"Where do you think you're going? You have school in the morning."

"Dad, let's get a few things straight. One, I'm not going back to that school. Ever. That place has nothing to teach me. I attend the most exclusive school in the galaxy, and it's far enough away that you never have to deal with the embarrassment of me fighting back against Miley ever again. Two, my DNA is special, and I'm the only one who can rescue Mom, so I'm going to go do that, and we can talk later."

John wasn't expecting to see this kind of strength in his little girl. Suddenly, his expression changed from the strong father she had always known to a broken little boy.

"Bring her back to me. Please, Livy, bring her back. I need your mom. I don't know how to be…without her." He covered his face with the crook of his elbow just in time to hide the flood that followed. In her whole life, Olivia had never seen her father cry, but now she watched as the strongest man she knew shattered into pieces, broken without his love.

21 A DARK PLACE

ONCE THEY WERE safely back in the ship and floating high above Saskatchewan, Olivia loosened her grip, freeing the brochure from its cage. On the front, an imposing three-storey building with a steep roof and a grand gabled entrance was framed by two words in capital letters: HEEM, MONTANA. AmmaNa set a course for Heem, but the ship didn't move.

Heem, Montana does not register as a valid location. There is a cluster of buildings in northern Europe named Heem. Would you like to peruse these locations and select one?

It was pretty cool that the ship was like an intergalactic Siri. Olivia could definitely work with this. "Europe is out. Let's try something else. Can you to connect to our planet's internet and search for a building in Montana that matches the picture on this brochure?"

Connecting... Scanning... The building that matches the picture on your brochure is located in Emerson Junction, Montana. Setting a course for Emerson Junction.

Olivia, Rama, and Tuatha crept through a dark thicket of trees on the outskirts of Emerson Junction. Tuatha could blind everyone, and Rama could blink into a human, but Keilte had no camouflage, so he remained on the ship with AmmaNa and her crew. He hadn't been happy about it until Olivia pointed out that it meant he wouldn't have to break any more rules.

The newly fallen leaves crunched underfoot, giving off the smoky odour of autumn decay. It felt welcoming, a comfy blanket Olivia hadn't even realized she was missing. They inched forward, unwilling to turn on a light and risk being seen, but it wasn't long before Olivia's eyes adjusted to the dark and she was able to pick her way around the fallen trees and large rocks blocking their path. As they crested a ridge directly north of the school, it was clear that the ship had done a superior job of choosing a lookout position. The front entrance was easy to see; anyone leaving or arriving was in full view. A dozen spotlights flooded the building, overlapping to destroy every last shadow. There was no way to sneak in unnoticed. Luckily, sneaking in was not the plan. They hunkered down for a better look. All the while, birch leaves, brittle as old paper, rained down on them in a constant flutter. Soon, Olivia's legs were hidden under a blanket of yellow.

"Look what I can do!" Rama blinked, leaving a pile of leaves where he had been sitting. Olivia tried to stifle a giggle.

"How about we get the scoop on what's happening inside those walls?"

Olivia shook her head. She was too wiped out from the last attempt with the fruit to try again.

"Come on, Carpenter, don't tell me you're scared. You're the bravest Terran I know!"

"I'm the only Terran you know."

"We're about to walk in completely blind. I mean, asking you for a head count might be a bit much, but you could sneak a listen to see if it's quiet in there…or really loud."

"What if the Greys use some kind of telepathic quiet mode and I think the place is deserted when it's really swarming?"

She was so busy trying to come up with her next objection to Tuatha's plan that she didn't notice two shadows approaching.

Rough hands grabbed her, stuffing a cloth over her mouth. Her lungs filled with acrid fumes that made her brain hurt. She tried to fight, but her muscles turned to rubber.

"The other one flew away. How is that even possible?"

"Jet pack? I dunno. Never mind. Won't be hard to find."

OLIVIA STOOD IN her circle, surrounded by corn. The warm breeze was relaxing, but she was confused. Why was she here? Wasn't she supposed to be somewhere else? It was like a dream, with fuzzy edges.

This place is comfortable, isn't it?

The voice was all around her. She raced around the clearing, searching behind cornstalks but she couldn't find its owner. It didn't seem to have a source.

Let's see how it all began, shall we?

Even though she was already in the field, she saw herself arrive. She threw her bike against the stalks, dropped to the ground, and hugged her knees, crying. When she had finished bandaging her ankle, she looked up at the sky, and made a wish: "I wish I could go to a place where people are like me."

She remembered saying that. She remembered being here. But this wasn't déjà vu. Déjà vu moments finished as soon as they started. This weird dream was holding her hostage.

How did I get here? What was I doing?

What did you do after you made the wish?

The voice pulled at her, shifting her focus back to the clearing where the other Olivia popped in her ear buds and danced to the music of her ancestors.

That's an interesting dance, Olivia. Where did you learn it?

The voice pulled her into the vision with a strength she couldn't resist. Her dance in the clearing began to change. It became more intense, full of passion. Her arms reached and twisted wildly, her body pulled by the song. Tendrils of light grew up out of the ground like vines, twisting around her dancing body and stretching up into the sky.

This wasn't right. She wasn't supposed to be in the cornfield. She needed to hide.

You can't hide from us. We see everything you see.

That was why she couldn't see the voice's owner. Whoever owned it was rummaging around in her mind. This moment was special, so there was only one thing to do. She found a shoe on the ground, made of soft leather, a shoe she'd worn to dance at the pow wow with Migitju. She picked up the shoe and thought of her special clearing in the middle of the woods, surrounded by massive trees. Daylight broke through, the dancer vanished, and she was alone next to a babbling brook flanked by wildflowers.

Aren't you clever? But it's only a matter of time before we learn your secrets.

It appeared only a few feet away, in front of a tall tree. It was a least a foot shorter than she was, bony, with a large, bald, egg-shaped head ending in a pointy chin that was almost too much for its neck to hold. Its grey skin was waxy and seemed to absorb the sunlight.

What about your wish? You wanted to live with others like you. What would that be like?

The question snapped through her focus, and she fell into another memory as the grassy clearing was suddenly replaced with walls made entirely of crystal. She had to get out of here. She had to stop this intruder from digging any deeper into her mind. It was time for Mindshield.

Where did you learn that word?

She ignored the question, forcing her mind to return to the clearing. She focused on the details: the smell of pine and cedar, her toes wiggling through a soft carpet of moss. The Grey appeared only a few feet away, following her through her mindscape. She had to keep him away from the important places.

What about the Jin? Have they been in your head?

Suddenly, the forest floor was replaced by the smooth, cold floor of the Jin ship. Olivia reached out, and as her fingers made contact with AmmaNa's sparkly wrist, she flinched into the collective unconscious.

The Jin used your brain as a storage bin, but we're the bad guys?

You are the bad guys. You snatched me out of the woods, away from my friends. Okay, Olivia, calm down. Control your thoughts. Don't give them any more information.

You can't stop us. If we want something, we'll take it.

But they couldn't take it if they didn't know what "it" was. She had no intention of being useful to these monsters.

She wiggled her toes, and the smooth floor gave way to a lush carpet of bugleweed and moss. Ancient maples burst from the ground around her and stretched their massive arms up into the sky. She only had precious few moments before it found her, so she did the only thing that made sense.

She ran.

She darted from tree to tree, around maples so large they could hide three of her, through the thick forest next to her grandmother's reserve, one of the few places that hadn't been chewed up by giant metal jaws in the name of the almighty dollar. She doubled back through the woods, and as soon as she reached the clearing, she built a fortress just like she and Keilte had practised. She ran inside and slammed the door.

She was safe.

She had less than a minute before she would begin to forget about the outside world. But the adrenaline in her veins carried her to the top of the stairs, where she found a marker and a stack of blank paper. As quickly as she could, she wrote messages to herself.

Remember to leave.

Keilte, Tuatha, and Rama are waiting.

Remember to leave.

A Grey is waiting outside. You need a plan.

Remember to leave.

She spread the notes over the floor in front of the chairs but thought twice about sitting down. She couldn't get comfortable. She had to make a plan. There had to be a way to watch what was going on outside. She needed a television and security cameras. As luck would have it, a small TV sat on a shelf, sandwiched between two stacks of books. But of course! This was her mindscape. In here, she could make anything happen.

Snow danced onscreen like it did on the old TV in Migitju's house. She always fixed that set by fiddling with the metal antlers until a picture appeared, but this set didn't have any antlers. What it did have was a remote, sitting on a pile of books nearby. Olivia snatched it up and clicked a button. The channel changed to Migitju, burning sweetgrass and making clover tea. If thinking about Migitju helped the TV find her, maybe thinking about the Grey would work the same way. She hit the channel button again, and there it was, searching along the wall. If the Greys used to be Jin, they knew all about the Mindshield fortress. Would he find the door? How long did she have?

We are the future of this planet, Olivia. You can either cooperate or be destroyed.

She scanned the spines of the books in front of her, hoping for something helpful. Finding one titled *Only One Way Out,* she flipped to the first page. It began:

> It seemed entirely logical that the surest way to get out of a situation was to retrace one's steps back to the place one came in. With that in mind, our heroine began crafting her escape.

She closed the book and put it back on the shelf. "This library is pretty great. I should come here more often. Maybe I'll stay for one adventure. There's always time to read."

The recliner was plush, comfy, the kind of comfortable you sank into and never wanted to leave. Strange… There were messages strewn about the floor. ***Keilte, Tuatha, and Rama are waiting. You need a plan. Remember to leave. A Grey is waiting outside.*** The last message snapped her back to her senses.

As long as you're hiding in here, your fleshy body is... unprotected. How long do you want to play this little game?

"Until I win," Olivia replied to nobody. "The surest way to get out is to go back to the place you came in." She pointed the remote at the television. "Show me where the Grey came in."

A figure slumped on a bed in a dark room. It seemed dead, except for a rhythmic breathing that filled the space. A rectangle of light, far, far off in the distance, shrank and shrank until it was just a thin sliver. With the click of a door, the light vanished. Lying in complete darkness, the figure shivered.

A pounding noise shattered the silence. It was close. Too close.

A crack ripped through the darkness opposite the bed, and a sickly light seeped in. The cracking intensified as the wall was pried open and finally gave way. A shadow stepped into the space uninvited. Now that she knew how he got in, it was time to kick his bony grey ass back out.

She turned off the television, and after re-reading all of the important messages one last time, headed down the stairs.

As soon as the fresh forest air hit her face, she thought of the black room with the door closing in the distance. The forest vanished, and she was surrounded by darkness, alone with her own motionless figure on the bed. A deafening crack, like an iceberg shearing away, let in a sick, greenish light. Moments later, the wall burst wide open, and a short, thin Grey with a large egg-head and huge oil-slick eyes climbed through the wall and into the room. Olivia clenched her jaw and focused on the intruder.

"GET OUUUUUTTTTTT!" she screamed, running full force into him. With all of her rage, she shoved the Grey backwards through the hole it had ripped into her psyche. The hole slammed shut, sealing him out.

22 OLIVIA'S TRIBE

A BONY FIGURE, hovering over a motionless girl with its hands pressed into her temples, suddenly flew backwards through the air. It crashed into the wall, slumped to the floor like a pile of wet laundry, groaned, and then went still.

It took Olivia a moment to adjust to her surroundings; she was no longer in her mindscape. This dark room was back in the real world, and she was still a prisoner. The door was locked with a keypad next to its handle, and Olivia didn't have the code. Either she was stuck until someone else showed up or until the thing in the corner came to.

If she could get inside the keypad, maybe she could cut the wires? But the screws on the casing had been painted shut. She tried but couldn't pry them open. She scrutinized the buttons, hoping the Grey had left behind some trace, maybe some residue from its long, waxy fingers. She grazed a finger over each button, but they were clean. Of course, that made sense. It had only used the code on the outside of the room.

Her attacker was still lying in a heap. In her panic, she'd almost forgotten that she could probably flinch the code out of its head. The idea of touching it made her nauseous, but she didn't know how long she had before it woke up and sounded the alarm. She had to do this. Besides, it had done the same thing to her. She grabbed it by the throat, just in case touching it caused it to wake up.

What is the combination to the door where Olivia Carpenter is being held?

The blackness around her shattered and reformed itself into a well-lit hallway. The Grey reached one of its three bony fingers to the keypad and punched the numbers 1-6-1-8-0-3. The door opened, and

Olivia yanked her hand away, ending the flinch. She raced to the keypad, entered the code, and moments later, light blasted in from the hallway. Shielding her eyes while they adjusted, she took a few steps and then stopped. She was free of that room but still a prisoner. When the Grey woke up, it would come for her. It would sound the alarm telepathically to everyone in this place.

The door slid open once again, revealing the monster. This was a time for survival, not for weakness. She marched over to her attacker, raised her boot, and brought it down firmly on the thing's skull, once, twice, three times. When a dark patch appeared under its head and began spreading across the floor, she knew the deed was done. She wiped her sole on the bare mattress, trying to forget the sound of its skull breaking like an egg, but the more she tried to forget, the more vivid the cracking noise became. Maybe once she was out of here, she'd tuck that memory away someplace that she'd never look again.

Back out in the bright lights of the compound, she chose a direction and crept along until she hit a T junction. Having no idea which way to go, she chose left. How was she going to find her mom in this maze? The question had her so distracted that she almost walked right in front of a long stretch of picture windows. Dropping to all fours, she crawled to the bottom of the first window and risked a peek.

The room beyond was large and full of screens. Some showed closeups, while others watched from a distance. Some were trained on important monuments, such as the feet of the Sphinx in Egypt, while others kept an eye on overgrown mountains. As fascinating as these images were, her mother wasn't in the room or on a screen, so Olivia put her head down and crawled quickly to the end of the hall. When she finally looked up, her stomach clenched. An elevator with another keypad blocked her way. She tried 1-6-1-8-0-3, but nothing happened.

Unsure of what to do next, Olivia sat in the corner to chew on some cheek. She stuffed her hands in her pockets. Her left hand found her MP3 player and her right hand clasped something hard and round —the piece of fruit Tuatha had been pushing her to eat right before she'd been grabbed. At the time, it had seemed like the worst idea in the world, but now, it was probably her only way to get out of this place alive.

Olivia sank her teeth into the fruit with purpose, knowing its crystal flesh would give way. A flood of deliciousness rushed over her taste buds, accompanied by the onslaught of negativity cutting through her brain like a massive razor blade. The pain was unreal. Grabbing at her temples, she visualized a remote and turned the volume down. The idea of an omnipotent god being able to hear every thought of every living person was overwhelming. If she had to listen to this crap full-time, she'd walk away. Peace the heck out. Abandon ship.

She took a deep breath and fixed her mind on her mom's voice: telling her to brush her teeth, telling her to say her prayers, reminding her to thank the Creator. Once she was locked on, she turned up the volume, listening for a match. The voices came rushing back in as much as the volume would allow, but none of them belonged to Brooke Carpenter. Olivia tried changing the channel like she had with the TV in her tower, but still, all she heard were the lamentations of people who didn't know how good they had it. Maybe she didn't know how to find specific people? Maybe her mother's voice was already gone? Why had she come on this mission so unprepared? Olivia wanted to cry, to scream, but she couldn't afford to grieve right now. Instead, she balled up all of the sadness, the anger, the fear, and pushed it deep down for later. Right now, she needed to be strong. She needed to focus.

Eating the apple on Sita hadn't flooded her brain with the complaints of eight billion humans. Why was that? Of course! Proximity mattered. Maybe she could use that to her advantage. Turning up the volume very slowly, the closest thoughts came through first. Her intuition didn't disappoint; the closest thoughts focused on quitting time. On going home. On having a beer. He wasn't thinking about elevator codes, and he wouldn't unless he had a good reason. On a whim, she tried the only thing that made sense; she imagined herself hovering right next to his ear, and whispered: *What's the elevator code?*

The elevator code is 3-1-4-1-5-3. That's weird. Why would I think about that?

Could getting secret codes from people's heads really be that easy? Easy, aside from the nosebleed that came with billions of complaints trying to pry their way in. She repeated the code to herself a few times, but before putting it to use, she turned the volume up enough to make sure that her whisper hadn't tipped off the guard to her presence. She was good. He was already back to thinking about beer.

She crossed her fingers, reached up, and punched 3-1-4-1-5-3 into the keypad. Ding. The light turned green and the doors slid open. She scrambled into the small metal box and considered which buttons to push next, but the elevator had other plans. It began dropping all on its own. The lights on the panel told her she was headed for B10.

Retchen knew she was here.

When the doors slid open, the acrid smell of vinegar assaulted her senses. Every breath burned her nostrils and the back of her throat. Even when Migitju pickled fiddleheads with vinegar, there was a sweetness in the air. This was different. This was putrid. Rotting.

The thick blackness beyond the elevator was more than just an absence of light. One candle, all by itself, is enough to chase away the darkness in a room, but the light seeping out of the elevator was swallowed up mere inches from the door. This kind of darkness was different. It consumed light.

The elevator closed, trapping her in obscurity. Olivia bent down to suss out her surroundings and was surprised to feel the cold of tile beneath her. She crawled forwards on hands and knees, feeling her way along a pattern that reminded her of the shower room at the community pool. What kind of hallway needed a tile floor? Her hand touched something metal embedded in the tile: round with slits. A drain?

"Tsk, tsk, Olivia. Did you really think I would let you walk away so easily?"

A single light flicked on twenty feet away. An unusually tall being stood in the solitary pool of light, cackling softly. It was definitely Retchen, but he had shed his fake hair, and tonight, his face didn't match any of the wide spectrum of human flesh tones. Tonight, his greenish-grey scales were on full display.

"Where's my mom?"

"Oh, in time, Olivia, in time."

Retchen snapped his fingers, revealing the room. Rows of workbenches stood between them, holding flasks and beakers full of multicoloured liquids that fizzed and bubbled, filling the air with a horrible stench that made the back of her throat raw like it had been scoured with sandpaper. The workbenches were far too short for humans. This was the workspace of the Greys.

"The time is now. Where is my mom?"

"You're in my house, and you will play by my rules. I could feel you searching for me from afar and for her just now. That's an interesting talent you possess." Retchen pulled a girl into the light, gently, not like someone he'd kidnapped. Olivia hadn't realized anyone else was in the room, but that's the thing about shadows, you rarely look at them long enough to uncover their secrets. The girl was middle school-aged, with a round face, strong cheekbones, and a tangle of fiery curls. It was like looking at a cousin, but none of Olivia's cousins had red hair. None that she knew of, anyway.

"You recognize her." He pulled more girls into the light until six identical faces stared at her. "This is what you've craved. This is your tribe, Olivia. Meet your sisters."

"I...I don't understand."

"The kids at your school call you a disease. It's hard being cast aside when you know that you are superior to your peers, is it not? Your sisters will never judge you. They will never cast you aside because they are just like you. Don't you want a family that accepts you as you are?"

He wasn't wrong. That was exactly what she wanted. Spending time with her tractor engines and her books was okay, but having zero friends was lonely. Her heart had always ached for friends who understood her. Maybe she'd found that with Tuatha, Rama, and Keilte, but she didn't have any experience trusting in these friendships. But these girls? How could they be sisters? What was this place?

"Go to her," he told them. "Go to your big sister."

The six redheads made their way around the workbenches and gathered around Olivia, hugging her and taking her by the hands, exactly like little sisters would do. They cocooned her in acceptance. It felt wonderful. Maybe the oracle wanted to save them as well. A quick flinch would tell her what she needed to know. She cleared her mind and closed her eyes.

Where did you come from?

The world shattered, but the flinch finished before it had even started, the blackness quickly reassembling itself into Retchen's lab. This wasn't possible. Flinching wasn't about seeing memories. Grampy Chester's totem was a block of wood. It didn't have memories, but it did hold an echo of the energy her grandfather had left behind. Even if the girls didn't remember their past, they still had one. How could this ten-year-old not have an echo?

"That smell again," Retchen chided, shaking his head. "If you have questions, Olivia, just ask."

"Where did you come from?" she asked the little girl whose face was closest to hers. But the girl just stared, dazzled by Olivia's attention.

"She hasn't learned to speak. She was only born yesterday."

"That can't be…"

"You left your bicycle in the clearing. There was blood on the chain. Once I had your DNA, this was easy."

He had to be lying. But maybe he wasn't? And that made their vacant looks all the more creepy, like dolls made in her image, with glass eyes that felt nothing. These spooks were all up in her personal space. She needed room. Olivia detached herself from the gaggle and, taking each one by the shoulders, arranged them in a line against the first workbench and then backed away, pretending to examine them, buying herself some distance. What was this? Retchen was all about eating kids, not raising a hockey team. For once, Olivia couldn't see the script.

"Hold on. You eat children. I know you do, so what is this…?" She waved her hand at the line of girls. "What is this!?"

"You are correct. My kind does eat humans."

Olivia could not hide her disgust as she imagined him sitting down to a meal.

He chuckled softly. “My forefathers showed humans how to farm corn and wheat to make you nice and sweet. You farm your food, and we farm you.”

“If human farms existed, people would know about it. We have the internet now.”

“Every city is a human farm, every skyscraper a chicken coop. We load you in, one on top of another, and the higher we build, the more you pay to live there. You’re the only species that doesn’t know it’s being farmed. Ironic, really.” He grinned, his teeth sharp like the tyrannosaurus at the museum in the Badlands, teeth made to eat flesh. “Humans are delicious.”

“That’s disgusting.”

“How is it any different from humans eating beef, or bacon, or chicken? You are below us on the food chain. That is how nature operates. Your slaughterhouses are much more violent than our methods. When was the last time you ate a juicy burger?”

“Humans are not food! We’re intelligent beings with emotions!”

“Perhaps, until the moment you consider something to be your property. And then you humans are just as ruthless as we are. Do you think a cow lacks the intelligence to know that a slaughterhouse is a death camp? Humans are so simple. You refuse to believe that any other life is intelligent. You fight wars with each other over ideologies that you cannot prove while the real threat walks among you. Most of you are too stupid to be anything other than food.”

“Exactly. So why make these clones? So you can eat them? So they can run the farm? I don’t get it.”

“My family knows about you, Olivia. They will hunt you and consume you, because to consume your flesh also consumes your power. That is not the fate I want for you. I want you to build me an army. Teach your sisters to be like you, and we will overthrow those who would destroy you. They will come for you, Olivia. I can protect you. I am your only salvation.”

So the clones had her DNA, but they couldn’t flinch. Despite all of his technology, his spooks were worthless without a teacher. That’s why he’d taken her mom as a replacement; he didn’t know that Brooke wasn't her teacher. She had to stall…to figure out a plan.

"These can't actually be my clones. I left my bike in the field a week ago. You can't make a batch of ten-year-olds in a week."

"My recent alliance with the Greys has created a myriad of new… possibilities."

He flipped a switch, lighting the entire room, revealing the true bone-chilling nature of the lab. Chambers similar to the Jin cocoons lined the walls from floor to ceiling, but they sat upright and were full of a greenish liquid, making the room look much more alien than anything she'd seen on Sita. A warning of danger spidered up her neck. The curls on her head tingled. Something about this place was very, very wrong.

In the chamber to Olivia's immediate left, a large membrane suspended in the liquid bumped into the glass. Something inside was alive. It began thrashing around like it was trying to break free, revealing a corkscrew tangle of red filaments, jellyfish stingers tossed by the tide. The filaments parted as a hand pushed through them, resting on the glass. From behind the hand, a pair of blue eyes peered through the membrane. It was a child. Even though it looked to be about five years old, it was still connected to its membrane by an umbilical cord. Its lungs had not yet tasted oxygen. Its eyes were blank. Olivia's gaze darted to another chamber, and another. Each one was growing a child.

The lab was filled with clones. Olivia's tribe.

Her stomach churned. The innocent girls gawking expectantly at her were suddenly more alien than anyone else, even the Greys. Each was a blank slate. They had zero knowledge of family or society. They had no reverence for the planet. They had zero connection. They were six lives dressed in human skin with no understanding of what it meant to be human. It was the scariest hall of mirrors that she had ever visited.

"They are exact copies of you in every way. Imagine what you can do to the bullies with a whole army."

She thought of Miley, the panic in her voice as the clones cornered her in the gym. It was the perfect revenge…but it was the stuff of fantasies. Having an army of clones wouldn't fix anything in Swift Current; it would just make her even more of a weirdo.

"You kidnapped my mom, and you think I'm going to help you?"

He vanished into the shadows for a moment and returned, wheeling a chair in front of him. Her mom was tied, gagged, and slumped forward, not at all conscious of what was going on. But she was here. She was alive. Hope welled up inside Olivia, making her feel as strong as a thousand-year-old tree. He believed these abilities were a family secret. She had to put him off of that trail, for Migitju.

"She's useless to you. She can't do what I can do. I learned my abilities from the Jin and the Yanisma." Hearing those names made Retchen recoil. He recovered his composure quickly, but Olivia saw his moment of hesitation. "You've heard of the Yanisma? Good. I did them a solid, and now they owe me."

"And yet, you came alone."

Olivia's confidence evaporated. He was right—her alliance with the Yanisma was a red herring. Percy wasn't here to back her up.

Retchen patted Brooke on the head. "She is insurance. To make sure you cooperate."

"What are you going to do with this army of clones? Take over the world?"

"Silly child, we already own this world. That is a birthright. I need the army to overthrow the despots currently screwing it all up."

"You think you can do a better job?"

"When I was in charge, humans knew their station. The new El have been letting too many of you survive. Letting you build up your numbers. They're abusing the program."

"The program? Could you be any more cliché?"

"We programmed the entire planet, naive little girl. We gave you televisions and movie screens, we gave you an endless symphony of hit songs, we engineered enough social media to bombard this entire planet with the thoughts we want you to think, but somehow our programming did not work on you. You do not believe what you should believe. Why is that, Olivia?"

"You think you've been programming the entire planet?" Olivia stalled. “Not likely. We’re not that gullible.” But in her heart, she knew he spoke the truth. For years, she’d heard people repeat what they’d seen on the news or the internet without actually checking the facts. She’d always wondered why. But maybe it wasn’t their fault. Maybe they were all being brainwashed.

“Humans are more like sheep than chickens or cows. As long as one of you behaves with conviction, the rest follow quite easily. You are all busy trying to get rich, and that makes you easy to control.”

“Not everyone wants to be rich.”

“True, we have had a few hiccups along the way. Every now and then, one of you tries to convince the rest that money is unnecessary. But you have such short lifespans. We just wait a few hundred years, release a plague, and in the ensuing chaos, we rewrite the story. It works like a charm. We install the shepherds, and the sheep follow without question.”

“You can’t brainwash an entire planet.”

“But we have. Whenever one of you somehow overcomes our programming, we give that person a choice. Get back in line, or be erased. Joan of Arc made the wrong choice, and I made a very public display of her demise. Wearing my human disguise, of course.” His yellow eyes filled with glee as he remembered the teenage girl he had barbecued. “I give you the same choice I gave her. Worship me as the god I am, or be erased.”

“I don’t believe in God. I believe in a Creator who gave us the skies, and the mountains, and the oceans, and the rivers. You haven’t given us anything. You came to Earth to take, to destroy what the Creator gave us. I will never worship you.”

“Then you will be replaced.”

The lights inside the incubators turned red. One by one, the liquid inside them began to drain. To Olivia’s horror, the first chamber opened, and an egg sack spilled out onto the floor, its contents thrashing around, fighting for freedom. A small hand clawed through the membrane, and a thick goop oozed across the floor as the slime-covered clone opened her mouth and gasped for her first breath. The clones lined up in front of Olivia were temporarily distracted, and she took the opportunity to back up to the elevator.

The newborn clone pulled herself to her knees and tried to stand, but her muscles were weak, and she teetered backward into her egg sack. She had no mother to wrap her in a hug, nobody to quiet the terror of being born onto a cold, tile-covered floor. But when she opened her blue eyes, they contained no fear, no love, no longing. Human babies were born with emotion. They cried for their mothers. They cooed when they were loved. This creature felt nothing. She was empty.

"You can't replace me with these…these things!"

"Who will stop me? You?"

"The Jin won't allow it."

"The Jin are not warriors. They are scientists."

The next chamber opened, spilling another goo-covered egg sack on the floor. The hatchling tried and failed to pull herself to her feet.

"Look at how pathetic she is, Olivia. She needs you. They all do. Accept your place as the leader of a new and far more superior version of humans."

The third chamber ejected its egg. Hands clawed at the inside of the membrane.

"How can you forsake your own self, Olivia? Each one of them is a part of you."

"They're not a part of me. They're nothing like me!"

"I'm sorry to hear you say that, but I'm not surprised. If you won't teach them, your mother will. She'll stay here with me for as long as it takes. I need someone to raise my army. And since you aren't up for the job, your usefulness has come to an end."

23 AWAKEN THE BEAST

"IF I AGREE to help you, to train your army, will you let her go?" She needed to stall long enough to find the invisible strings and pull her mother to safety.

"I already gave you the opportunity to make the correct choice. This desperation is…unbecoming. You beg for her life. Pathetic."

She blocked out his voice, listening instead for the low hum of the connection, but she couldn't find it. More incubators turned from green to red, going into hatch mode. Olivia needed to get her mom out now, before a swarm of clones hatched between them. She thought about Master Eldrin's private lesson. She could only find the strings once she was in tune. But she didn't have time to mess around with tuning forks. But maybe…

She stuffed her left hand into her pocket, grateful that her captors hadn't confiscated her stuff. She hit the play button on her MP3 player and stuffed an earbud into her left ear, praying that Beethoven would put her in tune quickly, her thumb hovering on shuffle just in case.

Dr. Retchen grabbed her mother's hair and yanked on it. Brooke woke up to the latest round of clones clawing through their membranes and writhing on the ground. The scream that left her lungs hit the rag filling her mouth and was transformed into a gurgling whimper that escaped mostly through her nostrils.

"Come, come. That's no way to treat your new owner."

In desperation, Olivia stuffed the second earbud in her right ear. The violins swelled, and finally, the strings showed themselves, flowing from her fingers like gentle waves across a still pond.

Thank you, Beethoven!

She directed the strings at her mother, wrapping them around the chair. Without the overwhelming panic that came with having the life choked out of her, the connection was strong. It felt like she could move anything. Three workbenches blocked the way forward, but the path around the outside of the room was littered with ooze-covered clones. The only way to pull her mother to safety was to lift her up and over the tables. Hoping her connection was strong enough to overcome gravity, Olivia threw her hand upward before yanking it back toward herself. To her amazement, Brooke's chair dusted over the benches, shattering beakers and flasks as its wheels mowed through the experiments. Foul-smelling liquids crashed to the floor, spewing plumes of smoke into the air. Brooke hit the ground next to Olivia and kept going, slamming into the elevator. She squirmed and struggled, tears welling up in her eyes. Olivia wanted to free her, to comfort her, to tell her she was sorry for running away, but first, she had to deal with Retchen.

"How dare you!" He tore around the benches towards her.

Olivia reached for him, commanding the invisible strings to appear. This time, they were so strong that everything else vanished. This time, there was only the music in her ears and the incredible strength of her claw. It clamped around him with a granite grip.

She whipped her hand to the left, and he flew across the room, slamming into an incubator. The egg sack that spilled onto his head was nowhere near ready to hatch. The flimsy membrane burst open, and a creature emerged with a huge head perched on a tiny body and four stumps that would have become arms and legs. It flopped a few times like a salmon out of water and went still.

Retchen flailed in midair, fighting and thrashing against stone. Olivia released him, and he crashed to the floor, crushing a hatchling trying to take its first steps. Retchen pulled himself to his feet, his yellow eyes full of hatred. "You'll pay for this!"

He lunged, but Olivia was ready. Her invisible hand grabbed him again and threw him to the right, smashing another incubator, then to the left, and back and forth, again and again, smashing up the lab like she was playing whack-a-mole with as many undeveloped clones as she could. But no matter how many blows she dealt, Retchen wasn't fazed or dazed. His eyes remained locked on her.

His prize.

Beethoven ended. Her grip began to weaken, and Retchen sensed the difference. He thrashed and struggled, breaking free and squashing another fully developed hatchling as he landed with a thud. He was badly bruised, green liquid oozing from cuts all over his body, but he climbed to his feet, ready for round three.

She raised her hand and called on the strings, but nothing happened. She shook her head, took a deep breath, and tried again. She couldn't do it without the music. She reached for her MP3 player, but her hand was sweaty, and the gadget slipped from her pocket, landing in a blob of clone goop at her feet. She snatched it back up, but it was fried.

"You're no match for me."

His sneer reminded her of Miley, of all the times Miley had backed her into a corner. She had never done anything to deserve that violence; Miley just hated anyone who didn't conform to her rules, as if, somehow, she was so important that she decided who everyone was allowed to be. Rage turned Olivia's blood to steam. It felt dangerous, like she was heading for an explosion, but she needed power, and here it was: raw and untamed. She gathered up all of the rage, the hurt, the anger, and the pain. She gathered it into a ball and shoved it down into her stomach, where she could hold it while she imagined herself transforming into a giant maple. She was as old as the Earth. She sent her roots down, down, deep into the ground, just like Migitju had taught her, and once her roots were firmly planted, she took that rage and pushed it as deep as it would go.

The earth trembled.

The lights hanging from the ceiling swayed back and forth, stretching shadows from one side of the room to the other, until the swaying became too much and they crashed to the floor, spraying cascades of sparks through the darkness. The trembling intensified. A great beast had awoken in the belly of the earth and demanded to be known. The incubators that had survived Olivia's game of whack-a-mole rattled. Cracks appeared in the glass, splintering into spiderwebs.

Unable to handle the stress, the glass exploded. More goop cascaded across the floor, adding to the slippery, slimy mess underfoot. The room shook so violently that every clone was thrown to the ground, but Olivia remained rooted as firmly as if she were a part of the earth itself.

SMUCK! A large chunk of concrete fell from the ceiling, crushing one of the defenceless hatchlings.

"STOP THIS NOW!" Retchen roared, dropping to all fours as if this were a normal thing to do. He scurried around the hatchlings, slipping and sliding through the goop. He was coming for her.

Keep him away from us!

The beast inside the earth obliged. A crack appeared a few feet in front of Retchen, cutting him off. As he tried to scurry around it, it ripped its way across the lab, opening a chasm between them. Another crack began five feet behind the first. Chunks of broken incubators and new hatchlings spilled into the bowels of the planet, swallowed by the beast within. As the room pulled apart, the ceiling burst open, letting in the morning's light.

"WHAT ARE YOU DOING TO MY LAB? I WILL DESTROY YOU!" He was furious. A pair of wings punctured through his cashmere sweater. They were much smaller than Enki's wings and without feathers, like a bat. He leapt across the chasm and landed ten metres away, baring his razor teeth. "You are more powerful than I thought. Absorbing you bite by bite will be...transformative." He chuckled softly, enjoying the look of horror punched into her face.

This was it. She was done for. She had used all of her tricks, but he was just too powerful. She'd failed. She didn't know what to do. There was nothing she could do.

Retchen lunged for her, his teeth sharp and hungry, but before he landed, Olivia and her mother shot upwards, through the layers of his underground base, pulled against gravity from the belly of the earth. He gave chase, flapping his wings, but they were constricted by strands of his shredded sweater. He snatched for Olivia's ankle, grabbing her shoelace, but she kicked and bucked until she broke free. Knocked off course by the struggle and unable to fully extend his wings, they shot upwards faster than he could chase, until they punctured the surface and were pulled into the Jin saucer. The hatch closed, and AmmaNa reengaged the cloak.

"Oh, my girl. My brave, brave girl. How are you so strong?" Brooke sobbed on Olivia's shoulder, wrapping her daughter in a hug that Olivia didn't ever want to end.

"Migitju taught me. She's so wise, Mom. And she misses you."

Brooke peeled away from the hug and looked around, losing her nerve all over again. "Is this a…?" Brooke couldn't bring herself to finish the question.

"It's a spaceship, Mom. The star people are real. They came back to save us."

Being inside a spaceship was too much for Brooke after the ghastly scene in the clone lab. She scurried to the edge of the room, shaking her head as she rocked herself, muttering at her own hands.

What can we do, Olivia,
to help your elder one?

"Do you have anything for anxiety?"

AmmaNa nodded, and one of her crew left to fetch a sedative. Brooke watched them all with suspicion.

"Mom, these are the Jin, and this is their captain, my friend, AmmaNa. They communicate with telepathy, so don't be surprised if you hear voices floating around." She directed Brooke's attention to the furry red being. "This is my friend, Keilte. He's from a planet called Teutonia. There are lots of star people, but the ones on this ship are friends, okay?"

"What about Tuatha and Rama?" Keilte asked.

"Things didn't go as planned," Olivia explained. "I got snatched at the lookout point, but Rama was disguised, and Tuatha flew out of reach. We have to go back for them before the Greys do."

A saucer whizzed by, pulling Olivia's attention towards the damage she'd caused below. A gaping canyon now ripped through the mountains, and the above ground portion of Retchen's lair was canted at an angle, teetering on the canyon's edge. Maybe it would slide in, taking Retchen with it. Her mom was safe for now, but he was still alive, still able to hunt her family. Three more saucers emerged from the new canyon, joining the scout. They whizzed up and out of sight as a squadron of fighter jets approached.

"We can't risk leaving the ship. AmmaNa, can you take us back to the lookout point and open the hatch?"

Tuatha, Rama, are you still down there? Can you hear me?

Tuatha shot up through the treetops, carrying Rama in a hug. "Seriously, Carpenter, what took you so long? I felt the rumbling and I knew that had to be you shaking things up, but what's with leaving us in the woods all night while you get to have all the fun?"

"It wasn't fun. We're only alive thanks to AmmaNa."

Tuatha and Rama were barely back inside the ship when the Grey swarm reappeared.

Hand over the humans or be destroyed.

The swarm of Greys that led the fighter jets away were back for Retchen's prize. Everyone heard them as clearly as if they were standing in the room, so it was a small blessing that Brooke was already asleep from the sedative. She had already lived enough trauma for one day.

"Keilte, can you please grab my mom? This is going to get dangerous. Everybody hold on!"

Keilte hoisted Brooke over his shoulder and secured himself as they shot up through the stratosphere, the Greys immediately in pursuit. Olivia punched the button to engage the quantum cloak.

Ship, evade the saucers. Make zigzag patterns. Do something they can't follow.

They whipped left. They zipped right. They rocketed up and down, but somehow, the saucers tracked every move.

"How are they following us?"

"Space is full of tiny particles," Keilte explained. "The friction we make when we pass them generates heat. If they have a heat sensor, they can follow our trail."

"So what do we do?"

"Can this ship fly through a star?"

In unison, the Jin all shook their heads no.

The saucers fired. Everyone was tossed around as the ship dodged the attack.

"Come on, Carpenter, how did you escape before?"

"Everybody hold on. I really mean it." *Ship, take us into the thickest part of the asteroid belt. Do whatever you have to do to lose those saucers.*

Many sets of knuckles heeded Olivia's warning, gripping hard and turning various shades of anxiety as they braced for what was to come. The ship lurched forward. Wondering if she'd ever get a chance to see it up close again, Olivia stared at Mars as they whizzed by, heading directly for the sea of giant boulders beyond. As they entered the realm of the asteroids, they veered around a small boulder and narrowly missed a very large one. Only three saucers followed them. Were they being boxed in?

The ship spun sideways, squeaking through a gap that was closing quickly. Seconds later, the boulders crushed into each other. Olivia shuddered. This place was a minefield of unseen dangers, each rock spinning with its own trajectory. She was glad the ship was keeping them safe, but the trio of saucers had also avoided the collision. The obstacle had created some distance, but the Greys were still in pursuit.

The Greys fired again, hitting a boulder in the wake of the Jin ship. The hit altered the asteroid's direction, sending it spinning faster towards them. They veered away, towards an asteroid that seemed to go on forever. They whizzed up, up, up… Olivia held her breath as they crested the asteroid and exhaled only when she saw clear space. If they had met another asteroid, it would have been game over.

That will not happen, Olivia. I have scanned the belt for all asteroids and calculated their trajectories. My survival depends on it.

It hadn't occurred to Olivia that the ship was more than a computer, that it had its own instinct for survival, but why not? The Jin were geneticists. It was comforting to know that the ship wanted to survive this as well.

For a few precious moments, the saucers were out of view. Olivia had an idea.

Hug this asteroid. Fly around it close to the surface and find a flat spot to land.

The ship changed course, dropping quickly and passing under another asteroid spinning along the surface of the immense hunk of rock. It hugged the jagged terrain until it found an indentation where it could safely land. Everyone was thrown into the air as it slammed into the rocky surface. Immediately, the entire ship went dark.

"What are we doing? Why did we stop?" Rama was confused.

"We know we can't outrun them. Maybe we can hide."

"But won't they follow our heat trail?"

"The asteroid we landed on already moved us away from the trail we left, and it must be creating a heat trail, too. It's hitting the same particles we were hitting—all of these boulders are. We're going to use the crisscrossing trails all around us as camouflage."

Olivia is correct. I have now calculated all outcomes, and her plan is our best chance to remain hidden.

The first saucer crested the apex of the massive asteroid, but it wasn't prepared for the smaller asteroid scraping along its surface. The boulder made contact with the saucer like a bowling ball hitting a strike. The explosion lit up the darkness around them. Fiery chunks streaked out in all directions.

"One baddy goes kaboom!"

The other two saucers appeared on either side of the explosion at a safe distance. They zipped around in many directions, avoiding asteroids and searching for their target, but the heat from the explosion coupled with the spin of their landing pad was the perfect combo disguise. The saucers doubled back, doing sweep after sweep of the area, but the heat trail of the Jin ship had long since spun away. Fully cloaked, the ship was a chameleon on a tree branch. Until it moved, it was impossible to see.

"It looks like we lost them," Rama declared as Olivia and Keilte settled Brooke into a chair with a harness.

"Only until we move," Olivia shot back. "We're stuck in the asteroid belt, being hunted by Greys who want to vaporize us. The danger is real. And now that they're watching for us, I don't know how we're going to get my mom back to my dad. The plan was to rescue her, not kidnap her all over again."

"Listen, Creepy McSlenderman was definitely working with the Greys. If we take Mama Carpenter back, they're just going to snatch her again."

The air in the control room was thick, like breathing honey. Was it this revelation, or was the air actually getting soupy?

Ship, is there any issue with our oxygen supply?

Yes. The plants that excrete oxygen for life-support are insufficient to support the number of passengers on board this ship. At your current rate of consumption, you have twenty minutes of oxygen remaining.

They were out of time. They couldn't stay. They had to return to Sita with Brooke. Her mother was going to meet the star people.

24 FOOD FOR THOUGHTS

THEY WERE GOING back to Sita. They had no other choice. AmmaNa equipped Brooke with the translation worms Olivia still had in her ears, and suddenly, it clicked. Olivia had been able to understand eight billion voices, all speaking in different languages, because of the worms. They must be able to translate on a telepathic level, like the Jin. These worms were likely a life form created by the Jin, customized to meet a purpose, but an independent life nonetheless. How many life-forms had they created that they had to be asked to stop?

The clockwork gadget tracking Sita's movements showed that Maia had just left Sita's sky and it was safe to return. They had to get back through the gate quickly, before Queen Tara sent more guards to the cave. Three Jin remained in the control room with the ship on survival mode while everyone else headed for the lab with the quantagate.

You shall not pass. You shall not pass.

On orders of our queen.

A squadron of eight Jin stood in formation around the gate, guarding its use, crystal-tipped weapons at the ready.

"Queen Tara doesn't have the authority to interfere with orders of the Council," Keilte warned them.

Our orders are to keep you here.

You will not use our quantagate.

You shall not pass. You shall not pass.

On orders of our queen.

Before Olivia could join Keilte in protest, two of the newly reformed guards stepped forward, obvious in their robes bearing Queen Tara's royal emblem: a hexagon made of bees. They raised their hands.

We have been captives of these rogues.

We thank you for releasing us.

We must share with you what we know,

in service to our queen.

What? The Jin were capable of a double-cross? How was that even possible? Olivia had felt the ripple of these guards becoming one mind with AmmaNa's crew. And yet, the betrayal played itself out right in front of her. The first two guards lowered their weapons and raised their palms, accepting the knowledge transfer from the captives. Once complete, they turned, passing the knowledge to the next two, and then the next, until all Jin had received the transfer. Great. Now, instead of having eight Jin against them, they had ten. Why did everything always have to be so complicated?

As soon as the transfer was complete, the guards faced Olivia. And to everyone's shock, they laid their weapons on the ground and stepped away from the gate.

"I'm confused," Olivia whispered to Keilte. "What just happened?"

Now that we understand your quest,

we will no longer block your way.

Now that your origins are known,

the gate is yours to use.

And just like that, the guards sent to stop them had become allies. Winning them over was as simple as duping them into a thought-share, and just in time. The air was almost gone.

"AmmaNa, will you come back with me?"

Of course I will return with you.

Why would you doubt my loyalty?

"But is that too much for me to ask?" Olivia remembered Miley's birthday. It wasn't until her dad had driven away that Olivia learned she was only there to be the butt of Miley's jokes. She'd gone home with her hair caked in icing and drenched in a funny-smelling yellow liquid that she told herself was only Gatorade. "I guess what I'm trying to say is that I've been the outcast. I avoid going where I'm not wanted, and I'd understand if you felt that way too."

Are you inviting me along to fill my hair with sticky goop?

"No. I would never do that to you."

You do not make me feel cast out. You make me feel brought in.

You saved my life. You are my friend. My place is at your side.

"I vote that the guards go first," Keilte chimed in, breathing heavily and anxious to get moving. "If they meet any more guards, they can do the thought transfer thing. Once they give the all-clear, the rest of us can follow."

Without hesitation, the guards turned, drew their weapons, and strode back through the gate. As soon as the last one was gone, Brooke began to stir. Keilte put her down carefully, backing up so that when her eyes opened, she'd see Olivia.

"Mom, I need you to focus on me. We're on a spaceship, but we're running out of oxygen. We have to go through that gate right there. See it? The big round thing? Do you think you can get up?"

Brooke shook her head and refused to move. She had experienced so much trauma that she was all locked up. It was understandable. She'd just been the centrepiece of a battle in a clone lab, had seen a human (who wasn't at all human) sprout bat wings, had been beamed up into a spaceship, and was now being asked to step through a stargate to destinations unknown. It was a lot for one life, never mind one day.

The Jin guards returned, nodding. Tuatha and Rama wasted no time stepping through. Keilte held back, ready to help Olivia.

"We have to go, Mom. We're running out of air."

Your daughter is correct. This ship has exactly two minutes and nine seconds of oxygen remaining at current consumption rates.

"What was that?"

"The ship is intelligent. It got us away from Dr. Retchen, and it's trying to save our lives." Without waiting for her agreement, Olivia grabbed her mom by the hand and pulled Brooke to her feet, leading her towards the gate. "Make sure to hold your breath," she said as she stepped forward.

The air on the other side of the gate was rich with oxygen. With every new breath, Olivia felt her strength returning, felt her mind waking up from a long nap. As she stepped forward and pulled back the vines for her mother, all Brooke could do was gasp.

"Pretty great view, isn't it, Mama Carpenter? Can I call you Mama Carpenter? Or Mama Terra? No, Mama Carpenter is good."

Brooke nodded weakly, overwhelmed by her surroundings and still not really sure about talking to aliens who looked like human-sized fairies, complete with wings and an aura of shimmer.

Olivia let her mom marvel at their surroundings for a moment before ushering her forward. The going was slow at first, with Brooke trying to walk off a sedative, but her strength and resolve seemed to return with each step.

"Are we really going to meet the star people?"

"Look around, Mom. You've already met the star people. They helped me rescue you. Migitju was right. She was right about everything."

Brooke walked the rest of the way in reverent silence, her gaze fixed on Bodie, its rings, three of its moons, and beyond them, a dark sky full of bright blue stars where there had only ever been tiny points of white light. She didn't see the crystal skyscraper grow taller and taller as they neared the limits of the canyon.

It was all new for Olivia, too. The first time she'd approached the hive, she'd been too focused on saving her friend. When they'd left to return to Earth, she was running to escape Maia. But now, as they approached, she saw the hive in all of its majesty. A sculpture carved into a cliff of opaque white crystal glinted high overhead, becoming one with the starry sky. It was at least a kilometre tall, its smooth hexagonal windows reflecting the blue-white starlight. The entrance was flanked on both sides by ornately carved pillars of bees tending to flowers on a tangle of six vines. The vines twisted upwards, creating an arch over the doorway that merged into a pine cone shaped fruit at the apex. Carvings inlaid into the cliff behind the pillars depicted a multitude of animals. Some were familiar, like the elephant and the lion, while others looked like they belonged in a fantasy novel.

Open.

The crystal door crawled away, but the tunnel was blocked. Hundreds of Jin stood shoulder to shoulder, pointing defiantly.

You shall not pass, you shall not pass,
on orders of the Queen.

Standing down was out of the question. "Queen Tara, if you don't let us in, you'll have to explain yourself to the Council." The threat of losing her seat was real.

The Jin who left may not return.
The Council has no vote in that.
This hive does not belong to them.
The rogue Jin shall not pass.

Having delivered the message, the Jin put their hands on the crystal walls, and the door grew back into a wall, shutting them out. Olivia wondered how AmmaNa could be so calm while her own siblings tossed her out like a used tissue.

We saw the greater good in you,
and we came back to show them too.
Our numbers grew to six from three,
and now eight more have eyes to see.
We are prepared to wage this fight,
ensuring all Jin see the light.

"AmmaNa, earlier, when I touched the crystal inside the hive, I could hear the Queen ordering the Jin to find me. Can you do that too? Can you download your knowledge into the hive?"

That skill is one we do not have.
The Queen alone ingests the comb.
The honey lets her transmit thoughts
for us to hear when we recharge.

A light breeze whistled across the canyon, coming from the orange flowers carpeting the canyon floor. The wind was sweet, like the honeycomb in the infirmary. Olivia could still feel the tingle of its power on her tongue. Her tummy growled, wanting more of the delicious food, but her brain was twisting on an idea.

"Carpenter's hatching a plan. I can feel it."

"When I woke up in the infirmary, I ate a bunch of the honeycomb."

The Jin all gasped together. Clearly, this was not allowed, but the deed was already done.

"If I can flinch with AmmaNa and download her message into the crystal, maybe we can convert the hive right under Queen Tara's butt."

"Aren't you afraid you might crack the moon open again?"

"Well, I wasn't even thinking about it until you brought it up, Rama. Thanks. You got a better idea?"

He looked sheepishly at his feet. He did not.

AmmaNa nodded to Olivia, who leaned one hand against the crystal tower and imagined roots growing from her fingers into its sparkling depths. Tendrils of light twisted like vines from under her hand, crawling up the wall and spiderwebbing out in all directions. In moments, the entire cliff was as blindingly bright as Maia. Olivia cleared her mind and reached for AmmaNa's hand.

What did you show the Jin that made them join your hive?

Blackness shattered into a blur of images, whizzing through Olivia's mind at a terrifying speed. She couldn't hold onto any of them —they were gone before she could even catch the slightest detail or outline. Both of her hands heated up from the transfer of energy until, like an overloaded computer, she couldn't process any more data, and her entire body shut down.

25 A HERO AND HER QUEEN

"CARPENTER, YOU STILL with us? Come on, Carpenter, you gotta wake up." Tuatha's voice cut through the soupy fog filling Olivia's mind, filtering sights and sounds. She propped herself up, still in a daze. Blood dripped from her nose and over her upper lip, hitting the crystal every second. Tuatha searched the ground for a specific plant, ripped off a leaf, and shoved it into Olivia's left nostril. Olivia didn't protest. Every part of her body ached. The last thing she remembered was flinching with AmmaNa.

"What happened? Did it work?"

"Were you trying to make the planet sing?" Rama asked.

"Huh?"

"It started the moment you passed out. There was a low hum, like someone was blowing on one of Master Yamma's horns, but super loud and all around us, like it was coming out of the crystal."

Olivia looked to AmmaNa, who seemed to be waiting for her.

Open.

The crystal parted. The horde of angry faces was gone. The tunnel was deserted. When they crossed the threshold into the central chamber, the silence was obvious above all else. If she'd been an explorer or a treasure hunter, she would have assumed this place had been abandoned eons ago. AmmaNa, however, looked right at home. Her skin was glowing. Returning in defiance of Queen Tara had given the Jin captain a newfound confidence. She was standing taller than Olivia had ever seen.

The team stepped onto the lift, and the crystal lit up all on its own. That was new. Before Olivia could think a command, the lift shot upward all on its own. It brought them up, up, up, but there were no Jin to be seen. They continued upward, soon reaching the floors damaged by the moonquake. Thankfully, the temperature in the hive had dropped, so the Jin must have been able to reroute the water needed for cooling, but Olivia expected to see crews pushing forward with the repairs. The active part of the hive, normally buzzing with life, was as silent as the entrance below.

"Where is everyone?" Rama wondered.

"Maybe they're investigating the sound you said was coming from the crystal after I passed out. Let's stop at the dorms to check in." Olivia tried to stop the lift, but it ignored her, travelling upward of its own accord.

"AmmaNa, can you stop the lift? It won't listen to me."

AmmaNa put her hand on the crystal railing to listen. How were her antennae suddenly at eye level? Was she growing?

We have been summoned to the Tree
to face Queen Tara and the hive.
We have created much unrest
by spreading what we know.

It was like being summoned to the principal's office, except the principal didn't invade people's minds and watch their most private moments for entertainment. There was no way to get off, and there were too many of them for Tuatha to fly them all to safety. The panic in her stomach grew as the lift took them headlong into danger.

"Take it easy, Carpenter. Whatever this is about, you have the support of the Council, and you have us."

Keilte, Rama, and AmmaNa nodded.

Brooke just stared at her daughter and hiked her shoulders. "I have no idea what's going on, but you're a smart girl. You'll figure this out."

"How are you doing with all of this, Mom? Meeting the star people is a big deal."

"I don't know, Liv. I really don't. It's all just too strange for me."

"If you feel yourself getting worked up into a froth, I can help with that," Tuatha offered. "My people's involvement in creating Terrans gave us the ability to, well, adjust your emotions."

"What?" Olivia was dumbfounded.

"Listen, Carpenter, don't get your tunic in a twist. You kept the whole I'm-a-Terran thing as a secret identity. I had no reason to divulge my connection with the Terrans until you came clean about being one. And then, I forgot."

It was a fair point. She couldn't get mad at Tuatha for keeping secrets, not after keeping some of her own.

The lift didn't stop until it reached the surface. Despite her dread, Olivia couldn't help but marvel at the sight. Thousands of students and ten thousand Jin were gathered, transforming the plateau into a tapestry of gold with small clusters of colour quilted throughout. As their platform emerged, a massive cheer erupted from the patches of colour. The Jin joined in, chanting through the cheer, growing louder with each pass.

All hail to our new Queen!
All hail to Queen Amma!
All hail to our new Queen!
All hail to Queen Amma!

Olivia looked to AmmaNa for some kind of explanation and was shocked to see that her golden friend had grown again. There was no doubt about it now. She was looking AmmaNa in the eye—they were the same height.

"What's happening?"

Now that all Jin have learned the truth,
we are upset with secrets kept.
Queen Tara has now been deposed;
we have been asked to take her place.
No longer are we AmmaNa.
We are now titled Queen Amma.

It was as if explaining it was akin to accepting the title, and Queen Amma grew taller right in front of Olivia's eyes. A group of Jin approached, carrying a throne. They set it down in front of their new queen, who climbed on. They carried Queen Amma through the sea of gold, which parted as they approached. Olivia followed, her mother's trembling hand in hers, her new friends right behind her. The procession led them across a bridge that had been built across the dry lakebed and onto the island where the Tree of Life sparkled like a chandelier in the twilight. It was covered with pale purple flowers, each containing a delicate silver bell. A wonderful aroma of maple-infused peaches filled the air. It reminded her of the honeycomb she had eaten in the infirmary, and her mouth watered.

As soon as Queen Amma was settled under the tree, the Jin began to hum. It started as a quiet, wordless chant but quickly swelled into a symphony of voices. It wasn't just a song; there was also a rhythm woven into the harmonies.

Da-DUM-Da-DUM-Da-DUM.

"Carpenter, get ready to see the coolest thing ever."

In a blink, dark clouds obscured the pale-blue twilight, moving in quickly and hovering overhead, as if the Jin were singing up a storm. The song moved into a higher octave and the clouds descended, shrouding the tree. That's when Olivia became aware of the buzzing.

These weren't clouds, they were bees, giant swarms of bees that lived with the Jin in their hive. They flew in a frenzy from flower to flower, feasting on the pollen of the tree. When the Jin finally dropped their song back to its original octave, the bees left the tree, once again forming clouds so thick that they blocked out the stars, then dove into the depths of Sita, vanishing. A group of Jin stepped forward to offer baskets of honeycomb to Queen Amma, who took two pieces. To everyone's shock, she gave one of the chunks to Olivia. Olivia waited for the Queen to eat first, then gobbled down her own helping, trying hard to look dignified despite the need to lick every morsel of melted honey from her hands. The Jin cheered. The coronation was complete.

It is now time to celebrate
our victory and our new friends.
Do any of the Councillors
have any thoughts to add?

Lord Harvarder stepped forward and raised his hand. "Jin of Sita, Queen Amma, Guardians-in-training, and guests. We have a special announcement, something I never imagined would happen in my lifetime, long as that lifetime is. You may already have heard the rumours, and I can now verify them. We have with us the very first

Terran." He motioned to Olivia as the crowd gasped. Whispers swelled through the crowd in waves, bouncing against the edges and returning back to the centre. "Olivia Carpenter is very dear to the Jin, as evidenced by the sharing of the sacred honeycomb. I have never heard of a Jin Queen sharing the sacred honey." He looked to Queen Amma for confirmation.

This Terran did not crack our moon;
the crack came from the former queen.
The Terran came with power bright
and ate the fruit and shone her light.
She amplified the rift within.
The Tree of Life sees her as kin.
We've learned to do things differently.
The time has come for unity.

AmmaNa believed that the Tree of Life could think, and it made sense. Migitju believed that all trees think like people; it was the people who forgot how to listen.

"Not only is this Terran a hero for saving Queen Amma's life, but she also rooted out an impostor within the Council. We are in your debt, Olivia Carpenter."

The Jin approached Olivia and her mother with shawls made of golden flowers and plates of delicious-looking fruit. Needing sustenance after such a draining battle with Retchen and overwhelmed by the wonderful smell of the food, Brooke dug into a purple cucumber, covering the front of her shirt with juice. Queen Amma giggled. The crowd cheered, and from somewhere on the main shore came an upbeat tune with a solid baseline. The students, interspersed throughout the sea of gold, began dancing. Queen Amma nodded, and the tapestry of Jin joined in the celebration.

Master Eldrin, who'd been waiting patiently for the other formalities to finish, couldn't wait any longer. "What news, Olivia? Were you able to hear anything near the Triad?"

"I'm sorry, Master Eldrin, we weren't able to get anywhere near the Centauri Triad. Queen Amma's ship is still trapped in my star system, pinned by the Greys."

Master Eldrin looked heartbroken. "I understand. You had to focus on your mission."

Wanting to avoid any more questions that would force her to lie, Olivia nodded toward the new queen. "I've been given quite the honour today. I really shouldn't be ignoring my hosts. Excuse me, Master Eldrin. I look forward to your next class." She returned to Queen Amma's side.

We'd love to celebrate all night,
but we don't have this luxury.
We must return our efforts to
repairs that are at hand.

The coronation of a new queen had been so unexpected that Olivia had completely forgotten about the crack splitting the hive in two. But the lakebed was still dry, a jagged wound cutting it in two. Barricades set up along its edges to keep the revellers away were easily hidden by the sheer number of Jin and students celebrating on the plateau. Everyone had survived, but the repairs were far from done.

"My queen, my friend. If you'll allow me to try, I think I may be able to fix the damage I've caused. At least some of it. Do I have your permission?"

As AmmaNa we trusted you,
but now we speak for everyone.
We ask therefore that you divulge
the details of your plan.

"Fair enough. Master Yamma, our Doggo instructor, told me that my head is out of tune, and Master Eldrin figured out that it affects my ability to use my gifts. I was thinking if we get Master Yamma to keep me in tune and I use the power from the honeycomb to speak with all of the entities in the crystal all at once like I did down at the entrance, maybe we can speed up the repairs."

We cannot see the danger in
allowing you to try this plan.
Our guards will bring the Doggo here
to help you get in tune.

Master Yamma arrived, eager to help however she could. "What is it you need of me, young Guardian-in-training?"

"I want to try to fix the crack from the moonquake and I need you to keep me in tune."

"Returning the water to its original course is a noble endeavour indeed. The Jin have created a holding pool for me since the moonquake, and while I very much appreciate the care they have put into serving my aquatic needs, I will also be very happy to leave such temporary accommodations behind."

Olivia produced the tuning forks and, with a nod from Queen Amma, helped herself to another serving of the energy-infused honeycomb. Master Yamma tapped the two forks and held them close to Olivia's ears. Olivia closed her eyes and focused on the sound for a few beats, then took a deep breath and placed her hands on the ground. Once again, she envisioned roots growing from her hands into the crystal, and this time, fuelled by the recent serving of honeycomb, the roots exploded from her palms. The whole plateau lit up just as if Maia had risen, and an accompanying tidal wave of nervousness broke across the crowd as everyone awed at the crystal glowing underfoot.

I know that this crystal is your home, and it is asking a lot to request that you uproot your homes and rebuild, but I ask this of you anyway. There is a giant crack in the Jin hive and it puts the entire city in danger. Could you please help me by stitching this crack back together, at least enough to reroute the waterfall to its original place? I am grateful to have your audience, and I appreciate any help you can provide.

Under her knees and hands, the crystal hummed with the same note her friends had heard earlier. The hum intensified, drowning out the tuning forks. It was all Olivia could hear. Her hands and knees heated up as the energy flowed, but this time there was no pain—the energy flowed without resistance. From somewhere deep below, the crystal began to rise, filling the crack in the island, filling the crack in the dry lakebed, filling the crack from its source all the way to the place where the waterfall was meant to be. Pink water pooled where the lake had previously been, quickly soaking the feet of Jin and students alike. They scrambled up its sides, albeit with glee, and when the first trickle of water reached the head of the waterfall and spilled over into the hive, the crowd erupted once again into revelry.

Thank you, thank you, thank you.

Olivia repeated her thanks three times to ensure it was heard, but couldn't imagine any words expressing how grateful she truly was for the sacrifice made by the crystal dwellers. She collapsed, spent from the effort but still aware. Instinctively, she reached for another chunk of honeycomb, and as it warmed down her throat, she regained enough strength to sit up. The relationship between the Jin and the bees and the crystal was deep and multifaceted. Queen Amma watched these revelations in Olivia with love and astonishment.

You have amazed us once again.
We are infused with gratitude.
Our celebration will go on
until the daylight comes.

"If you don't mind, highness, that wore me out. I'm going to head down and take a nap, but I'll be back before the party ends."

Getting back to the shore from the island was easy enough now that it was full of water and not people, but once on shore, everyone wanted to meet the Terran who had just performed a miracle. As the students pushed towards her, Jin near the edge of the lake dropped into the water. It was clear they couldn't swim. More Jin reached down to save their siblings, and as they did, the push of the crowd sent more tumbling back into the lake. Olivia saw Tuatha nearby and called out, desperate.

"Tuatha! Can you lift me out of this? Someone's going to get hurt!"

Happy to play the hero, Tuatha swooped in and pulled her up and above the crowd. Instantly, the crowd stopped pressing towards the lake and Jin stopped falling in. Tuatha put them down on the platform where Olivia had first surfaced, quickly joined by Keilte and Rama.

"I'm glad you're all here. We need to talk."

"What's going on?"

Down.

Olivia waited until they were well into the belly of the deserted hive before she dared to say another word. "Can I swear you all to secrecy?"

"What does that mean?" Rama asked.

"It means that if I tell you this thing, you're not allowed to tell another living soul or even write it down. Can you handle that?"

They all nodded.

"Rama, seriously, if you blab, no more missions."

"Fine, fine. This must be really juicy."

"When we were on Terra, I had to eat a crystal apple to find my mom, and I heard their voices. Thousands of them. Trapped somehow."

"Whose voices, Carpenter? Who's trapped?"

Olivia produced her oracle, the smoke now a swirling indigo. The projection was of a city made of multiple rings connected by bridges, surrounded by steep walls of water.

"You must rescue the City of Atlantis," it said.

Olivia looked at them gravely. "This looks really bad. This looks like my people put the City of Atlantis in a prison. I can't believe that's true, but I don't know what the Atlantians might do if they saw this oracle. I don't want anyone to get hurt. Will you help me rescue them?"

"Of course we will," Keilte affirmed for the group. "We are Team Olivia."

She beamed. She had no idea how she would find and rescue an entire city, but it didn't matter. She had already accomplished what she never thought she could—she had found her tribe. Together, they'd find the lost Atlantians and bring them home.

IF YOU LOVED PROJECT HUMAN,
GET READY FOR OLIVIA CARPENTER'S
NEXT EPIC ADVENTURE:

ATLANTIS RISING

FOLLOW THE JOURNEY AT:

WWW.PROJECTHUMANBOOKS.COM
SIGN UP TO OUR EMAIL LIST
FOR INSIDER BONUSES!

JOIN OUR FACEBOOK GROUP:
@PROJECTHUMANBOOKS

ON INSTAGRAM:
@MOSHKINSGAMES

ABOUT THE AUTHOR

Bea Waters was born and raised on the north eastern coast of Turtle Island, a massive chunk of land known by European colonists as North America. She chooses to identify her location this way in order to honour ten thousand years worth of history and culture of the people who originally named this land. She lives with her husband Mark, their daughter Emily, and their two cats, Rupert and Sadie in a small city along the Wolastoq River. By identifying the river by its ancestral title, Bea is choosing to be the change she wants to see in the world.

Bea enjoys playing board games with her husband and inventing new games that may someday be published. She likes acting, creating recipes, singing, playing music, and is fascinated with learning about other cultures, both current and ancient.

Milton Keynes UK
Ingram Content Group UK Ltd.
UKHW041939170823
427061UK00004B/40